R G Barnes
Bristol

3 Novr 1857 St Andrews N.B.

COMMODORE R. F. STOCKTON.

United States Navy.

DECK AND PORT;

OR,

INCIDENTS OF A CRUISE

IN THE

UNITED STATES FRIGATE CONGRESS

TO

CALIFORNIA.

WITH SKETCHES OF RIO JANEIRO, VALPARAISO, LIMA, HONOLULU, AND SAN FRANCISCO.

BY

REV. WALTER COLTON, U. S. N.,

AUTHOR OF "SHIP AND SHORE," ETC.

NEW YORK:
PUBLISHED BY A. S. BARNES & CO.,
NO. 51 JOHN-STREET.
CINCINNATI:—H. W. DERBY & CO.
1850.

Stereotyped by
RICHARD C. VALENTINE,
New York

F. C. GUTIERREZ, Printer,
No. 61 John-street, corner of Dutch.

TO

THOMAS I. WHARTON, ESQ.

OF PHILADELPHIA,

This Volume

IS MOST RESPECTFULLY DEDICATED

BY HIS FRIEND

THE AUTHOR.

PREFACE.

On joining the United States frigate Congress, fitting for sea, at Norfolk, and destined to the Pacific, I commenced a journal, in which I sketched down the incidents of each day, as they occurred. It was more a whim of the hour, than any purpose connected with the public press. It was a diverting experiment on the monotony of a sea-life; was continued because it had been begun—and the present volume is the result. The streamlet flows from gathered drops.

I send it to the press as it was written, except the division into chapters, which has been made at the suggestion of the publishers, who perhaps, think the yarn will reel better if the thread be broken. It undoubtedly contains passages which may seem light and irrelevant; but a diary has privileges, in this respect, which are not extended to compositions of a graver character. He who gathers what the chance wind may shake from the trees of his garden, will find some leaves as well as fruit in his basket; and he may find there the nest of some insect that has a sting in it, but this he has no right to send to market. He may send the leaves—perhaps their sear hues may set off the bloom of his fruit, as a wrinkle the rouge through which age sometimes seeks to blush back again into youth.

The members of Congress are responsible for any typographical errors which the volume may contain, for they so lumbered the mails, between Washington—where the proofs were sent—and New York, with their speeches, that my publishers had about as little chance of getting a corrected copy through this travelling Babel, as they would have had in finding a righteous man in Sodom after Lot had left. I know it seems cruel to roll the responsibility of blunders on a body of men who have errors enough of their own to answer for. But the evil one himself is held accountable for the sins of half the world.

Having thus conveniently disposed of all responsibility, I leave my Deck and Port to the wave and strand, where they belong. Wreckers will receive no salvage from me—they must make the most of the floating planks. I only ask them not to scuttle the craft before she strikes.

W. C.

NOTE.

The incidents which connected the officers of the Pacific Squadron and of the army, and many other prominent persons, with public events in California, are not reached by the Diary of this volume; they fall within the three years which are reserved for another work, entitled "*Three Years in California.*"

CONTENTS.

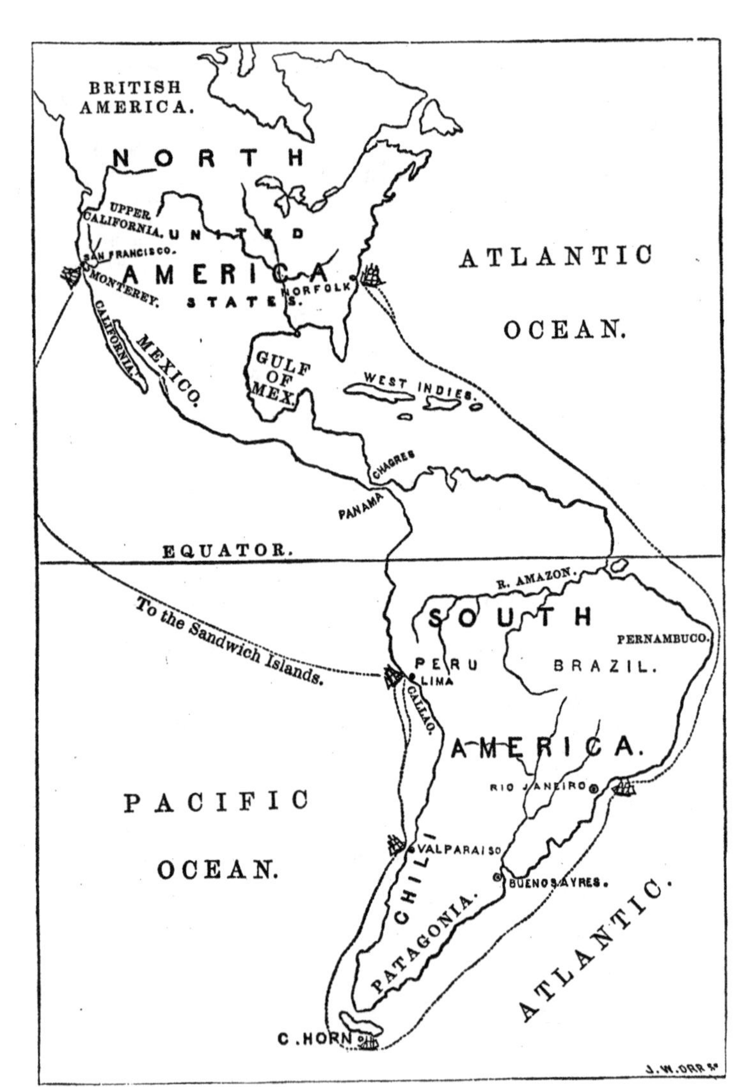

BRITISH AMERICA.
NORTH AMERICA.
UPPER CALIFORNIA.
UNITED STATES.
SAN FRANCISCO.
MONTEREY.
NORFOLK
CALIFORNIA.
MEXICO.
GULF OF MEX.
WEST INDIES.
ATLANTIC OCEAN.
CHAGRES
PANAMA
EQUATOR.
R. AMAZON.
To the Sandwich Islands.
SOUTH AMERICA.
PERNAMBUCO.
PERU
LIMA
CALLAO.
BRAZIL.
RIO JANEIRO
PACIFIC OCEAN.
VALPARAISO
BUENOS AYRES.
CHILI
PATAGONIA.
ATLANTIC.
C. HORN
J. W. ORR Sc

DECK AND PORT.

CHAPTER I.

PREPARATIONS FOR THE VOYAGE.

ORDERS TO THE CONGRESS.—PASSENGERS' POOP-CABIN.—PASSING U. S. SHIP PENNSYLVANIA.—DIVINE SERVICE.—WAITING THE WIND.—RIP-RAPS.—INTERNAL ARRANGEMENTS.—LIBRARY OF THE CREW.—SHIP CHEERED.—DEPARTURE OF THE PILOT.

To sea! to sea! thy soft shore life
Must wrestle on the deck,
Where winds and waters meet in strife,
To revel o'er the wreck.

WHILE enjoying the luxury of sea-bathing at Sachem's Head, I received an order to report for duty on board the U. S. Frigate Congress, fitting for sea at Norfolk. The order came as unexpectedly as thunder out of a cloudless sky. But never having declined an order of the department during the many years that I have been in the navy, I determined not to dishonor a good rule on this occasion, and informed the secretary that I should report agreeable to his instructions, but requested the indulgence of a few days in which to make my preparations. The reply was, that the ship was ready for sea, that the other officers were on board, and I must hasten at once to my post. My trunks were immediately packed, my books boxed, and in twenty-four hours I was on board the Congress. Home, and all that makes that home dear, exchanged at once for the bustle of a man-of-war! It was like throwing a bird from its nest upon the whirlwind: not that I have any thing in common with a bird, unless it be a sort of involuntary cheerfulness when the storm-cloud has passed. I have never yet met with a picture all the features of which were dark. There is a star even in the night of the grave.

I found the frigate nearly ready for sea. The honorable secretary, as if to hasten our departure, paid us a farewell visit. We returned the compliment in a parting salute. We were now ready to weigh anchor and make sail, when an order came for us to take out as passengers a commissioner and a consul to the Sandwich Islands, with their families, twelve individuals in all. The question was, where shall they be accommodated? Every part of the ship was already occupied. Another order soon came for the construction of a poop-cabin. Some thirty carpenters were immediately set at work, but its completion occupied three weeks. In the mean time some of the officers, whose homes were less remote, had an opportunity of visiting their families. I was enabled to finish my preparations, complete my wardrobe, and take a decent leave of one from whom I had been hurried away as the culprit,

> "Who fitted the halter and traversed the cart,
> And often looked back as if loath to depart."

SATURDAY, OCT. 25, 1845. The poop-cabin being finished, commissioner, consul, and families, quartered in it, stores laid in, the commodore on board, an order was given to unmoor. In a few minutes our anchors were up and we were proceeding under a light land-breeze towards the sea. Passing the Pennsylvania, where she lay in her majesty and strength, we gave her a parting salute, which she returned in thunder from her frowning batteries. She frowned not on us; she seemed to grieve, "if aught inanimate e'er grieves," that she must lie there and rot, and we be bounding over the billows. She seemed like a daring eagle that has never been permitted to soar into its element and unfurl its strong pinions on the storm. The Titan chained to the Caucasian rock stayed his proud heart on his past triumphs, but this noble ship perishes without a solitary achievement to relieve her indignant doom. On reaching Hampton Roads the wind came out ahead, and we were obliged to let go our anchors. An air of disappointment was visible among the crew. I once started on a journey in a splendid carriage, broke down in sight of my own home, and learned a lesson of submission that will never wholly desert me. Calamities are our best instructors.

Sunday, Oct. 26. The wind still ahead. This being the sabbath, we had divine service. The crew were attentive: not the rustle of a hand or foot disturbed the stillness; the speaker's voice only broke the silence of the deck. The text was the injunction of the prophet, "Go up now, look towards the sea." The object of the speaker was to sketch the stern magnificence of the ocean as illustrating the majesty of God; to exhibit the effects of an ocean life on the social and moral character of man; and to inculcate the great lesson, that into whatever climes we may penetrate, through whatever seas we may pass, we cannot escape from the presence of the Deity. The effects of our moral teachings may in many instances never be revealed in this life, but the time will come, when they will be fully recognised. They are like underground streams which will yet rush to the light.

Monday, Oct. 27. Still in Hampton Roads. The day has passed with scarce a breath of wind from any quarter. The sun has set in gorgeous splendor. Evening has spread its purple light over sea and land. Only here and there a cloud floats through the star-lit depths of heaven. The fortress of the old Rip-raps lifts its giant form in savage grandeur from the wave; and yet the moonlight sleeps upon it so lovingly, you half forget its chained thunder. It seems as some submarine monster that had shoved its head up through the sea, to glance at the wonders of earth. Gaze on, thou Titan of the deep! Thou hearest not the death-knell which shakes the heart of nations: thou seest only the verdure which waves in fragrant life and beauty over the dust of ages. Thou heedest not the sorrows of the millions that have sunk to the silent shroud. Earth is a charnel-house, but thou knowest it not. It is death's empire. Go look into some world where sin hath not been, and where man has not marred the works of his Maker.

Tuesday, Oct. 28. Our ship still riding in the Roads, with forty sail around wind-bound like ourselves. We went to general quarters at ten o'clock, exercised the guns, passed powder, called away the boarders, and went through all the forms of a real engagement at sea. It is singular what an enthusiasm even a mimic battle can create; what then must be the excitement of the reality! The sailors are proud of our frigate; and well may they be; she is a splendid specimen of naval architecture. For capacity, strength, and harmony of proportions, she stands in her class without a rival in the world.

She is so much a favorite in the service that one old sailor travelled all the way from Pensacola to Norfolk in the mail stage, and at his own expense, to join her. We had our complement of seamen, but his was so strong a case he could not be denied.

We number about five hundred souls, all told; have laid in provisions and fuel for five months, with fifty thousand gallons of water, and sails and rigging sufficient to replace what is now in use, should emergency demand. How such a mass of life and material can be brought within a frigate's capacity, and yet leave "scope and verge" enough for action and repose, is a mystery which can be comprehended only by those who are versed in nautical economy. The housewife who grumbles over the intrusion of an additional piece of furniture, should look into a man-of-war, and she will go home with the conviction that she can sleep quite comfortably in the cradle with her infant. How beautiful is an infant waking out of its sweet slumber, and opening its soft blue eyes upon the face of its mother! But what has this to do with our getting under way?

Wednesday, Oct. 29. Our anchors still sleep in the sands of Hampton Roads—a slumber which we now think the morrow will break. The wind has been light and varying, but inclining towards the right quarter, though hesitatingly, as a diffident youth in his first declaration of love. How the words on such an occasion will stick in a man's throat!—worse, indeed, than Macbeth's prayer, trying to struggle up from the grasp of his guilty conscience.

I have been occupied to-day in arranging in suitable cases the library of the crew—a library comprising between three and four hundred volumes. For many of the miscellaneous and religious books in this library I am indebted to the Presbyterian Board of Publication, to the Sunday School Union, to the American Tract Society, and to the liberality of Commodore Stockton. My acknowledgments are also due to the American Bible Society for a donation of Bibles adequate to the wants of the crew. No national ship ever left a port of the United States more amply provided with books suited to the habits and capacities of those on board. This desideratum has been supplied, so far as the crew is concerned, with comparatively little aid from the department. The government furnishes the sailor with grog to burn up his body, a Christian liberality with books to save his soul. The whisky ration is a curse to the service, and a damning blot on our national legislation.

THURSDAY, OCT. 30. The long looked for breeze came at last. It was a south-wester; and at daylight this morning we weighed anchor and got under way. When we had cleared the capes of Old Virginia, all hands were called, and Commodore Stockton delivered the following brief and appropriate address to the officers and crew:—

"Captain Du Pont and officers—

"Your reputation in the service is a sufficient guaranty that the cruise before us will enlist your highest energies and zeal.

"Men—

"Your conduct since you have been on board this ship justifies the strongest confidence in your fidelity. Above us floats the flag of our country; to your patriotism and undaunted valor I intrust its honor, dearer to me than life. We now sail for California and Oregon, and then, where it may please Heaven."

Then, turning to the chaplain, he said—

"You will offer up our prayers to Almighty God for his protection."

This service performed, the broad pennant was saluted, the ship cheered, and the band struck up "Hail Columbia."

The whole ceremony was well calculated to inspire a jealous regard for the honor of our flag, and impress sentiments of dependence on the divine protection—

so well becoming those who go down to the sea in ships, who do business on the great waters, and who see the wonders of the Lord in the deep.

Commodore Stockton invited the officers into the cabin to an elegant entertainment. Sentiments connected with country, home, and those left behind, passed feelingly around. The pilot now took his departure with our letter-bag. How many affections, hopes, and fears, that little hasty mail took back! If you would know how dear home is, start on a three years' cruise. How the heart clings to the living, recalls the dead, and restores the forgotten! How all animosities die and give place to love! I do not wonder the Greek and Roman dreaded exile more than death. What is earth without a home?

Farewell! the shore is fading fast,
  The wind is piping free,
The pennant, from our gallant mast,
  Points to the dark blue sea.

CHAPTER II.

PASSAGE FROM NORFOLK TO RIO DE JANEIRO.

A CULPRIT.—CORPORAL PUNISHMENTS.—DIVINE SERVICE.—A BIRD.—A GALE.—GRANDEUR OF THE GULF STREAM.—MAN MISSING.—TRACTS ON BOARD.—WATER-SPOUT.—LIFE AT SEA.—AN ECLIPSE.—THE SICK BAY.—MORAL MECHANISM OF A MAN-OF-WAR.—SPEAKING A BRIG.—DEPARTURE OF MR. BEALE.—DEATH OF SPILLIER.—ASTOR-HOUSE SAILOR.—UNIVERSALIST CHAPLAIN.—A PETREL.—SPEAKING A SHIP.—DEPARTURE OF MR. NORRIS.—CROSSING THE EQUATOR.—SOUTHERN CONSTELLATIONS.—A MAN LOST.—LAND HO!

"The ship was cheered, the harbor cleared,
And merrily did we drop
Below the kirk, below the hill,
Below the lighthouse top."

Friday, Oct. 31. A brilliant soft atmosphere; a light breeze from the southwest; average log, three knots; sounded in thirty-six fathoms; a sand and shell bottom; exercised the men at the guns from 10 to 12 o'clock; loaded the guns a little before sunset. One of the crew, after nightfall, watched his opportunity and knocked down a marine. The aggressor is one of those hardened fellows where the hope of reformation seems to despair in its work. He was flogged but a few days since for an aggravated offense. He has cruised before, and been notorious for his bad conduct. The best thing that could be done with him would be to turn him out of the ship, but the law don't allow this. The next best thing is to try him by a court-martial, and award him a punishment that will linger with terror in his memory. I am opposed to severity when milder measures will avail; but leniency to the incorrigible is destructive of discipline.

Corporal punishments are opposed to the spirit of the age; but he would be worthy a monument who could invent an adequate substitute on board a man-of-war. It is easy to pull down a house, but not so easy to build another on its ruins. Still the power to inflict corporal punishment is so liable to abuse, and *is* so often abused, I do not wonder public sentiment seems to demand its abolition. Could sailors be brought thoroughly under moral influences, it might be easily dispensed with. Virtue has motives and impulses to good conduct stronger than those ever wielded by physical force. The best obedience is that which flows from moral rectitude.

Saturday, Nov. 1. The high temperature of the water, which my boy brought me this morning for bathing, indicated that we were in the Gulf Stream. On inquiry, I ascertained that during the night we had penetrated near to its centre. This great river of the ocean holds its majestic course in seeming independence of the vast and violent elements through which it moves. Storms may howl over it, and conflicting currents fiercely assail it, but it moves on in the tranquil greatness of its unabated strength. It never stops to parley with its adversaries, proposes no terms, accepts none; but like a brave champion of truth, moves steadily to its goal. In its equanimity, its fidelity to one great purpose, and its triumph, the God of Nature utters a moral lesson in the ear of nations.

Our coursers, topsails, top-gallant, and studding-sails are set to a free, fresh wind from the southwest, and we are making ten knots the hour. Our ship has been too much by the stern, but the removal of four of her spar-deck guns from her after to her forward ports, has brought her more by the head, and she sails better. Her constructor conjectured that if deep, she would sail better by being at least fifteen inches by the head. His conjecture turns out to be correct. She is now moving through the waters as if she had an exulting pride in her occupation. I do not wonder sailors regard a fast ship as a thing of life, and speak of her with an affection applicable only to the higher attributes of humanity. She is indeed the highest triumph of human skill—the noblest representative of art.

SUNDAY, NOV. 2. The Sabbath. The force of the wind and the roll of the ship might have excused divine service with those disposed to find an apology for such omission. But we have commenced the cruise with the determination to have service every Sabbath when it is at all practicable. Regularity in this duty promotes regularity in every other. The discipline of a man-of-war lies in the fact that nothing is omitted that ought to be done. Besides what more appropriate for men, tost on the howling waste of the ocean, than a recognised dependence on that Being who binds the elements at his will; who can say to the rushing storm and chainless wave, hitherto shall ye come and no further, and here shall your proud strength be stayed.

Last evening a bird flew on board. He had been driven far out to sea in a gale, and now timidly sought our spars as a place of rest. No one was allowed to molest him for the night; in the morning, turning his eyes in that direction where the land lay, though some three hundred miles off, he bade us adieu and disappeared in the distant horizon. A safe passage to him and a speedy return to those left behind. He too has his home, and those there who make that home dear; and though but a bird of the wild wood, he shares the benevolent regard of One whose care extends to the falling sparrow, and who hears the young raven when it cries. If the bird whose wing is thrown on the wind to-day, and is furled in death to-morrow, may share the guardianship of the great Parent of all, much more man with his boundless sympathies and immortal hopes.

MONDAY, NOV. 3. The wind last night hauled several points to the east, and forced us north of our true course. We have been waiting for it to haul back, but it seems to have settled down as if determined to make itself at home in its new quarter. Well, let it stay there, if it will, and I will ponder these lines which I find inclosed in my last letter from home.

THE SAILOR'S WIFE.

Thou o'er the world and I at home,
But one may linger, the other may roam,
Yet our hearts will flee o'er the sounding sea,
Mine to thy bosom, and thine to me.

Thy lot is the toil of a roving life,
Chances and changes, sorrow and strife—
Yet is mine more drear to linger here—
In a ceaseless, changeless war with fear.

I watch the sky by the stars' pale light,
Till the day-dawn breaketh on gloomy night,
And the wind's low tone hath a dreary moan
That comes to my heart as I weep alone.

With the morning light, oh! would I could see
Thy white sail far on the breaking sea,
And welcome thee home, o'er the wild wave's foam,
And bid thee no more from my side to roam.

TUESDAY, NOV. 4. The sun rose this morning with that look of darkness and flame which the monarch of the seasons puts on when tempests are abroad in his domain. Yet he drove his flashing chariot up the lowering steep of clouds with a fleetness and force which indicated no disposition to resign his sceptre. The glance of his eye kindled the ridges of the black masses around into lines of fire, and revealed the caverns of darkness which stretched away in their unfathomed folds. The roused ocean threw up its howling billows as if in stern defiance. It was evident we were to have a conflict of the giant elements. They rushed into the battle like foes who neither give nor crave quarter.

The roar of the tempest above, the thunder of the sea below, the careering squadrons of clouds, and the dark defiant waves, as they rushed into combat, added sublimity to terror. Our ship was not an idle spectator; she plunged into the thickest of the fight, and with wings furled and a steady keel, presented her frowning mass of exulting courage and strength; she trembled but not with fear, she wavered but not from want of valor. Wave after wave of the great ocean rolled its massive strength against her, but she met each successive shock with dauntless intrepidity. Night at last closed over the conflict, and the lightnings lit the watch-fires of the hostile squadrons. The moon broke through a rift in the black masses, and cast her soft light on the savage features of the scene. So rose she over Thermopylæ, and Waterloo, and blushed at the havoc of human ambition.

Wednesday, Nov. 5. The gale of yesterday increasing at night-fall, we sent down our fore and mizen top-gallant masts, and put our ship under close-reefed main top-sail, fore storm stay-sail, fore and mizen try-sails. Thus she lay like a crouched lion. Darkness was on the face of the deep, save here and there, where a falling meteor threw its transient light on the foaming crest of some towering wave. As the soaring billow combed over, sheets of lighted foam rolled down into the intervening gulfs of night, and then succeeded a darkness that might be felt. As the heavy bell struck the hours, the voices of the watch from different parts of the ship came like broken tones from unseen sources. The hollow sound of the storm through the rigging, made it seem as if the very winds were pouring our death-dirge.

But a little after midnight the gale broke. It broke suddenly as the hope of the wicked at death. But the driving waves still remained, dark and tumultuous as the convulsions of guilt in despair. Our ship, without wind or sail to steady her, plunged blindly about. She had scarcely a dry foot of plank in her, and yet multitudes slept soundly that night.

Such is life at sea. The resistless gale and the dead calm follow each other with the fickleness of an unweaned child over its toys. And proud man submits, as well he may; for he cannot help it. We are always reconciled to that which is remediless. Even death seems to lose its terrors in its inevitability.

THURSDAY, NOV. 6. At quarters, this morning, one of the crew, John Amey, was missing at his post. His name was called through the ship, but there was no reply. All the decks and the hold were searched, but he was nowhere to be found. He was last seen between seven and eight bells of the mid-watch. He had not been well since we left Norfolk, had complained of his head, of an oppression on the brain, and had evinced at times, in the incoherency of his remarks, symptoms of insanity. He had most undoubtedly, in a paroxysm of this disease, jumped out of one of the ports, and perished. The watch might perhaps have heard him as he fell into the water, but for the high sea that was running at the time.

He had shipped from Philadelphia, where he left a sister, of whom he often spoke with tenderness and affection. He was prompt and faithful in the discharge of his duties, and had been promised promotion. But he is now where the frowns or caresses of fortune can never reach him. His sister will long wait and watch for his return, and will long doubt in her amazement and tears the story of his death. But he has gone to that silent bourne from which nor wave, nor sail, nor mariner, has e'er returned, nor one fond farewell word traversed the waters back. He will reappear no more, till the signal-trump of the archangel shall summon the sea to give up her dead. He will then, wrapped in the winding-sheet of the wave, appear at that tribunal where infinite rectitude will sit in judgment on the deeds of men.

Friday, Nov. 7. All hands were mustered this morning on the spar-deck by order of the commodore, and the untimely death of poor Amey was announced to the crew. The chaplain was called upon for such remarks as the melancholy event suggested. After briefly sketching the characteristics of the deceased, his fidelity to duty, his love for his sister, the awful malady of which he died, he told the crew that the sad event impressed one lesson with fearful force upon all, and that was the necessity of a preparation for death and the scenes that await us beyond, while life and reason remain,—that as no one knows the hour or circumstances of his death, his only security lies in that thorough preparation which no event can surprise. The crew listened with attention, as they always do on such occasions; but impressions connected with death are often transient with the sailor. His wild adventurous life is so full of tragedy, that the dead drop through it like pebbles through a stormy wave.

If you would see the most deep and wide impression that death ever produces, go to a quiet country village. You will hear it whispered from house to house, that Henry or Mary is dead! No long array of mourning-carriages darkens the street; but a silent train is there, moving in sympathy and grief to the grave. All gather around that narrow cavern, and as the coffin rumbles down to its rest, tears from the aged and the young fall thick and fast, and each, as he returns to his home, feels that a joy has been extinguished, that a light has fled from his own hearth.

SATURDAY, NOV. 8. Last evening, while a fine breeze was filling our sails, and the white caps were dancing under the light of the stars, a cloud was seen emerging above the bright line of the horizon. It sailed steadily up the blue cope, and at last stationed its dark distended form directly over our ship. All eyes were turned to it, expecting a storm to explode from its folds. But its contents fell in a sheet of water that instantly drenched us all, and utterly annihilated the breeze. The poor dog-vane fell motionless, as if suspended in a grave. The cloud now dissolved, the light of the stars streamed down through the radiant depths of air, and the crushed wind, like an unhorsed rider, resumed its career.

Man, when frustrated in his purposes, slowly, if ever, recovers his courage and force; but nature instantly moves on again in her exulting strength. What to her are crumbling temples and mouldering pyramids? She spreads her verdure over the ruins of nations! In her august domain empires rise and fall with as little sensation as leaves put forth and perish. She hushes the great dirge of human sorrow. Her winds waltz over the graves of ages. All are hers, and all, from the stars that tremble in the blue vault of heaven to the groves of coral which wave over the pavements of the unsounded sea, feel the pulses which throb in her mighty heart. What, then, frail man, is thy pride amid these stupendous attributes and achievements of nature?—a bubble that breaks amid the eternal thunders of the deep.

Nov. 9. Sunday, and a soft breeze from the southwest. The sparkling wave disturbs not the even tenor of our keel. Our ship swings only to the slow and solemn undulations of the ocean. No flapping sail disturbed the quietude of our worship. We sung "old hundred," the band performing the instrumental part. How impressive on the sounding sea is that old majestic tune! It seems in harmony with the many-voiced waves around. The organ-tones of the mighty deep roll it to heaven with a fullness and power which no cathedral choir can pour from its melodious recesses. Nature through all her vast domains awakens and sustains the devotions of the human heart. Our pilgrim fathers worshipped in the sanctuary of the forest. The aisles of the deep wood rang with their hymns of gratitude and praise.

What to them were stately shrines,
Gorgeous dome or towering spire?
'Neath their sturdy oaks and pines,
Rose their anthems, winged with fire.

I distributed tracts to-day to the crew—to all who came to me for them; and few remained behind. It would have encouraged the hearts of those who supply these sources of salutary instruction, to have witnessed the eagerness with which our sailors took them. In a few minutes there were three or four hundred men on the decks of our ship reading tracts; each catching some thought which lures from sin, and throws its clear and tender light on the narrow path which leads to heaven.

Monday, Nov. 10. Our sweet southwest breeze still continues, and we are moving on under an easy sail seven knots the hour. There is not a greater folly on the ocean than for a man-of-war to be crowding on sail, as if speed were the all-predominant motive. This will do for a merchantman, when a market is to be reached as soon as possible; but for a national ship, bound on a three-years' cruise, it is a miserable exhibition of impatience. Indeed, in all the affairs of human life moderation is true philosophy. Our energies will give way soon enough without any forced action. A spirit of restlessness and discontent is one of the most striking faults in the American character. We rush with rail-road speed even on ruin. It is as if a man on his way to the scaffold were to put his horse into a gallop.

We have been for several days past in the vicinity of water-spouts. One of them rose close upon our larboard bow. It towered through several strata of clouds, preserving through each its columnar form till its summit was lost in the sky. We attempted to near it sufficiently to bring it within the range of a cannon-ball, but it seemed to elude our approach as the rainbow the flying footsteps of childhood. Its apparent vicinity was undoubtedly one of those optical delusions so common to the phenomena of the sea. The wonders of the deep belong to their Maker. Man may survey them as a worshipper, but when he attempts to appropriate them, they fly his profane grasp, disarm him with their terrors, or overpower him with their magnificence. We filled away and were again on our course.

Tuesday, Nov. 11. This has been inspection-day. Once a month each sailor is required to exhibit his clothing to the officer who has charge of the division to which he belongs. The object of this inspection is to see that his clothes are in good condition, to see if he wants any thing further for his comfort, and to see that every article of apparel is marked with his name. In this respect sailors are to be treated as children. They require the same constant care. They are the most thoughtless, improvident beings in the world; and if left to themselves, will be, in some instances, without a decent article of clothing, and in others with their whole wages in their clothes-bag. There is no subject on which officers of the navy should exercise so much patience, and such sound paternal judgment. It is a work which brings its own reward in the consciousness of the benefits conferred.

The life of a sailor is brief enough at best. Even with all the care which you can bestow upon his habits, and with all the restraints you can exert upon his headlong career, he soon reaches his goal. You seldom meet with a grayheaded sailor. Long before age can have frosted his locks, the icy hand of death has been laid on his heart. He dies in the midst of his days, and often in his full strength. He perishes like his ship, which the tempest hath cast on the rocks. Could the wave which sepulchres his form be the winding-sheet of his soul, our solicitude for him might be less; but he has a spirit that will sing in worlds of light or wail in regions of wo, when the dirge of the deep sea is over.

Wednesday, Nov. 12. Last evening we had another tropical shower. It fell as if some atmospheric lake had burst its cloudy boundary. In a moment all exposed to it were drenched. It passed, and the moon circled up out of the sea full of mellow light. I love that orb on land, but more at sea. On shore, other objects relieve your solitude, but on the ocean it is all that seems to break the desolation which would else be universal. I have seen sailors sit and look at it by the hour. Few of them understand the laws which regulate its phenomena, but all feel its influence. Nature unrolls her treasures to the simplest of her children.

This morning a fine breeze visited us from the northwest, the first that has cheered us from that quarter. We have been on the starboard tack ever since we left Norfolk. We who occupy the larboard state-rooms, now congratulated ourselves that in the event of a blow, we should have dry quarters, and our starboard companions would take their turn at leaking ports. But this self-gratulation was hardly over, when the wind chopped about to its old quarter, and our exultation, like most exhibitions of selfish delight, proved premature. Our frigate, with a breeze that scarcely crisps the sea, knots her hundred miles a day. This, before steam began to annihilate space, would have been considered very fair travelling. But now it is a tortoise by the side of an antelope. Four bells have struck—my light must be extinguished, and I can either walk the deck or turn in for the night.

THURSDAY, Nov. 13th. I rise with the sun, and, like that stern old monarch, from a salt bath. Like him, too, I take another on retiring to rest. Here, I suppose, ends the resemblance between us, except that both have some spots. They who go to sea for their health should rise with the sun, bathe in salt water, and inhale the fresh atmosphere an hour before breakfast. They should also bathe before they retire to rest. Salt water, the chafing towel, and fresh air, are the restoratives most to be relied on, and the very restoratives which a lazy invalid will first neglect. Were I to omit these, I should hardly live long enough to reach our next port. The invalid should confine himself to a spare diet, and take no stimulants. His only tonic should be the pure salt atmosphere of the sea. Wine, brandy, and porter are sufficiently injurious on land, but at sea they carry disease and death in their train.

We have had this evening an eclipse of the moon;

only a narrow rim of the orb escaped the dark shadow of our earth. Our sailors, not anticipating this eclipse, could not at first account for the disappearing light. They saw the slender spars and tracery of the ship becoming momentarily less distinct and visible, but knew not from whence the shadow fell. A few of them, better versed in lunar observations, explained to the rest the phenomenon. They said the earth had shoved a part of her black hull between us and the moon. But when asked why she had done this, the reason assigned was, that the moon had probably got a little out of her reckoning, and in attempting to tack had missed stays.

Friday, Nov. 14. We have now been fourteen days at sea, and have sailed eighteen hundred miles. A vast sheet of water spreads between us and our homes, but a greater between us and our port of destination. Our fresh provisions still hold out, but the appearance of a junk of corned beef on our table every day indicates the gradual approach of short commons. Still it will be some time before we reach that last dish of gastronomic desperation—lobscouse. We have an experienced caterer, a provident steward, and an ingenious cook. With the three we feel pretty safe. I have been at sea in four or five national ships, and have never found in any, after the second week out, a table so well supplied as ours. Still our variety is effected in a great measure by the ingenuity of our steward and cook.

The culinary art is forced into its highest degree of perfection, and achieves its last triumph at sea. The cook, who, in a Parisian restaurant, can make a palatable soup from the carcass of a crow that has perished of inanition, is entitled to but little praise in comparison with him who can raise a good soup at sea after the third week out. The nautical cook has seemingly nothing left for his pot but the recollections of his coop. Recollections make very good poetry, but they simmer badly into a soup. The attenuation is too fine even for homœopathic gastronomy. It would do, perhaps, for Bishop Berkeley's ideal world. I rather think the worthy bishop must have formed that theory at sea after the third week out. It certainly suits man in that condition. The unstableness of a thing entitles it to faith.

Saturday, Nov. 15. To-day our ship has been holystoned from stem to stern. A person who has stood in the silent excavations of Herculaneum, and heard the carriages rattling overhead, can have some idea of the sounds which those rumbling stones produce on the decks of a ship. The whole ship is converted into a floating Babel, and worse indeed, unless the strokes of the gravel be comprehended in the vocal jargon of the tower. But we shall have our compensation for this in decks so clean that a handkerchief might be swept over them without soiling its whiteness.

Nothing on board a man-of-war requires such unremitted attention as cleanliness. It puts to the last test the most indomitable purpose. Without it, a ship soon becomes intolerable. Without it, sickness would ensue; some epidemic would sweep half the crew to the grave. And yet nine-tenths of our sailors are so inconsiderate, that if left to themselves they would exercise no precautions on the subject. This renders the most careful supervision of officers indispensable. Negligence in this department soils every laurel he can win on the deck. It is like that louse which Burns saw climbing up a lady's bonnet in church. This allusion reminds one of an anecdote related of Lord Byron and Lady Blessington. Her ladyship had taken something that the poet had said in high dudgeon, but dismissed it with the fling that she "didn't care three skips of a louse for his lordship." To which the sarcastic poet retorted in the couplet—

> "I forgive the dear lady what she has said,
> A woman will talk of what runs in her head."

Sunday, Nov. 16. The Sabbath has returned, and we have had divine service. Last night we discovered a sail on our starboard-bow, close hauled upon her wind. This morning we tacked ship and brought her to. She proved to be a brig from Norfolk, bound to Rio de Janeiro. She had been fifty-two days out, with light head-winds. We wished the captain a pleasant voyage, and parted company. We were in hopes she might prove a craft bound to some port in the United States, and that she would take letters back from us. We were disappointed; our friends must wait for letters from our port of destination. It will probably be six months from our departure before they will get a line from us.

You who cannot leave your wives and children for a week, without intelligence from them, go to sea with the prospect that we have, of not hearing from them for a year. The truth is, none but old bachelors and hen-pecked husbands should go to sea. The latter flies from persecution, the former from that wretchedness which a sight of real domestic happiness inflicts. The bliss of Eden made even Satan more wretched than he was before. But the ocean is itself a rich domain. The treasures of empires lie in its depths. The wrecks of the richest argosies are hers; and her waves roll over the unsurrendered forms of matchless beauty. She gives back nought that comes within her vast embrace. Her great seal of proprietorship will be broken only by the thunders of the last trump.

MONDAY, NOV. 17. Our ship has been tantalized all day with a light head-wind—just one of those winds that are but little better than none; the only advantage it has over a dead calm is the air it affords. As for progress, we might as well be

"A painted ship upon a painted ocean."

How dependent is a ship on the elements! Let the winds refuse to visit us, and this noble frigate would never move from her present position; she would rot down piece-meal where she is now lying, with the bleaching bones of five hundred men on her decks. But the winds are at the bidding of Him whose pavilion is in the clouds, and whose mandates are nature's resistless law. May we ever live in humble submission to His will, and rejoice that He reigns; feeling fully assured that His measures are dictated by infinite wisdom, and by an unerring regard to the happiness of His creatures.

I found in the sick-bay to-day a patient laboring under a typhoid fever, and apparently near his end. He spoke to me of his mother and his sisters, and tears filled his eyes. The first being that rushes to the recollections and heart of a sailor, smitten with disease at sea, is his mother. She still clings to his memory and affection in the midst of all the forgetfulness and hardihood induced by a roving life. The last message he leaves is for her; his last dying whisper breathes her name. The mother as she instills the lessons of piety and filial obligation upon the heart of her infant son, should always feel that her labor is not in vain. She may drop into her grave, but she has left behind influences that will work for her. The bow is broken, but the arrow is sped and will do its office.

TUESDAY, Nov. 18. Another day of light airs. Our sails hang as pertinaciously to our masts as a veil over the features of one whose imaginary beauty has touched your heart. We discovered another sail to-day over our weather-bow, hull down. Conjecture makes her the Courier, which sailed from Hampton Roads two or three days before us. There is an interest in speaking a vessel at sea, which they who dwell on land can hardly realize. These nautical greetings are all that break the vast solitude of the ocean. Without them a ship would be more lonely than the solitary traveller on the desert of Sahara, for *he* will now and then encounter a gazelle.

A sailor's life is one of constant privations. He makes his meals from bread which the hammer can scarcely break, and from meat often as juiceless and dry as the bones which it feebly covers. The fresh products of the garden and the fruits of the field have all been left behind. As for a bowl of milk, which the child of the humblest cottager can bring to its lips, it is as much beyond his reach as the nectar which sparkled in the goblets of the fabled divinities on Ida. When Adam went forth from his lost Eden, under the frown of God, he had still a confiding companion at his side, to share with him the sorrows of his lot, and he still found some flowers amid the briers and brambles which infested his path; but the sailor finds no flowers springing up along the pathway of the sea, and he has no consoling companion there, except in his dreams of some far-off shore.

Wednesday, Nov. 19. We have three sailors in the sick-bay to-day, in a very critical condition. They are all good men, so far at least as ship duty is concerned. Their death would make a serious breach in our crew. Our intelligent surgeon and his faithful assistants are devoted to them. They are not left night or day, for an hour, without a medical attendant. Commodore Stockton went into the sick-bay to-day to see them. He never forgets the sailor. He pities when others might reproach, forgives when others might denounce, and never abandons him even though he should abandon himself; and yet he exacts prompt obedience. His discipline, and that of Capt. Du Pont, is derived in a great measure from moral influences, the power of correct example and the pressure of circumstance.

Make the moral mechanism of a ship like a piece of well-contrived machinery, and but few blows will be required to keep it in order. But this requires energy in the details. It is much easier to flog a man who has committed an error, than it is to train him to avoid that error. Indolence flies to the lash, enlightened activity to a system of correct training, which is to be pressed at all points. And this training must be consistent with itself. It will not succeed if it is to be broken in upon constantly by brute force, or by language as disreputable to the officer who uses it, as it is unjust and provoking to the men to whom it is addressed. Profane or opprobrious epithets are a mockery of all discipline, except that which is enforced by the lash. An officer incapable of enforcing any other discipline, is a calamity to the service.

THURSDAY, Nov. 20. We discovered, this morning, a brig on our weather-beam, standing down for us, and hove-to with our main top-sail to the mast. She run up Danish colors, and in an hour hove-to at a cable's length under our lee-quarter. We lowered a boat and boarded her. She proved to be the brig Mariah, forty days from Rio Grande, bound to Hamburg. We inquired for fruit, but she had none. The captain wished to correct his reckoning, and well he might, for he was seven degrees out of his longitude.

Mr. Beale, our second master, took passage in her for the United States. It was arranged between him and the captain of the brig, that he should be put on board the first vessel that they might fall in with bound to an American port, and if they fell in with none before that, he should be landed at Dover, England. The captain must have had a very flexible policy. When it was understood that letters could be sent back, pens that had slumbered for weeks woke up. In half an hour the commodore had finished his communications, our home-letters were written, and Mr. Beale was passing over the side. In reaching the boat, a box of segars and a revolving-pistol fell overboard. Strange as it may seem, the pistol floated a moment, and was saved, while the segars were lost. I watched the letter-bag, saw that safe in, thought of the satisfaction it would give, and forgot the Havanas. Though the sea was running high, Mr. Beale reached the brig safely, and our boat returned. The little vessel then squared away, and we made sail; and thus we parted, the one for Hamburg, the other for Rio. How the paths of life cross each other!

FRIDAY, Nov. 21. Poor Spillier, whose critical condition I have watched for several days in the sick bay, has passed beyond hope. His disease has passed into pneumonia, and his lungs have already ceased, in a great measure, to perform their functions. I told him to-day he could not live. The sad intelligence brought tears to his eyes. He said it was dreadful to die away from his friends, and be buried in the sea. I told him his mother died a good Christian and had gone to heaven, and he could go there and meet her. But he must bring all the errors and sins of his life, and with sincere sorrow and contrition, lay them at the foot of the cross, and implore divine forgiveness. He was silent for a few minutes, and then uttered a brief and appropriate prayer, confessing his manifold transgressions, and casting himself on the compassion of Christ.

He was silent again, and seemed absorbed in thought. The expressions of mental anguish and hope alternated over his pale features like cloud and sunlight over a landscape. He now became composed, and opening his large swimming eyes upon me, thanked me for my attentions to him, and requested me to write his sisters; to give them his dying love; to say that he died in Christ and hoped to go to heaven, where he should see their mother. He told me that the dread of being buried at sea had left him; that it was no matter where his poor body was laid, if his soul was saved; that his blessed mother would know him and would be the first to greet him. How the ties of a mother's love fasten upon her child, soothing the couch of pain and triumphing over the terrors of the grave!

Saturday, Nov. 22. We have a stiff wind to-day from the southeast, and we are running, close hauled, under reefed top-sails. The sea is high, and every now and then a huge wave throws its curling crest through some half-closed port, as a wolf pounces into a sheep-fold, or as the arch adversary o'erleaped the green wall of Eden. Though we are any thing but Eden, with its beauty and its bliss: our first parent would have had but little cause of regret, if, in resigning Eden, he had relinquished only the habitudes of a sea-life. A wigwam might have consoled him for his loss. No Milton had sung—

> "Of man's first disobedience, and the fruit
> Of that forbidden tree, whose mortal taste
> Brought death into the world, and all our woe,
> With loss of Eden."

The truth is, man was never intended for a nautical being. He was made perfect, but he has sought out many inventions; and this going to sea is one of them. His pathway on the deep is hedged about with storms, icebergs, water-spouts, and breakers. But, in the strange perversity of his nature, he perseveres through the whole of them. He knows and feels that he is a fool in his nautical obstinacy, and yet he clings to it, as the inebriate to the cup that consumes his vitals. He seems to court hardship for its own sake, and to court peril for the excitement which it bestows. But for the indecency of the thing he would toll, in advance, his own funeral-bell, that its fearful monotone might tremble on his heart before it should be cold. And he would almost dig his own grave, that he might hear his coffin rumbling down to its rest.

SUNDAY, NOV. 23. Another Sabbath morn has poured its holy light on land and sea. On land, the stir of the village and the tumult of the great city have ceased. Men walk softly in the prelude of that rest which remains to the good. Sacred truth melts on their hearts like dew. No community in a Christian land can be utterly bereft of moral influence. If it has none from within, there is a pressure from without. The moral as well as physical atmosphere tends to an equilibrium. Righteous Lot may have fled from Sodom, but his warning voice rolled back upon the wind to the doomed city.

But a ship is cut off by its position from all extraneous influences. It is like a ball suspended in the centre of a hollow sphere. This isolation has placed it beyond the reach, and seemingly beyond the sympathies, of those who dwell on the land. They have regarded it as a thing apart from themselves, a thing with which they had no common bond of brotherhood, and they have abandoned it to its calamities and its crimes. When guilt and misery have done their worst, when the pirate-flag has been unfurled where the insignia of commerce streamed before, instead of accusing their own apathy and negligence, they have seemed to regard the terrible spectacle as some singular exemplification of divine justice—as some malignant star accursed and made

"A wandering hell in the eternal space."

MONDAY, NOV. 24. Yesterday morning, as the men left their hammocks, the ominous whisper went round—"Spillier is dead!" He had died during the night, while storm and darkness rested on the face of the deep. Last evening, as the sun was going down, we consigned him to his floating grave. The deep-toned call, "All hands to bury the dead!" went like a knell through the ship. The body, wrapped in that hammock in which the deceased had swung to the force of the wind, was borne by his messmates, preceded by the chaplain of the ship, from the gun-deck up the forward hatch, and round the capstan to the lee-side; the band, with muffled drums, playing the "dead-march," and the marine-guard presenting arms. The commodore, the captain, and officers of the ship, took their position near the main-mast; the crew were stationed forward.

Then commenced the burial-service: "I am the resurrection and the life, saith the Lord; he that believeth in me, though he were dead yet shall he live; and whosoever believeth in me shall never die." When the solemn sentence was uttered, "We commit this body to the deep," the inner end of the plank was lifted, and down its steep plane moved the hammocked dead, and a hoarse hollow sound followed the heavy plunge. The waters closed over the disappearing form—the ship glided on as before. Then, with impressive effect, came in the words, "Looking for the general resurrection in the last day, and the life of the world to come, through our Lord Jesus Christ, at whose second coming in glorious majesty to judge the world, the earth and sea shall give up their dead, and the corruptible bodies of those who sleep in Him shall be changed, and made like unto His own glorious body, according to the mighty working whereby He is able to subdue all things unto Himself." The benediction followed, and the crew returned in silence to their stations.

Reader, when you die, it will be, I trust, in the sabbath calm of your hushed chamber; but the poor sailor dies at sea between the narrow decks of his rolling vessel. The last accents that will reach your ears will be those of kindness and affection, such as flow from a mother's care, and a sister's solicitude; the last sounds that reach the ears of the dying sailor are the hoarse murmurs of that wave which seems to complain at the delay of its victim. You will be buried beneath the green tree, where love and grief may go to plant their flowers and cherish your virtues; but the poor sailor is hearsed in the dark depths of the ocean, there to drift about, in its under-currents, to the great judgment-day. Alas, for the poor sailor! the child of misfortune, impulse, and error: his brief life filled with privation, hardship, and peril; his grave in the foaming deep! Though man pity him not, may God remember his weaknesses and trials in the day of his last account.

TUESDAY, Nov. 25th. We have had for two days past a steady breeze from the southeast, and have run an average of seven knots the hour. We are now in the hope of making Rio in twenty days from this time. This will make our whole passage forty-six days,—not a bad run. The Columbia was ninety-three days making the same passage; but it was at the most unfavorable season of the year. To take this as a specimen of her sailing would be doing great injustice to that noble frigate.

WEDNESDAY, Nov. 26th. We are to-day in lat. 18° 49 N., long. 33° 46′ W., with a light steady breeze from the southeast. We are knocked off to the west of our course. We ought to head east of south, even with the variation in our favor. We are anxious to cross the line at twenty-seven or eight, to avoid the head winds of Cape St. Roque. We are where we ought to have the northeast trades, but we have not yet had a puff of wind from that quarter. Unless our present breeze hauls or dies we shall be obliged to tack, which will be about as agreeable as running back in a railroad-car to make way for a locomotive ahead, when you are in haste to get on. But we have one thing to console us, it is all in the cruise, so let the winds blow as they list.

The hammers of our blacksmiths are heard this morning, the first time for some days. They have been silenced on account of the sick; but they are now going as if determined to make up lost time. Iron takes almost every shape under their blows. A ship's blacksmith has no such word as can't in his vocabulary. He takes his order, and tries to shape his iron accordingly, though he may know it to be utterly impracticable. We had on board the Natchez an old time-piece which had broken its main-spring. The first lieutenant, for fun, told the blacksmith to take it to the anvil and put a new main-spring in it. Hearing the puff of the bellows and the click of the hammer, I went forward, where I found the old watch taken to pieces, and the worthy representative of Vulcan, beating with his full force a piece of iron. "What are you doing with this time-piece?" I inquired. "Making a kinked-up sort of a thing, sir, to make it go," was the sardonic reply.

THURSDAY, NOV. 27. The wind hauled round into our teeth last evening. We tacked to the east, and headed east by north through the night. But the wind soon became too light for us to make much progress in any direction. Instead of trade-winds, these fickle puffs ought to be called the variables. No coquette was ever half so inconstant. The only certain thing about them is the lightning, which has been throwing its cables of flame from its aerial craft. I have often thought a thunder-cloud might be the chariot of the prince of darkness. But let that pass: digression is my besetting infirmity.

This morning, large masses of cloud broke the horizon in the east with their dark distended forms. The sun coming up behind them, converted their jagged outline into fire, and poured over their steep precipices torrents of flame. We predicted a strong wind from that quarter. But one battlement after another tumbled from this cloudy fortress, till only a few tottering bastions remained, and these soon dissolved,

> "And like an unsubstantial vision faded,
> Left not a wreck behind."

We felt as much disappointed as a confident lover

getting a blank refusal. How singular it is that the enamored youth always ascribes the first negative to female delicacy, and the second to the hostility of some one of her friends. He still believes she loves him, and would say so if her heart could only speak out. Perhaps this amiable weakness has been placed in our nature to relieve disappointment, and suppress an indignant tone from wounded pride.

FRIDAY, NOV. 28. This morning our vanished clouds reappeared on the eastern horizon, and as they lifted, a strong wind streamed down from that quarter, and we were able to lay our course. We shook the only reef out of our top-sails, and at seven bells set our top-gallant-sails. The sky had that light haze upon it peculiar to the tropics. The sun melts through it, instead of throwing its full burning beams. The appearance of the atmosphere resembles in some respects that of the Indian summer in other climes, but it is more humid and softer. In the afternoon the wind became so stiff that our ship fairly staggered under it. Her lee-guns knocked the caps from the waves. We now took in our top-gallant-sails. At sunset we took a reef in our top-sails and courses; but still plunged ahead sufficiently fast.

Our frigate returned from her last cruise with a brilliant reputation for speed,—a reputation which she has not sustained thus far with us. Some ascribe this loss of character to a foul bottom; but the three thousand miles which we have run, must have pretty well scoured her copper. Others ascribe it to her lying so deep; but this difficulty every day is removing in the consumption of provisions and water. We shall soon be able to settle the truth or fallacy of this supposition. The truth is, a ship often loses her sailing and recovers it again without any satisfactory reason. The United States, one of the best sailors in the service, once lost her reputation entirely, but recovered it again; and our frigate will, I doubt not, regain her laurels. Our commodore and captain are studying her points as anxiously as a gentleman of the turf those of a race-horse that has had the misfortune to be beaten once.

Saturday, Nov. 29th. Our east wind still holds steady and strong; we are running nine and ten knots on our course. This has put us all in fine spirits, notwithstanding the wet condition of our frigate. Only give a sailor a good ten-knot breeze on his course, and he wont complain, if he wades in water to the chin. Some of us had a fine shower-bath to-day. We were reading on the half deck between the weather guns, when we shipped a tremendous sea through the ports, which half buried us in its surge. Our chairs slipped up, and we were tumbling about like porpoises. One of the crew, at least, laughed in his sleeve.

This reminds me of an occurrence on board the Vincennes. We had been in a gale for two days, which at last broke suddenly, leaving a high sea. Governor V. S., of Santa Cruz, whom we were taking out as passenger, when the gale had broken, sent an invitation to the wardroom officers to come to the cabin and take a glass of whisky-punch with him. Total abstinence not being at that time the order of the day, we all went up. The governor stated that he had one bottle of very old Irish whisky with him, which would make a capital punch. Tumblers were ordered; the hot water, whisky, and sugar, in due proportions, mixed and stirred. Now, said the governor, please take your glasses, gentlemen, and I will propose one sentiment; each lifted his glass, when a tremendous sea struck us under the counter, and pitched us all in a mass together on the floor. Whisky, glasses, and sentiment all came down in one crash. The first thing I heard was the exclamatory inquiry of the governor, —"Captain Shubrick, are we still afloat?"

SUNDAY, Nov. 30th. We were apprehensive that our sabbath worship would be broken in upon, by a dash of rain from some of the clouds that were driving over our ship. But only a few drops fell.

Sailors have but very little respect for fair-weather Christians. They believe the course to heaven lies through a stormy sea, and that a man to get there must battle with hostile elements. They like plain, direct preaching, full of heart and strength. They cannot tolerate a display of literature, or metaphysical acumen, in a sermon. They know they are wicked and unfit for heaven, and they wish to be told so. The man who should tell them otherwise would at once forfeit their confidence.

A gentleman of the Universalist persuasion was once appointed a chaplain in the navy, and reported for duty on board one of our ships fitting for sea. His creed soon became known to the sailors, and was freely discussed in their messes. "If we are all so good that we are going to heaven," said an old tar, "what is the use in overhauling one's sins? it only gives a man a bloody sight of trouble for nothing." "If we are all on the right tack," said another, "and must bring up at the right port, what is the use in preaching and praying about it?" "If we trust this doctrine, and it don't turn out true, there'll be hell to pay," exclaimed a third. These sentiments were shared in by the whole crew, and soon became known to the newly-appointed chaplain. He resigned his commission, and showed a considerateness in doing it which entitles him to respect. Sailors, ignorant and wicked as they are, can never be made to believe that the good and bad bring up at last in the same port.

MONDAY, DEC. 1. Our fine east wind, which has been shoving us on at the rate of two hundred and thirty miles a day, was crossed this afternoon by a squall from the south, and knocked under. We watched its overthrow with grief, and expected for some time that it would rally and overpower its antagonist. But victory remained with the foe, and we were driven from our course. In the mean time, a tropical shower, falling without premonition, has drenched all on duty to the skin.

These reverses fall hardest upon the *gentlemen* among the crew. We have one, an Englishman by birth, who was living a few months since at the Astor House, drinking the choicest wines the hotel could furnish, and promenading Broadway in white kid gloves, with gold-headed cane and quizzing-glass. But suddenly, from some freak of nature, he threw himself into our ship as a common sailor. He is about twenty years of age, full six feet high, and extremely well proportioned. He has a small foot and hand, an open cheerful countenance, large floating eye, and hair that falls in showering ringlets. He is willing and prompt in the performance of every duty. But what a transition! The Astor House for a wet rolling deck, its beds of down for a hammock, its rich viands and desserts for salt junk and hard tack. The last London cut in coat, pants, and beaver, for a blue roundabout, ducks, and tarpaulin, and a gold-headed cane for a tarred rope! And yet he is cheerful, and seemingly ambitious of excelling as a sailor. How nature accommodates herself to circumstances!

Tuesday, Dec. 2. Poor Lynch, one of our crew, from the state of Maine, died last evening, and we have to-day, as the sun was setting, committed his remains to the deep. He has left a pious mother, of whom he often spoke to me in his last sickness. She seemed to be the strongest tie that fastened him to earth. Her early lessons of piety awoke with singular power as his end approached. They crowded thick and fast upon his heart; he clung to them as something that could stay him, something that could lift him above present suffering and future apprehension. He died under the light of these sentiments, and in an humble hope of the happiness which they promise to the pure and meek.

At the call, "All hands to bury the dead!" the officers and crew took their stations. The body, wound in its hammock, and preceded by the chaplain, was brought up the fore hatch and round the capstan to the waist, the band playing the "dead-march," and the marine-guard presenting arms. The service was read, and the hollow sound of the hammocked dead descending through the sea, told that another of our crew had left us for ever. This is the third that we have lost within less than thirty days. The death of a man in a crowded town is little felt, but in a ship's crew it leaves a vacuum which all observe. Still, these bereavements are so blended with the vicissitudes of a sea life, that they fail to make a permanent impression; they are felt deeply for the moment and then glide away.

> "As from the wing the sky no scar retains,
> The parted wave no furrow from the keel,
> So dies in human hearts the thought of death."

WEDNESDAY, DEC. 3. Our trade-wind has left us utterly. We have had a regular Irishman's hurricane—up and down. The rain fell in a perfect avalanche; with all the scuppers open, the water became, in a few minutes, almost knee deep on the spar-deck. The rolling of the ship threw it over the combings of the hatches, and down it came upon the gun-deck, and then took another leap below, flooding the ward-room, steerage, and berth-deck. With the hatches covered, and the external air excluded, the heat below soon became intolerable. Our choice lay between being roasted or drenched. Most of us preferred the latter, and emerged into the drifting sea above.

In the midst of these troubles, our cook came aft

and informed our caterer that the water came in such floods into the galley, that he could not keep fire enough alive to light his pipe by. This was good news for our last pig, who looked out from his gratings as one that has another day to live. I always pity the last tenant of the coop and sty. He looks so lonely, so disconsolate in the midst of that voiceless solitude, which the untimely death of his companions has spread around him, that I could never have the heart to kill him. It seems like extinguishing the last of a race. Indeed, I would never take the life of any thing, unless it was in the way in which the Irishman thought his squirrel might have been killed. Two of them were gunning, and had treed a large squirrel upon a very high limb. One of them, a little more experienced at the business, lifted and fired his old Queen's-arm; down came the squirrel with a bone-breaking crash; when the other exclaimed, "An' faith, you might as well have spared your pooder, the fall itself would ha' kilt him."

Thursday, Dec. 4. We caught, two days since, a stormy petrel. As the bird was brought on board, the old sailors around shook their heads with ominous looks of dissatisfaction. "We'll have a blow for that," said an old salt; and sure enough, before the wings of the petrel were dry a storm set in. "We'll have no more fair weather," said another, "till that petrel is put back into the sea." "I knew a ship," exclaimed a third, "that had a forty days' gale for having killed a petrel; and if that bird dies on board, we'll escape a wreck by the skin of our teeth, or we'll rot down in a dead calm." Our storm continued without any token of abatement, and last evening the ominous bird was returned in safety to its element. The clouds soon swept past, the sun emerged into a bright sapphire sky, and a leading wind from the southeast sprung up.

How far the return of the petrel to the sea influenced this auspicious change in the elements, I leave to the decision of those who have more or less philosophy than myself. I must confess I was glad to see the petrel go back. There is a sacredness attached to this bird that should exempt it from violence. It is supposed to be the form in which the spirit of some one, who has been sepulchred in the sea, still floats in troubled light, and that when its penance is passed, it will be translated to some higher form which the gale and the breaker can never reach. This may all be superstition, but it is a glimmering of the great truth of man's immortality. He who believes that man can survive death in the shape of a bird, is more than half way to the belief that he can survive in the form of an angel.

It is a tranquil eve; our ship is gliding quietly on;

my thoughts, unoccupied here, run warmly back to those left behind—to the loved and lost

CATHARA.

The evening star sleeps in the moon's pale rim,
 And slumber rocks the weary world to rest;
Nor wakes a sound except the vesper hymn
 Of pines, that murmur on the mountain's crest;
And now, at this lone hour, fond thoughts of thee
Melt o'er my heart as music on the sea.

But thou hast gone, hast winged thy silent flight
 O'er Death's dim waters to the spirit-land;
Thy faith discerned its hills of purple light
 Ere yet thy footstep left our mortal strand;
As closed the shadows on thy farewell track,
A whisper of thy bliss came floating back.

It came too soft and low for Echo's breath,
 And died, with tender transport in its tone;
But ere it ceased, it reached the ear of Death,
 And shook the sable monarch on his throne;
He knew the omen, which that whisper gave,
Would burst one day in thunder from the grave.

Friday, Dec. 5. We are to-day in lat. 3° 23′ n., long. 28° 20′ w. We have a steady but light breeze from the southeast, and are heading south by southwest, with half a point westerly variation. We shall cross the line if this wind holds, and there is now little prospect of change, at 30°. This is three or four degrees further west than most ships bound to

Rio de Janeiro venture to cross it at. Still, unless we encounter westerly currents on the other side of the line, we expect to be able to double Cape San Roque, and proceed directly to our port. Should we be disappointed, we shall be obliged to make a long tack to the northeast, which may keep us many days longer at sea. But we are going to make the experiment, and must bide the consequences. Nothing can be less certain than a ship's progress. Even those winds deemed regular and almost infallible by mariners, seem now and then infected with the last degree of fickleness and perversity.

We have now been thirty-six days at sea without an isle or promontory to break the dim horizon, or relieve the vast rolling waste of waters. Harmony and good feeling prevail among the officers. There has not been the slightest clash of feeling between our Captain and those who carry on duty under him. And yet the most energetic forms of discipline have been maintained. The crew are cheerful and active. Punishments have been very rare. The cats have been used but once since we weighed anchor. Efficiency has been secured by a thorough attention to details on the part of Mr. Livingston, our first lieutenant, and the watch officers.

SATURDAY, DEC. 6. We are now within one degree of the equator. But the wind having hauled round one point east of south, we have been obliged to go upon our starboard tack to avoid crossing it too far to the west. We shall probably have made sufficient easting by to-morrow noon to make a dash over it. Then for a new hemisphere and new constellations. But we have a splendid moon to-night, directly in the centre of the great dome of heaven. Our masts cast no shadow. This position gives the moon a much greater apparent distance than it has when near the horizon. It now seems as some heaven-born sphere, that, having in vain tried to win you from the cares of earth, has gone back with melancholy countenance to its choiring sisterhood on high.

> "There's not the smallest orb, which thou behold'st,
> But in his motion, like an angel, sings,
> Still choiring to the young-eyed cherubim."

We had a visit, a few evenings since, from a whale. We were lying in a dead calm, when this monster saluted us like a locomotive blowing off steam. The column of brine which he threw up with his great forcing-pump, fell in a sparkling shower. Man constructs his fountain with great cost and pains, and when all is done, it can play only in that one place: but the whale moves about, throwing up his brilliant cascade at will in every zone. The springs may fail, the streams forsake their channels, but this showering column still soars from a source exhaustless as the mighty deep. Give me the whale and ocean for a fountain, and you may do what you please with your drizzling pipes and frog-ponds.

Sunday, Dec. 7th. At eleven o'clock, the tolling of the ship's bell announced the hour of worship. The officers took their accustomed station on the starboard-quarter; the marines on the poop-deck; the crew on the larboard-quarter, stretching back to the waist and circling the main-mast to the opposite side; the band and singers between the after-hatches; Mr. Ten Eyche and Mr. Turrel, with their families, forming a group between the officers and marines. The commodore, being informed by the captain that the crew were assembled for worship, appeared and took his station on the left of the officers. The chaplain then took his station at the capstan, which was covered with a large flag, when the band played the impressive air to the words, "O come and let us worship."

We sung the missionary hymn—"From Greenland's icy mountain"—a hymn for which sailors have the greatest partiality. The splendid imagery of this hymn, and the rich melody of the music, always take hold of the sailor. It has something of the same effect on him, which the impassioned eloquence of Peter the Hermit must have had, when he poured the population of Europe, in tumultuous crusades, on the bosom of Asia. If sailors could win their way to heaven with weapons of war, there is no act of hardship or daring from which they would shrink. But when you throw them back upon their own hearts, and confine them to the enemy found there, they are too apt to make a truce; still, so far are they from being unsusceptible of religious impression, that could I at all times select my auditory and place of worship, I would take a ship of the line with her thousand sailors on her spar deck; and, if I failed of making an impression there, I should despair of making it anywhere.

Monday, Dec. 8th. The watch in the main-top discovered this morning, at break of day, a sail just peering up over the swelling sweep of the sea. She was hull down; indeed, the little canvas that loomed to the eye might easily have been mistaken for one of those small sheets of vapor which seem blent with the spray of a wave. But sail after sail emerged into vision till her hull broke with its dark mass the bright line of the horizon. She came down to us before the wind, with her royals and studding-sails set, and with the American ensign flying from her mizen-peak.

She proved to be the whale-ship Jason, of New London; twelve days from St. Helena; bound home. She had been out on her whaling expedition seventeen months, and had secured in that time twenty-eight thousand gallons of oil, and forty-six thousand pounds of whalebone. The second mate, a noble tough tar, who came on board, told us that his portion of the spoil would be eight hundred dollars. He wanted some powder and shot to keep off the Mexicans. We told him there was no war with Mexico; still he should be welcome to some ammunition, certainly enough to fire a salute as he wound into the harbor of New London.

All pens were now put in motion to dispatch letters home. Go where you would, fore or aft, nothing was to be heard but the scratch of these pens. What surprised me most was the number of sailors who were driving the quill. How they can carry paper in their clothes-bags unrumpled, where every thing else is mussed up, is more than I can explain. But of all beings the sailor is most fertile in expedients. He stows away every thing in his clothes-bag, from a mirror to a marlin-spike, from a cable to a cambric needle, and has plenty of room remaining.

The captain of the Jason kindly offered to take any officer to the United States whom the commander-in-chief might wish to dispatch. Our commodore fixed on Mr. Morris, his secretary, who was very desirous of going; and having given him an outfit, in the shape of provisions and funds, equal to all emergencies, instructed him to get the President's message, the proceedings of Congress, all the news of the day, with letters for the officers of the ship, take the first packet to Chagres, cross over to Panama, and join him at the nearest point practicable. The letters now being bagged, a boat was called away, Mr. Morris took leave of us, and was soon on the deck of the Jason. The sturdy whaler squared round before the wind, we filled away, and when the sun went down were once more alone on the ocean.

Each seemed lost in thoughts of the surprise and pleasure which the letters he had thus unexpectedly been able to send back would awaken. One of our best young sailors told me his mother would weep for joy over his letter, and sleep for a month with it under her pillow. No eloquence that ever flowed from human lips affected me half so much as the simple remark of this dutiful sailor. There was a tenderness, a truthfulness, a moral beauty in it, which made me forget the rough exterior of the being from whom it came. He seemed as a brother whom I could take to my heart, and whose hard lot I could most cheerfully share. That man who can forget his mother, who can forget the sorrows and solicitudes which she has endured for him, and the lessons of piety which she instilled into his young mind, has sundered the last tie that binds him to virtue and a reasonable hope of heaven.

TUESDAY, DEC. 9. Our painters commenced to-day painting our gun-carriages black. They had a coat of white paint when we left port, but it soon became dingy and defaced by the rough-and-tumble of sea usage. Black paint can easily be restored; a few coats of varnish will make it shine like a Congo under his native sun. The objects to be aimed at in the use of paint on board a man-of-war are neatness, preservation, economy in money and time. There is nothing fantastic, but all is substantial and enduring. It is in harmony with the solid oak out of which the storm-defying fabric is itself constructed.

I have been attached to ships where the belaying-pins, the midship-stanchions, and even crowbars, were bright work. The amount of labor bestowed upon them during a three years' cruise, might, if properly directed, have almost constructed another ship equal to that of which these are mere blacksmith appendages. Were sailors merely unthinking machines, it might do to keep them employed on such work; but as it is, the idea will often force itself upon them that their labor is a frivolous waste of time. This renders them impatient and remiss, and this impatience and remissness soon extends to their other duties. Keep sailors employed, but let them feel that their employment is working out some adequate ends. No man will continue to roll an empty wheelbarrow, however liberally paid for his services.

Wednesday, Dec. 10. This morning, with our royals set to a steady southeaster, we dashed across the equator at longitude thirty. That great circle, cutting the continents, mountains, oceans, and islands of the globe asunder, now threw its steep plane between us and the thousand objects to which memory clings with affection and pride. The sunset clouds on which we had gazed, the towering crags where morn first broke, and the brilliant constellations which faith had peopled with the spirits of the pure and meek, all went down in dying pomp over the dim horizon. What now to us Niagara's thunder, or the rush of the Alpine avalanche! Even the polar star, that has poured its steady light for ages on the ruins of pyramids, the wrecks of temples, and the graves of empires, has left its watch-tower in darkness,—all are lost in the shoreless ocean of night.

Old Neptune formerly saluted every ship that crossed the line. He appeared in the shape of some tall sturdy tar, in ox-hide mail, with a long beard of yarn falling far below his chin, and locks of the same flowing in drenched ringlets down his shoulders. His trident was a huge harpoon, his pipe the coiled hose of the fire-engine; thus accoutred, he hailed the ship over her bows, and mounting a gun-carriage, was drawn aft to the quarter-deck. Here he summoned the green horns to his presence, and after lathering them from a tub of grease and tar, shaved them with a ship's scraper. Having thus introduced the novice into his service, he returned in triumph to his watery realm. This ceremony was found such an infraction of discipline, that it has been discontinued on board our national ships. Our sailors were allowed to splice the main-brace as a substitute.

THURSDAY, DEC. 11. A delicate question of discipline occurred to-day. The master's mate of the gun-deck, finding the captain of the main-top behind the rest in lashing and stowing his hammock, ordered him to clean the bell,—a menial service, and intended as a punishment. The captain of the main-top, knowing the order to be illegal and derogatory to his position, declined compliance. He was reported to the officer of the deck and confined. All this had taken place without the knowledge of the first lieutenant or the commander. When known to them, the facts were promptly inquired into. I felt some interest in seeing how Captain Du Pont would dispose of the question.

The illegality of an order, though it may mitigate the offence, cannot for a moment justify disobedience. Such a doctrine would make every man a judge in his own case, and overthrow discipline. He must obey the order, and seek redress at its proper source. The offender saw his error, as exhibited to him by Captain Du Pont, and said he should submit to any punishment which the government of the ship required. That was enough; he was one of our best men, this his first offence, and Captain Du Pont very properly at once restored him to duty. Now what would have been the moral effect of inflicting chastisement on that man, as some, in a spirit of haste, might have done. It might have broken his ambition. It would certainly have reduced him to a lash-level with the hardened culprit. It would have relieved punishment of some portion of the shame which attaches to it. The bad always exult when they see any portion of their disgrace transferred to the good; therefore never punish a good faithful sailor for the first offence into which he may be betrayed, if there is any way of getting round it. Let his virtues

"Plead for him like angels, trumpet-tongued."

Friday, Dec. 12. We have had, for three days, the regular trade-wind from the southeast, and have been running under royals and studding-sails, from seven to ten knots the hour. The thermometer has ranged at 75, the air has been balmy, and the sky free of clouds. What a contrast to the weather of the line,—where a cloud gathered before you could turn your eye, and where showers fell like water from some vast reservoir, with the bottom suddenly knocked out!

A flying-fish, hard-pressed by a dolphin, took refuge

on the deck of our ship. He might as well have remained in the sea, for he was instantly secured by one of our sailors, and presented by him to a lady passenger, who, with too little feeling, fried and ate him. It is true he had the satisfaction of being eaten by a lady, which was perhaps preferable to being swallowed by a dolphin. How many frantic lovers there are who would like to be eaten up by their mistress! Besides, it is in much better taste to dispose of one's self in this way, than making a plunge into the sea to feed a hungry shark. Still, for one, I should not like to see a woman coming at me with a frying-pan.

Our batteries, in their black paint, look solid and uncompromising. Their threatening strength reminds one of the terrific lines of Campbell, in the Battle of the Baltic:—

> "When each gun,
> From its adamantine lips,
> Spread a death-shade round the ships
> Like the hurricane's eclipse
> Of the sun."

SATURDAY, DEC. 13. A booby was seen last evening, at sunset, circling around our masts. He was looking where he should light when it should become sufficiently dark. He lives on what he can find in the sea, but prefers a spar to a wave on which to roost. He has sense enough to know that when asleep, the fish may avenge upon him some of the wrongs which he inflicts. But he is, after all, a very stupid fellow. He secures his prey often at the expense of his life, and that, too, when there is no necessity for it. If a little billow casts a dead fish on a rock, he poises over it for a moment to be sure of his mark, and then plunging down, head first, dashes his own brains out; very much like a politician who rushes so hard upon an office that he destroys himself in its attainment. The senate is, in this case, the rock on which his little craft splits.

We are now approaching the region of dolphins, porpoises, sharks, and small whales. Our sailors are rigging their hooks and harpoons. It will be difficult for any thing that comes near us to escape their glittering steel. Their hostility falls mostly on the shark. They regard him as a graver robber. He can expect no mercy. The loudest note of exultation I ever heard on board a man-of-war, was when one of these fellows was brought on board. "There," said a rough salt, "you have been prowling about here to get a nab at us, and have got nabbed yourself—you old blood-sucker!" There are three beings that can expect no mercy in misfortune,—a rat, a tyrant, and a shark. Of the three I would soonest spare the rat; I always associated something respectable with his long tail. But let that pass.

SUNDAY, DEC. 14. We have had the awning spread, and have held divine service. All joined in, and sung Old Hundred to the hymn commencing with the lines—

"God of the seas, thine awful voice
Bids all the rolling waves rejoice."

The impressiveness of a service at sea is owing, in part, to the isolation of those on board. There is nothing around to distract the attention, or win a diverted thought. Around rolls or rests the melancholy main—above stretches the blue heaven, and over all reigns that Supreme Intelligence, at whose fiat resplendent worlds rolled from chaotic night. All is vast and awful, like that state of being into which we are ushered at death. It is this that makes the sailor religious, and inspires him with respect for all the great truths which throw their light through the night of the grave.

The errors and vices of the sailor seldom result from skepticism. I never met with one who denied or doubted the existence of a God, the wickedness of the human heart, or the realities of a future state. They attach a much higher offence to a disrespect to the Bible, than the use of profane language. They seem to think a man's impulses may be wrong, while in the main he is good. The spirit is willing, but the flesh is weak. They have a law in their members warring against the law of their mind, and bringing them into captivity to Satan ; and yet they are free to denounce that captivity, and brand it as the source of all their degredation and misery. Their loathing spirits, touched with a diviner life, often exclaim, " Who shall deliver us from this body of sin and death ?"

Monday, Dec. 15. We were to-day, at 12 o'clock, in lat. 15° 46′ s., long. 36° 58′ w. We have run within the last five days a thousand miles, and are now within six hundred and sixty miles of Rio. Three or four days more, and we shall probably be at rest in one of the most magnificent bays in the world. Our ship is in prime condition for displaying her symmetry and strength. She is indebted for this to the experience and activity of our captain and first lieutenant. They are thorough in the details of ship duty, and are sustained by efficient officers. To keep a man-of-war trig, taxes the profoundest patience and energy. It requires an eye that sees every thing, and a fidelity that neglects nothing.

I saw this morning, at daybreak, an old tar standing alone on the forecastle. His stalwart form rose in bold relief on the brightening sky. His dark locks flowed out from under his tarpaulin upon the wind. His large deep eye was fastened on the sun as it came whirling up in splendor out of the sea. His large sinewy arms were extended, as if to welcome some being that inspired reverence and love; when Milton's sublime apostrophe to light rolled in solemn emphasis from his lips:—

> "Hail, holy Light! offspring of Heaven, first born
> Or of the eternal co-eternal beam!
> May I express thee unblamed? since God is light,
> And never but in unapproached light,
> Dwelt from eternity, dwelt then in thee,
> Bright affluence of bright essence increate."

TUESDAY, DEC. 16. This is beautiful sailing; a soft, balmy atmosphere, a smooth sea, and a breeze that carries us seven and eight knots the hour. We have not taken in our studding-sails for several days; while our royals seemed to have entered into an agreement with our broad pennant to stand or come down together. The day is not darkened by clouds, and the night is filled with the soft light of the moon. The stars come out from the blue vault of heaven, and blaze with a distinctness and force that makes each one seem some central source of exhaustless and unquenchable splendor. Of this high host Jupiter leads the way; to him the eye of the sailor turns as that of the Moslem to the crescent that glows on the minaret of his prophet.

An officer to-day, after reprimanding a sailor for some alleged neglect of duty, told him to go forward;

that he was such a perfect nondescript that he did not know what to do with him. So forward Jack went, muttering to himself *nondescript*—what does that mean? "Here, Wilkins," said he, "can you tell me what nondescript means? the officer of the deck called me a nondescript, and I want to know what it means—something bad, I suppose, for he was mighty angry." "No," said Wilkins, "I don't know what it means; call Tim Shades, he can tell you." Now this latter person was a sort of ship's dictionary, and though perhaps as ignorant as any on board, had a meaning for every thing, and a reason for it besides. So Tim Shades came. "What does nondescript mean?" inquired the aggrieved sailor. Our lexicographer seemed at first a little puzzled; but soon settling his features into oracular solemnity, replied:—"Nondescript means one who gets into heaven without being regularly entered on the books." "Is that all it means?" ejaculated the offended sailor; "well, well, I shall be glad to get there any way, poor sinner as I am." Were there more of the spirit of this sailor among sectarians, there would be less altercation about the right road, and quite as much speed.

Wednesday, Dec. 17. Another hundred miles of the distance that separated us from Rio has been left behind. Four hundred miles more remain to be traversed. The breeze is extremely light, directly aft, and our studding-sails on both sides, below and aloft, are out. We are under a cloud of canvas, which hangs over our frigate like the brooding wings of the cherubim over the sanctuary of the ark. But here I fear the parallel must stop. We have the sacred tables, it is true, and the commandments inscribed on them, but where is the soul-absorbing reverence they should inspire ?

All hands are at work getting our ship ready for port. She is being scoured from stem to stern, outside and in. Every soil on her paint is obliged to yield to soap and clean water; and every weather-stain on her rigging is removed. She will look neat as a bride approaching the nuptial altar. What is there more beautiful on earth than a young and guileless being thus timidly intrusting her destiny to the hands of another,—leaving her home, her father, mother, brothers and sisters, for a hearth which another love has lighted, and where other hopes are to bud and bloom? He who can betray the confidence thus reposed in him, and break the heart that has treasured its last trust in his, is callous alike to crime and shame. But this is digression.

Thursday, Dec. 18. As we were exercising today at general quarters, our ears were startled by the cry, "Man overboard!" The life-buoy was instantly cut away, the ship hove-to, and a boat lowered. The missing sailor had fallen from the steps of the lee gangway, and was discovered before he had passed the ship's counter, but immediately disappeared. He was known to be a good swimmer; the cause of his sudden disappearance is left to conjecture. His head may possibly have struck the ship's side with sufficient force to have stunned him, or he may have fallen a prey to an enormous shark that has been hanging around our ship all the morning. A protracted and most diligent search was made, but not a trace of him could be found. The boat was at last recalled, and our ship filled away.

The deceased was one of the most intractable and dangerous men we had on board. He had knocked down one of the crew in the dark, and stamped on the face of another at night, with the apparent intention of inflicting a mortal wound. No punishments, no counsels had the slightest effect upon him. Captain Du Pont had tried his utmost to reform him. He seemed proof both to the language of kindness and rebuke. When it was known among the crew that he was the one that was lost, not a sentiment of sorrow or regret was evinced. But on the contrary, the crew seemed as if relieved of a calamity by a mysterious Providence. This death carries one moral lesson with obvious effect to all, and that is, to have the sympathy and regret of others in death, we must command their friendship and respect in life. No eloquence can proclaim this truth with half the effect that this death has done. But the appearance of one at the bar of God so utterly unprepared for his last account, is a thought inexpressibly awful, and should strike the deepest alarm into a guilty breast.

FRIDAY, DEC. 19. We were to-day, at 12 o'clock, in lat. 21° 36′ s., long. 38° 55′ w., 200 miles from Cape Frio, and 260 from Rio. The breeze which for several days past has often died into a calm, has freshened to-day, and is carrying us along with studding-sails below and aloft, some six and seven knots. We may perhaps get in on Sunday evening, but not before. We have seen nothing of the strong westerly winds which prevail in the North Atlantic during the winter months, and very little of the northeast monsoons found to the south of the equator. These winds, like broken-down politicians, have blown themselves out.

A large ship, which, if our glasses speak truly, is armed, and bears a broad pennant, is in sight. All hands have been called to quarters, the breeching of the guns cast loose, the match-buckets stationed, cutlasses and pistols belted, the magazines opened, and every thing ready for an engagement. Our commodore will never be taken by surprise. His ship is ready at any moment for action. To this subject he gives his personal attention. Every division of the guns is exercised under his immediate supervision. His presence, and the interest he takes in the exercise, encourages and animates the men. He has an enthusiasm himself which he infuses into others.

> " Our bosoms we'll bear to the glorious strife,
> And our oath is recorded on high,
> To prevail in the cause that is dearer than life,
> Or crushed in its ruins to die."

SATURDAY, DEC. 20. " Land-ho!" This cry from the man in the fore-top sent an exulting thrill this morning through our whole ship. We have been on the ocean fifty-two days, and not an island or even desolate rock have we seen. Our eyes have rested only on the sky and melancholy main. But now a towering headland welcomes us to a new clime and the wonders of a new shore. Mr. Morgan, our master, calculated that we should discover land this morning at half past eleven, on our starboard bow. Within ten minutes of the time, and bearing precisely as he had calculated, Cape Frio was announced by the man in the fore-top. This, after an absence from land of more than seven weeks, and the sailing of more than six thousand miles, speaks well for our chronometers, and the scientific accuracy of our sailing-master,

We have been running, for several hours past, twelve knots, with the wind on our quarter. We shot past a Brazilian brig on the same course, as if she had been at anchor. The line of coast is now but a few miles distant, and heaves its soaring peaks into the sky. The sun is setting in splendor. As the night deepens apace, sheets of moonlight descend through the rifts of the floating darkness above, while a long train of phosphoric light flashes behind our keel. The storm on the lofty coast becomes still more grand and awful. Every mountain-peak becomes a blazing fortress, and shakes with the heavy thunder. The very sea trembles under this artillery of the sky.

> "And this is in the night:—most glorious night!
> Thou wert not sent for slumber! let me be
> A sharer in your fierce and far delight,—
> A portion of the tempest and of thee!
> How the lit wave shines a phosphoric sea,
> And the big rain comes dancing to the earth!
> And now again 'tis black,—and now, the glee
> Of the loud hills shakes with its mountain-mirth,
> As if they did rejoice o'er a young earthquake's birth."

CHAPTER III.

RIO DE JANEIRO.

BAY OF RIO.—SCENERY.—ASPECT OF THE CITY.—ROYAL PALACE AND CHAPEL.—LANCERS AND BABY.—MISERACORDIA.—AQUEDUCT.—MORNING RIDE.—BOTANIC GARDEN.—TEA-PLANT.—THE SABBATH IN RIO.—MUSEUM.—NUNNERY.—JEALOUSY OF HUSBANDS.—A POMPOUS FUNERAL.—THE PLYMOUTH.—HON. HENRY A. WISE.—SLAVE-TRADE.—MARRIAGES AND DOMESTIC ARRANGEMENTS.—POLITICAL CONDITION OF THE BRAZILIANS.—TREATMENT OF THE SLAVES.—RELIGION.—WASHER-WOMEN.—SAN ANTONIO.—CLIMATE.—THE UNKNOWN COUPLE.—DIAMONDS.—FAREWELL TO RIO.

Land-ho—from the mast-head swelling,
On the breeze its music throws,
Like the tones of angels, telling
Where the soul may find repose.

SUNDAY, DEC. 21. We found ourselves on Sunday morning off the harbor of Rio. The first object that here arrests the eye is a rocky isle swelling abruptly from the sea, and crowned with a pharos, that had thrown its light some thirty miles to us the night before. Between this and the main land on the left, soars another mass of rocks, while a corresponding one rises with a savage aspect on the right. These wave-encircled bastions resemble those posted by nature on either side of the Dardanelles, through which the grim spirits of Europe and Asia challenge each other.

Within the entrance on the left rise the steep

sides of Sugar-loaf mountain, while on the right frowns the lofty fortress of Santa Cruz. Further in looms the fortified isle of Lagem, commanding the central passage, and throwing its protection over the romantic cove, from which Bota Foga looks out upon the waters. As the eye wanders further up the bay, it encounters the island of Cobras, buried under its frowning batteries, and the Ville-Gagnon with its castellated summits; while on the opposite side a giant rock has walked out into the waters, and taken up its lofty, independent position.

The bay, studded with picturesque islands, circles up bold and beautiful some thirty miles into the main land. The shore presents here a glittering beach, which retreats into the green recesses of a deep ravine, and is there overhung by some stupendous cliff, which throws its dark shadows below. The whole bay is like a resplendent lake looking to heaven amid Alpine pinnacles. High above all soars the steep Corcovada, where plays the first blush of morn, and where the dying day lingers; while the Organ mountains, with their sharp peaks, pour down the harmony of the winds. All between these lofty barriers and the quiet bay presents a forest of fantastic cones; while swinging depths of shade wave over the glad rills that leap down their sides, and make music at their base. It would seem as if some volcano had thrown up these hills in a frolic; or as if some Titanic spirit, imbued with a love of the wonderful, had been permitted to work out its conceptions in these wild shapes.

The city descends from mountain coves to the strand of the bay, like a spreading stream, which encounters here a rolling hill and there a projecting bluff. Some of the elevations are crowned with public edifices, but no princely palace, gorgeous dome, or glittering spire, strongly arrests the eye. The architecture of man here is so inferior to that of nature, it ought to make an apology whenever it shows itself. It is like the tent of an Arab throwing up its dirty cone beneath the magnificent umbrage of the palm. It is said the genius of a people is in harmony with the scenery in the midst of which they have been reared; but here is scenery that might almost throw sunbows over the dreams of the dead, and architecture sombre enough to send even a Quaker to sleep. Such is the aspect of the city as seen from our frigate, swinging at her anchors in front of the imperial palace. A nearer view may possibly bring out some concealed beauty. But cities, like fashionable women, are very apt to betray their charms at the first blush.

Monday, Dec. 22. I visited the shore to-day, in company with Dr. Mosely and Mr. Spieden, our purser. We landed in front of the palace-square. A flight of broken wood steps took us to the top of the sea-wall, where we found ourselves on a paved parapet, presenting an open area of several hundred feet, which was broken only by the dark form of a fountain, from which the water fell in profusion. We here encountered a swarm of half-naked slaves, sufficiently diversified in their features to represent every African tribe from which they were stolen. Some had not lost their first look of wonder, while others seemed as those in whom grief and hope had long since perished. They were engaged in transporting merchandise, and seemed to be the walking drays of the city. They carry these enormous burdens on their heads, and trot along with a sonorous grunt, which works itself off into a sort of song. You wonder how they can have so much wind to spare for their tune.

We next encountered a little carriage, with a child in it, drawn by a diminutive pony. You might almost put the whole establishment into a good sized market-basket. It was attended by some half dozen slaves, who seemed extremely anxious about their charge. Where they were going I know not; but the whole group presented a striking picture of the extremes of human life. That child would have been just as happy in the strong arms of its nurse; the globe would probably have turned on its axle just as long; but parental pride and folly would not have been gratified. This is a small outbreak of the aristocratic sentiment—a sentiment not primitive.

> "When Adam delved and Eve span,
> Where was then the gentleman?"

The royal palace has no charms of architecture. It is a long, low, and rather heavy-looking building, with ballustraded windows, and stuccoed walls. Within the iron gratings of the court the form of a black soldier moved to and fro, on guard; while others stretched at length on benches, or sitting in the corners of the walls, were sound asleep. The whole was a breathing type of that listlessness and slumber which falls on the soldier guarding in a time of profound peace an empty palace. This palace might be converted into a warehouse without ever awaking in the visiter a suspicion of the regal use to which it had been put.

We passed on to the royal chapel, which stands near by, and which communicates with the palace through the silent halls of a monastery. The exterior of the chapel presents only its front to the eye, surmounted by a cross, and relieved by a mimic crown which reposes in a central niche. The interior is adorned with a profusion of gilding, and contains several private boxes, where the occupants may conceal themselves behind crimson curtains. We found in the oratory a dozen priests or monks, chanting their devotions. Two of them were laughing most immoderately. They seemed to make every effort to suppress their risible impulses, and would now and then succeed so far as to present for a moment a grave countenance, but the ludicrous would immediately gain the ascendency, and the laughter burst out. I once saw the gravity of a whole congregation in one of our largest country churches irretrievably disturbed. An owl had perched himself on the key of the arch directly over the choir; the clergyman had given out the hymn commencing with the words,

"Hark from the tombs, a doleful sound."

As the singers rose, and just as the leader was going to pitch the pathetic tune, the owl, as if taking this duty on himself, gave a solemn hoot! They who were troubled with a quick sense of the ludicrous, couldn't hold in for a moment, and the infection spread to the whole congregation.

Tuesday, Dec. 23. I came near being captured to-day by a troop of lancers. They were riding at full speed before two carriages, in one of which lay the infant emperor, in its nurse's arms, and in the other chatted the servants in attendance on the baby. The lancers had the important bearing of Roman cohorts, ushering Cæsar into the imperial city after the triumphs of his African campaign. How far the baby was benefitted by this military display, or the lactant provisions of its nurse increased, I was not informed.

Turning away, I soon encountered a woman with her infant lashed to her back. The little fellow reposed in the bunt of a shawl, the corners of which were fastened over the breast of his mother. He kept his eye on me, as I walked behind him, but with no signs of fear; he well knew that the love which carried him would protect him. His mother was still in youth, moved with an elastic step, and evinced her cheerfulness of heart in her animated face. How strikingly this group contrasts itself with that in the imperial carriage! Pomp was there, but heart here. Between a venal homage of soldiers and a mother's love who could hesitate? The last will live and throb with undying strength, when the other is a breathless mockery.

Wednesday, Dec. 24. We visited to-day the Miseracordia, a noble monument of Brazilian humanity. Hundreds, who would otherwise have died unnoticed and unknown in the streets, have here experienced, in their last hours, those attentions which religion and benevolence bestow upon the destitute and helpless. A statue of the Emperor, in the finest Carrara marble, is being executed by an Italian artist, for this institution, at the private expense of a wealthy Brazilian.

Long may that statue stand on its pedestal, a true symbol of the humanity of him whom it represents. One king in an hospital has more true glory than a thousand on the field of carnage. It is a false view of the moral characteristics of our nature, to find more honor in killing a man than comforting him. It is doing homage to the thieves, who robbed the traveller and left him for dead, instead of the good Samaritan, who bound up his wounds and took him to an inn.

We passed on to the Aqueduct, which is brought over this section of the city upon a succession of lofty arches, which sweep high over the dwellings. This national work, constructed under the viceroyalty of Vasconcellas, is in imitation of the Alcantra aqueduct at Lisbon, and reflects lasting honor on its projector. It is supplied with water from artificial lakes in the Corcovada mountain. The summit of this mountain is covered with wild forest-trees, which being cooler than the surrounding atmosphere, condense the vapor, which falls in showers into these lakes. To this beautiful law of nature Rio is indebted for that refreshing element without which she would be but little better than a desert.

In giving a community pure water to drink, you take from the tippler his standing apology for putting rum in it. You reduce him to that pain in the stomach from which he finds no relief except in the minted toddy. When among the temperate, this perpetual colic will sometimes twist him almost double. Poor fellow! to have such a pain, and no relief except in rum, and even this very much embarrassed by the refusal of others to drink it. What business has a man to stop drinking himself, if doing so makes it disreputable in others? He should be held responsible for bringing odium on that horn of poor human nature's dilemma. Let whisky be as plenty as water, and it would be a beastly disgrace to get drunk on it. Can three cents turn vulgarity into gentility, shame into honor, and guilt into innocence?

"O would some power the giftie gie us,
To see oursels as others see us."

THURSDAY, DEC. 25. Mr. Livingston, Dr. Mosely, Mr. Spieden, with myself, chartered this morning a carriage-and-four for the day. Our first drive was to the residence of the American minister, some three miles out of the city, and in the centre of a vast variety of rural charms. We found Mr. Wise listening to the grievances of two American sailors, who had been unceremoniously thrown ashore by their captains. His action was prompt and energetic, as it always is when there are rights to be vindicated, or wrongs to be redressed.

We spent a very agreeable and entertaining hour with him, and called for our carriage, when we discovered that our postillion had unharnessed his steeds and put them very quietly to the manger, thinking, no doubt, that as the fodder would cost him nothing, it was by no means best to let it pass. While he was harnessing up, a servant connected with the imperial palace came in for his Christmas token. He had called, it seemed, on the morning of the happy day, and wished the American minister a merry Christmas, and had now come for his fee. The same call, with the same salutation, had been made on all the foreign ministers, and all were expected to "shell out" very liberally on the occasion. Usage is law, and the result is very expensive merry wishes. I intend next year to wish the whole world a merry Christmas.

Seated once more in our carriage, we found our postillion whirling us back to the city, instead of taking the rode to the Botanic Garden, to which we were bound. We explained our wishes to him, thinking he labored under a misapprehension; but a shrug of his shoulders convinced us that he was acting from obstinacy. We then poured our remonstrances, reproaches, and threats upon him, in half a dozen different languages, creating quite a little Babel. Shaking his head like one whose purpose, but not will, is broken, he turned into the right road, and drove his horses, at the top of their speed, under a broiling sun, to Bota Foga, about half the distance to the Garden, but then brought up in front of a restaurant, declaring his horses could proceed no further.

We ordered for them a bucket or two of fresh water, and after resting a few moments, directed the postillion to drive on; but not a step would he budge. Here was a poser, a sort of crisis in our affairs, as political leaders say when they wish to rally the strength of their party. We gave our postillion one minute in which to decide whether he would drive us to the Garden, or be ousted from his seat to make room for another who would drive us there. He waited till the last second, and then started off sulkily, as one in doubt whether to fight or yield. At last we reached the little hotel near the Garden, where we alighted, and directed the keeper to take the best care of the horses. In the mean time, we pushed into a neighboring grove, where we indulged in the luxuries of a lunch, which our provident purser had brought from the ship, and for which our ride had given us a keen appetite. This finished, and a few segars whiffed off, we directed a dinner, and proceeded to the Garden.

This refreshing retreat from the heat and dust of the city, derives its leading attractions from its location. Beyond rolls the sea, and over it towers the lofty Corcovada. It occupies some fifty acres, and is intersected by winding walks, which are overhung with forest shade. Several of the plats are devoted to the cultivation of the tea plant, which had been introduced by the father of the present emperor. Although the plant has never succeeded to perfection, it has approached it sufficiently to have satisfied the good ladies of Boston, whose husbands had thrown their Chinese dreams into the sea. What a scene such an interference with the phlegathontic weed would create around our hearths! Think you our ladies would so quietly have taken to spearmint and sage? But let that pass.

In other plats we met with the cinnamon, the red pepper, and the clove, all in fruit. But aromatics are the last plants that will consent to carry their fragrance with them into foreign climes. The walks are overhung with the mango, the orange, the marmosa, and dark olive, while the croton and plantain cast in every coppice the deep umbrage of their forest gloom.

On one side of the garden a silver-footed streamlet dashes down the steeps of the Corcovada, like a girl escaping from a crabbed aunt for Gretna Green. Near this rises an elliptical mound, crowned with a beautiful bower of the arbor vitæ. This vivacious shrub allows itself to be twisted into a thousand fantastic shapes, without a thought of dying. In this bower, which is so thickly interlaced as to exclude the sun, I sought a wicker couch, and, lulled by the lapse of the waters, and the melody of a mourning bird, fell asleep, and dreamed of

> "Groves, whose rich trees wept odorous gums and balm,
> Flowers of all hue, and without thorn the rose."

We returned to the hotel, discussed a very indifferent dinner, ordered up our carriage, and started on our return to the city. The evening came in with a soft beautiful twilight. We passed many family groups seated in the front yards of their houses enjoying the hour. Here and there was one who had deeper thoughts than her younger sisters, and whose large black eyes were often turned to the climbing moon.

We called on our return upon Mr. Furgeson, our naval store-keeper at Rio, a situation which he fills with a fidelity and business tact, which have the merited confidence of the department.

The evening had well advanced when we reached the city. We discharged our postillion in the same sulky humor in which he had been all day. He had the look and air of an old pirate, thrown by some freak of fortune into livery, and upon the box of a coach instead of the scaffold. All his ill temper arose from the fact that we had not promised him a gratuity. We had engaged to give his employer twelve dollars for the carriage, and we should not have forgotten him had he been civil and obliging. His conduct, like that of most people when they get out of temper, worked him only evil.

Ill fortune rides ill will where'er it leads.

Friday, Dec. 26. The United States frigate Columbia, commanded by Capt. Richie, and bearing the broad pennant of Commodore Rousseau, arrived this morning from Norfolk. She has had, by a singular coincidence, the same passage as the Congress—fifty-two days. I was right glad to find on board of her, as chaplain, my esteemed friend, the Rev. T. R. Lambert. A portion of her crew are down with the smallpox, which broke out in the person of one of her marines several days after she had sailed. All direct communication with her has been interdicted; but we met her officers, who are very agreeable associates, on shore. We expected letters by the Columbia, but her departure followed so fast on our own that very few were sent.

The Columbia is a fine frigate, combining speed, strength, and grace of architecture. Near her swings the frigate Raritan, under the command of Captain Gregory. She has less beauty than her sister, is low between her decks, and her spikes, with their black heads, disfigure her planks; but she rides the water gracefully, and is a swift sailor. For this, however, she may be indebted, in some degree, to the skill of her commander, whose sagacity in detecting and bringing out the latent qualities of a ship is seldom baffled. Her wardroom, though dark from without, has light from within ; not that which strays from a few dim tapers, but from the spirit that is in man, and which will still stream on when life's taper itself is out.

SATURDAY, DEC. 27. Her Britannic Majesty's frigate President, under the command of Rear-Admiral Dacres, entered the harbor to-day, and let go her anchors within a few cables length of us. She is the new-fledged phenix of the old one, captured from us in the last war. The parent has perished, but her memory still survives in the glorious triumphs of Decatur, as well as in this fledgling which bears her name. The old bird was captured by an overwhelming superiority of force ; not by greater tact or courage. No laurels were won or lost.

The offspring which has arisen from her relics, is now bearing the pennant of one who was himself, while commanding the Guerrier, captured by the Constitution, under Commodore Hull. But he fought his ship well ; it was no want of courage that allowed victory to perch on our flag. He had no resource but to surrender, or sink in a dismantled hulk. The English journals affected to prefer the last catastro phe; but this does very well for those who are not themselves in the hulk. The bubbles which brim the watery grave of the sailor may break and disappear as other bubbles; but when they ascend from our own strangling gasps, they carry with them agonies which should shake a world. The capture of the Guerrier, and the triumphs which followed, broke the charm of British invincibility. That dream of supremacy fled the ocean, never to return,—

> "That spell upon the minds of men,
> Broke, never to unite again."

SUNDAY, DEC. 28. Were a stranger to the religious habits of a Catholic community thrown into Rio on the Sabbath, he would think he had mistaken his sabbatical calendar. He would think he had arrived on some holiday, in which the serious concerns of life yield to gayety. He would see this spirit of social mirth pervading all classes. Even the bells would have a glee in their tones. He would find the priests in the promenade instead of the pulpit, with their large-rimmed hats rolled up over the ear, and the solemnity of their sable gowns in singular contrast with the levity that runs through their manner.

Such is the Sabbath where the principles of Protestantism have not obtained, and where its spirit is not felt. It is a day of amusement and recreation. Such it has ever been in every country where the genius of papacy has been paramount. Such it is now in Italy, France, Portugal, and Spain. Let the see of Rome roll its waves over the Protestant institutions of the United States, and it would sweep the sanctity of the Sabbath from the land. There would not be enough of its vitality left to embalm the memory of our pilgrim fathers. To rebuke those who abuse religion is not to disparage its spirit.

"All hail, Religion! maid divine,
Pardon a muse so mean as mine,
Who, in his rough, imperfect line,
Thus dares to name thee;
To stigmatize false friends of thine,
Can ne'er defame thee."

MONDAY, DEC. 29. Visited the Museum of Natural History. Here the beautiful birds of Brazil speak in dumb show, and her minerals seem to mourn their mines. But the specimens are not extensive. The Public Library, in another building, contains some twenty thousand volumes, which slumber in dust on their shelves. The Academy of Fine Arts has a few specimens in statuary and painting; but none that would kindle an eye that has once gazed on the triumphs of a Phidias or a Raphael. The Opera House has elegant and ample accommodations for spectators, but no performers.

All these institutions were established by Don

Pedro I., but have been on the decline since his abdication. It was his ambition to make Rio a second Lisbon; but his plans outran his means. Mafra Castle alone, with its time-honored towers and their hundred and twenty bells, rolling out their anthems on the airs of old Portugal, leave all that Rio can present, like an afterpiece from which the auditory has escaped.

The great mass of the laboring classes in Rio subsist on the farina of the jatrapha-plant, made into a coarse bread, called *pan de tierre caliente.* It is manufactured from the same plant of which the tapioca is obtained. This, with the black bean, which grows in great abundance, is with them the staple of life. The more luxurious bread-stuffs are imported. Even meat, amidst all this teeming vegetation, is scarce and dear. Every thing here runs to coffee, of which a hundred and thirty millions of pounds are exported annually, which goes to foreign markets, and brings back, in the great circle of commerce, the products of every other clime.

Tuesday, Dec. 30. Visited the queen's garden, which covers some six acres, and lies within the environs of the city, between the Miseracordia and Gloria Hill, and opens by a broad terrace on the bay. The gravelled walks, which sweep around in every direction, are over-arched by swinging masses of shade. The cassia waves here by the side of the silver-leaved myrtle, and the imperial laurel—the shamrock of Brazil—turns its green yellow-striped leaves to the sun; while two small pyramids of granite stand as grim sentinels over the proprieties of the place. A tough job, it is said, they have of it, when the young of the city flock here in the evening, though their watch duties are aided by conjugal jealousy and parental vigilance.

Not far removed from the garden, and in harmony with some of its associations, stands a nunnery, which, considering the uses to which it is put, might with propriety be called the bridal prison. Husbands, leaving the country or the city for any length of time, are in the habit of shutting up their wives and children in this nunnery. A beautiful exhibition of conjugal love and confidence! But where are the confessors all this time with their compulsory vows of celibacy, and that latitude of conscience which compulsion always leaves? Better to trust a wife to her own affections than the guidance of men whom superstition has invested with the power to pardon the errors of human frailty, who can commit sin one hour, and cancel it with all parties the next. Ecclesiastical rules and regulations, which deprive any portion of the community of the privileges of the marriage state, pave the way to crime. They are a violation of the laws of nature and nature's God.

On our return we stopped at the imperial chapel, where preparations were making for a sumptuous funeral. The chapel was brilliantly lighted; the priests were in their gorgeous robes; and the dark carriage of the dead soon arrived, with four black horses, and postillions in sable plumes. The body was placed near the great altar, candles were placed in the hands of those who crowded the nave, and amid a shower of light the chant for the repose of the soul began.

One of the candles set fire to the long locks of a fashionable youth standing near the bier. The priest who was sprinkling the holy water, dashed a shower of it upon his head, while a suppressed laughter shook the whole crowd. The prayers finished,—the bier was removed to the enclosure in the rear of the church, the body taken from the coffin, and thrown up into a niche in the wall, resembling a baker's oven. It was tossed in head first, and the aperture being small and high, it required no little tact in the swinging and cant to secure it a proper lodgment. Lime and holy water were then cast upon it, and the orifice closed. Sooner than have such a burial as this, with scorching hair, laughter, an oven, and dissolving lime, let me glide from earth unnoticed and unknown, as a flower falls in the pathless wilderness, and let my grave be a sunless cave of ocean, only let me have there as mourner:—

The mermaid, whose elegiac shell
Shall pour its tender stave,
In many a wild and fond farewell
Around my sea-green grave.

WEDNESDAY, DEC. 31. Visited to-day the Plymouth, under the command of Capt. Henry. She is one of the most finished specimens of naval architecture afloat; and the neatness of her internal appearance corresponds with her outward grace and beauty. Her light spar-deck, running flush fore and aft, unencumbered by a gun; her bulwarks sweeping from stem to stern without a breaking beam, and clouded into the hue of the pearl; her gun-carriages exhibiting through their hard varnish the native grain of the oak, and the guns presenting the hard polish of their cylinders; her stanchions of burnished iron, her sides and bends without a weather-stain, and her hammocks rising above their netting white as the snow-rift,—all have the finest effect. She reflects, in every aspect in which she may be viewed, the highest credit on the taste and professional skill of Captain Henry and his officers.

She came here from the Mediterranean, after having visited most of the ports in that sea, and paid her respects to the grand sultan at Constantinople. She was there, as she is here, the admiration of all who visited her. Such a ship as this, with the soft clime of Italy, the storied shores of Greece, and the classic associations of the Ægean isles, would be the perfection of cruising with the scholar, and would involve nothing incompatible with the sterner purposes of a man-of-war.

THURSDAY, JAN. 1, 1846. This is new-year's day, and the anniversary of the discovery of the bay of Rio by Salis. The Brazilian flag is flying from the public buildings and the masts of all the vessels in the harbor. Salutes from fortifications and national ships are pouring their reverberating thunder among the hills.

Commodore Stockton has graced the occasion in the shape of a splendid dinner to the Hon. Henry A. Wise. Many ladies and gentlemen of Rio, with the officers of the English and American squadrons, were present. The most perfect good feeling prevailed; many patriotic sentiments went round; and many recollections of home melted their way into our hearts.

The honor of the occasion was for Mr. Wise; nor was it unworthily bestowed. He has been a firm, devoted friend to the navy; he has stood by her in her darkest hours, and found, in the triumphs of the past, a bright prophecy of the future. He has been, at the court of Brazil, the fearless champion of the rights and claims of humanity. He has shrunk from no efforts and no responsibility in crushing the slave-trade. Where selfish ease suggested silence, he has spoken; where timidity urged a temporizing indifference, he has resolutely acted. His moral firmness has made him the terror of every slaver, and of all connected with this accursed traffic. If he resigns his present post, may his successor, in this respect at least, tread in his footsteps.

Friday, Jan. 2. A Brazilian lady was pointed out to me to-day who is but twelve years of age, and who has two children, who were frolicking around her steps. She was married at ten to a wealthy merchant of sixty-five,—a spring violet caught in a curling snow-drift! But ladies here marry extremely young. They have hardly done with their fictitious babies, when they have the smiles and tears of real ones. Their parents make the matches, as well they may at that age; and they ought in conscience to retain still the spanking privilege, and exercise it down to the third generation.

The evidences of consideration here turn upon a two or four wheeled vehicle, which is kept in the basement story of the house, and throws the sheen of its varnish on the eye of the passer. Whether there is a horse to draw it or not, is a matter of comparatively little importance. It answers its essential purpose without. It is a quiet indication of rank, and all the better that its slumber is seldom broken.

In the parlors and apartments above, you find the

transmitted furniture of past generations. Antiquity has a charm against which novelty cannot prevail. The same chair in which the departed ancestor trembled between this life and the next, still stands by the verandah, where budding beauty breathes and throbs. The same old harp, which was swept by a hand that has long since forgotten its cunning, now wakes to melody under the touch of one in whom life's earliest pulses play. Its music ever floats between the cradle and the grave.

Saturday, Jan. 3. This is a holiday at Rio, and the calkers from shore, who are at work on our frigate, knocked off last evening, refusing to come this morning unless their per diem should be raised fifty per cent. As we are anxious to get to sea, their demand has been complied with. Conscience, it would seem, has no concern in the matter, though it is a saint's day, and one of the most sacred in their calendar. How very convenient when that little inward troubler can be tied up in a man's purse, and stowed away in his breeches pocket!

Rio is a city without chimneys, and strikes one as a regiment of soldiers without caps. A vein of smoke is never seen circling up over its red-tiled roofs. The mildness of the climate dispenses with all parlor fires, except the gleam of the braséro. The houses, which rarely exceed two stories, are built of fragmented

10

stones and a species of mortar, which the air indurates into the solidity of a cement. The parlors are in the second story, and open out on a verandah. The servants divide the ground-floor with the old spaniel, who looks out from the dusky background like the lion of Agamemnon, still keeping stern watch over his master's gloomy shrine.

The domestic habits of the Brazilians, and their household economy, are closely shrouded; yet now and then, like guilty love, they betray themselves through their very disguises. They have but little confidence in their own virtue, and still less in yours; and, as might be expected, betray and are betrayed. Redress for such grievances is seldom sought through the forms of law. The stiletto makes less noise, and is more certain in its results. Don Pedro I. put his very throne in jeopardy by his profligacies. He brought ruin and indignant shame into some of the first families in Brazil. His victims were in every circle. The conditions of office involved their marriage, without interfering with this illicit relation. He was abusive to his wife, as false husbands generally are, and went to his grave with but little which friendship itself would not conceal.

Sunday, Jan. 4. The slave-trade is still carried on in the ports of Brazil. The government, though committed by treaty against it, connives at the traffic.

From ten to fifteen thousand slaves are imported annually. Of these the Mina, from the north interior of Africa, brings with him the greatest force of character. He never trifles with the misfortunes of his lot, and submits indignantly to a state of servitude. He speaks his deep-sounding Arabic, and looks with contempt upon the twattle of the other tribes. He has the bearing of one conscious of resources in himself. His energy and industry often procure him his liberty. His presence in Brazil puts the stability of her institutions in peril. It is apprehended he may one day strike for unconditional freedom. He is not a being who will crave quarter, or be very likely to grant it. It will be with him a life and death struggle.

MONDAY, JAN. 5. The United States frigate Raritan has arrived from La Plata, and reports that the English and French are still engaged fighting their way up the Parana for the purpose of opening a permanent communication with the interior provinces. The general opinion here is, that Governor Rosas will be obliged to abandon the blockade of Monte Video, and consent to the commercial communications demanded by England and France. Popular opinion here runs strongly in favor of free trade the world over.

The Brazilians do not like the interference of European powers in the affairs of this continent, but they dislike anarchy and despotism still more. They are the advocates of free constitutional government, and have embodied its most essential principles in their political institutions. The Emperor of Brazil has but little more power than the President of the United States. Law take its shape from the national legislature, and from that branch of it which expresses the popular will. This branch can at any time force a joint vote with the senate, and carry a measure by its numerical strength. This can indeed be vetoed by the emperor, but it would be an exercise of prerogative seldom resorted to, and never, I believe, where the popular will has been clearly expressed.

The condition of the slave population here is much less abject and wretched than I expected to find it. Slaves are generally treated with kindness and humanity by their masters. Their color operates less to their prejudice than with us. Their freedom, in many cases, lies within their reach, and may be obtained, as it often is, by industry and frugality. The owner who should demand an exorbitant price for a slave, who wishes to earn his freedom, would be severely censured. When free, he goes to the ballot-box, and is eligible to a seat in the national legislature.

Nor would anybody here go into hysterics should he

marry a woman whose skin should be a shade whiter than his own. It is for us Americans to preach up humanity, freedom, and equality, and then turn up our blessed noses if an African takes a seat at the same table on board a steamboat. Even in our churches he is obliged to look out some obscure nook, and dodge along towards heaven as if he had no business on the "narrow way." The misery is, that they who preach equality the loudest, are generally the last to practice it. They are generally for levelling downwards; but give me the man who tries to level upwards. Give me the man whose smiles are like the rays of the sun—if they strike the loftiest objects first, it is only that they may glance to the lowest.

Tuesday, Jan. 6. The religion of the Brazilians, as seen in their legislative policy, is less trammelled by superstition than in most countries where Papacy prevails. The Pope, a few years since, sent a legate to this court. It is expected, in such cases, that the salary of the legate will be paid by the country to which he is accredited. But the Brazilian legislature, not having the fear of the Vatican before their eyes, voted that his holiness might pay his own representative. He was of course recalled. Such has been the abuse here of ecclesiastical supremacy, such its interference in political affairs, and such its onerous pecuniary exactions, that there has been a sweeping reaction, and the civil power of the Pope is openly set at defiance.

As for the priests here, should they attempt to set up any secular authority, they would only expose themselves to derision. There is vastly more reverence for the decisions of the Papal see among the Roman Catholics of our country, than there is among the Brazilians. Were a bishop here to interfere at an election, it would cost him his episcopate. It is for us Americans to submit to such an outrage on the sanctity of the ballot-box.

WEDNESDAY, JAN. 7. I encountered to-day, on a large public square within the environs of the city, a washing-scene, which was rather primitive. The square is carpeted with green grass medallioned with flowers, and shaded here and there by clusters of forest trees. In the midst stands a fountain, from which the water falls in light showers into an immense basin. In this basin some two hundred females, of every age, clime, and color, were dashing their clothes, and rubbing them on the great sweep of the curb-stone. Their apparel, what little they had on, was fastened above the knee; the water in the basin was a pool of foaming suds, and they were jumping about in it like the Nereids of the Nile. The younger ones were full of mischief, and dis played their agility in tripping each other up. The fall of one into the suds was followed by a general shout. How they escaped having their clothes inextricably mixed up in this general melée of the great wash-tub, was a mystery to me.

On the green were hundreds of others occupied with their clothes. Some were snapping them in the wind; some spreading them on the grass to dry; some folding them up and depositing them in baskets, to be transported on their heads home; and others were under the shade of the trees asleep. Some trick, however, such as a dash of water from the bowl, was sure to await the dreamer; and then another laugh would be thrown on the wind. As twilight came on, all this panorama of life, with its breathing forms, its triumphs in laundry, and its merriments, disappeared. Nothing but the whisper of the leaf, or the bubble which still floated on the fountain, remained to tell where such a bustle had been.

What a magnificent washtub one of our great western lakes would make! It would hold all the clothes, clean and unclean, which cover the human race. There is only one difficulty in the way of this arrangement: it would be a little awkward to have the lake freeze over in the dead of winter. This, however, might be prevented by introducing under it the volcano of Vesuvius, which is of no use where it now stands. This done, and Whitney's railroad to the Pacific finished, and we shall truly be a great nation. But our women will never consent to have the *small clothes* perilled in Lake Superior; so there is an end to the whole business.

Thursday, Jan. 8. Rambled on shore to-day with Lieut. Gray, and returned several calls. Every family in Rio, where superstition asserts her sway, has two things, an image of St. Antonio and a whip. If the saint, after being duly invoked, still refuses to grant the boon craved, he is taken down from his niche and soundly whipped. This chastisement is repeated till the prayer is answered, or some priest interferes, and consoles the disappointed with the persuasion that the blessing sought has been, or will be, conferred in some other form. This compulsory process with a saint, accounts for the maimed state in which you always find poor Antonio here. There is something unique and interesting in this mode of obtaining benefactions. If a saint wont shell out, when he has the power, why should he not be whipped as well as a sinner?

We encountered to-day a Brazilian lady of rank in her palankeen. She was carried by two sturdy slaves, and followed by a retinue of servants. She was evidently bound on a visit to some female acquaintance, with whom she expected to spend the day. Her attendants must also be provided for.

Such an arrival in a quiet family would turn the whole house topsy-turvy. The further we get from the heart, the more bustle we make. The forms of fashionable etiquette, like feathers in a lady's bonnet, are full of flare and flutter.

Friday, Jan. 9. On shore to-day with Lieutenant Tilghman, rambling through the environs of the city, and on the green hills which overlook the bay. Capt. Wilkes, in his history of the exploring expedition, calls this place St. Salvador. The Brazilians laugh at the misnomer, and enjoy it the more as the captain's comments are deemed by them censorious and unjust. It was an unfortunate slip of the pen to write St. Salvador for St. Sebastian, and still more unfortunate to stereotype it into immortality.

The primitive name of this splendid bay is Nitherohi, which means concealed water, and is beautifully significant of its phenomena, as they unroll their wonders on the eye. And what a liquid name is that Nitherohi! it fairly melts on the tongue. It is Indian in its origin, and should never have been dropped for any saint in the calendar. But in Catholic countries, Eden itself would soon cease to go by its proper name.

I do not wonder the Brazilians are deficient in enterprise and energy. No physical force can withstand the enervating influences of this climate, and that listlessness which it induces. Not one exhilarating pulse heaves the heart. You feel as one walking in a half-exhausted receiver. The heat at this season is intense; the atmosphere often humid, and your whole frame yields to lassitude. How can a man attempt any thing great, when the least exertion throws him into perspiration, and even to dream seems an effort! It is as much as I can do to muster up resolution enough to pen this feeble page; and as for the reader he will probably fall asleep over it.

Saturday, Jan. 10. We had to-day a forcible specimen of Rio showers. We were in Rua d'Ouvidor, which is lined with the most fashionable shops in the city, when a black cloud, sailing down from the Corcovada peak, rolled out the lake, which lay in its bosom. The street was immediately filled with a flood of sufficient depth to float a family canoe. The inclined plane of the street carried it off in a rapid torrent. The sun again struck the pavement, and we were at liberty to renew our walk. Were such a flood to rush down Broadway, our New Yorkers would think their Croton reservoir had burst its last boundary. But here it creates as little commotion as the breaking of a bubble on the public fountain.

The fruits of Rio are delicious; richer oranges and bananas the houri never shook from the blooming boughs of Mahomet's horticultural heaven. But the milk here, or the liquid sold under that name, has less of the lacteal element in it than water filtered through the "milky-way." For this attenuated dilution our steward pays twenty cents the quart. Rumor says it is procured from the maternal functions of a tribe of slaves, who are wonderfully endowed in this particular, and who act as a class of wet-nurses to the community. Be the rumor true or not, it was very difficult to use it after this idea had once entered the imagination. It was hurrying one rather too fast into his second childhood. Would it bring back our first infancy, with its innocent glee, it would do. But life's current has no refluent tide.

Sunday, Jan. 11. Mr. Wise and family, with several other ladies and gentlemen from the shore, attended divine service on board. We assembled on the spar-deck under an awning that protected every one from the sun's rays. The leading points in the discourse turned on the value of the soul, as asserted in the nature of its powers and capacities, and in the humiliation and sufferings of the Son of God in its behalf. At the close of the service we all joined in singing the missionary hymn; the sacred music swelling up full and clear from so many deep-toned voices, floated far and wide over the still waters of the bay.

The Protestants in Rio have but one place of worship—the English chapel. They have been very unfortunate in the appointment of their chaplains. These appointments, and those of a diplomatic and political character, emanate substantially from the same source. Warm, devoted piety, in its unobtrusive meekness, seems to be overlooked in the glare of other qualities, or the erring partialities of private friendship. The last chaplain who served here for a time and left, went into one of the West India islands and set up a gaming-table. The English chaplain at Trieste, as I had occasion to observe, was one of the most accomplished waltzers in the place. Such men have their place, perhaps, in this varied world, but it is not in the missionary field. He will bring very few sheaves home with him who has converted his sickle into a fiddle-bow; and he will find even these few made up mostly of those tares which the devil sowed while he frolicked or slept.

MONDAY, JAN. 12. A Brazilian gentleman of some note sent his card over the side of our ship this morning, and was invited on board by Capt. Du Pont, who received him and his lady at the gangway. He was tall, well-proportioned, and in his carriage combined dignity with ease. His dark locks rolled out from under his chapeau in rich profusion. His face had that calmness and strength in its features which express force of intellect and benignity of heart. His dress was rich, but not gaudy; sable in hue, and well fitted to his stately person. He spoke in French, with a slight Brazilian accent. His questions were relevant and shrewd; his admiration of our frigate undisguised.

His lady was slightly below him in height, and more delicate in form. There was something peculiarly feminine in her air, and yet something which betrayed strength of character. Her small foot rose and lit on the deck with precision and airy lightness. Her countenance constantly changed in the tide of its expressions. The features were extremely regular, but you forgot their well-defined lines in the harmony of the whole. Her eyes were large, soft, and floating, and were shaded by long silken lashes, from which light and darkness seemed to fall. When some thought of deep animation struck her, the emotion flushed in her cheek like the blush of morn on a soft cloud. Her voice, though not deep, was musical, and flowed like the low sweet warble of a bird. Such was she, and such the one in whom her affections confided. They left the ship as they came, without ostentation. I have been told since that he is one of the first statesmen in Brazil.

Tuesday, Jan. 13. Visited the shore for the last time, as we are to weigh anchor to-morrow morning. Walked through Rua d'Ouvedor, the

Broadway of Rio, which displays in its fancy shops the fabrics and fashions of foreign capitals; and where you can purchase every thing from a camel's hair shawl to a shoe-string, and from a Damascus blade to a toothpick.

Crossed into the Rua d'Ourives, which flashes with all the jewels of Brazil. Their rays bewilder the eyes, and sometimes the wits. Doubloons, that are wanted for bread, are here parted with for a little pebble, that has nothing to recommend it but its light, and even that is a stolen ray. When Franklin's niece wrote to him at Paris to send her some ostrich feathers for her winter bonnet, the republican minister wrote her—"Catch the old rooster, my child, and pull the feathers out of his tail, they will do just as well." What is true of the rooster's feather, in comparison with the plume of the ostrich, is equally true of the common pebble by the side of the diamond. The brightest ray is that which flashes from intellect; the warmest that which melts from the heart.

Of the hotels in Rio the best is the Pharoux—an extensive establishment, under Parisian arrangements, and evincing a great want of cleanliness. If by good fortune your tester-bar keeps out the musqueto, you fall into the hands of a still worse enemy in the shape of the flea. Besides these annoyances, the night tubs, emptied on the beach of the bay, waft to your window odors which make you prefer heat to air. The goddess Cloacina ought to visit this place and order her altars under ground, where they belong, instead of having them transported on the heads of negroes, under the shadows of night, and sending up their exhalations, which are enough to make the man in the moon hold his nose. But let that pass. Flowers spring from corruption. Man pollutes, but nature purifies.

A spirit of freedom is gradually working its way into the heart of the Brazilians. They have made a vast stride in constitutional liberty within the last twenty years. Their government has ceased to be a despotism. Its functions now embody the energies of the public will; its measures look to the welfare of the great masses. The throne merely holds in check the leaders of factions, without wantonly impairing the freedom of the patriotic citizen. Should the period arrive, when monarchical forms can safely be dispensed with, and the public will tranquilly work itself out in the shape of law, Brazil will take her station among free republics.

As the old cathedral clock struck eleven, and the lights in the balconies grew dim, the barge of our commodore, in which we had been invited to take a seat, parted from the strand of Rio. Again on deck, a farewell look was thrown to its hills, sleeping in the soft moonlight. On those hills a Byron, a Cook, a Magellan have gazed. The morn still breaks over them, but they know it not. The world may still retain a faint echo of their fame, but where are they? and where, in a few years, shall we be? where are the millions, whose voices rang through the past? Death has hushed their exulting tunes, and their monuments have crumbled under the footstep of time. And we are passing to the same silent shore. As the furrows of our keel pass from the face of the deep, so will the strife, the sorrows, and the triumphs of our being, glide from the memory of man.

"What shadows we are, and what shadows we pursue!"

CHAPTER IV.

PASSAGE FROM RIO TO CAPE HORN.

GETTING UNDER WAY.—THE LETTER-BAG.—RUNAWAY SAILOR.—ISLE OF ST. CATHERINE.—PAMPEROES.—THE SHOTTED GUN.—LOSS OF OUR COON.—THE SAILOR AND SHARK.—GENERAL QUARTERS AT NIGHT.—FIREWORKS IN THE SEA.—THE PHANTOM SHIP.—PATAGONIANS.—THE FALKLAND ISLANDS.—THE CAPTURED ALBATROS.—TERRIFIC GALE.—CONDITION OF OUR FRIGATE.—THE SAILOR'S BURIAL.—THE CAPE OF STORMS.

All hands unmoor—the captain's brief command;
The cablè round the flying capstan rings,
The anchor quits its bed, the sails expand,
The gallant ship before the quick breeze springs.

WEDNESDAY, JAN. 14, 1846. This morning as the first rays of the sun lit the Corcovada peak, we tripped our anchors, and, under a light land breeze, stood down the bay of Rio. It being understood that we were to take our departure at this hour, the officers and crews of the national ships, which lay moored around us, were on deck to see us get under way. This being the first time we had gone through with these evolutions on the cruise, a slight solicitude was felt, lest some awkwardness in executing the orders, some want of perfect harmony and dispatch, should be evinced. The liability to those errors which we wished to avoid, was perhaps only enhanced by the presence of so many professional eyes. But the successive orders were executed with admirable promptitude and accuracy. We left our berth with the grace of the swan gliding from the place of her cradled sleep.

We left at anchor the U. S. frigate Columbia, bearing the broad pennant of Commodore Rousseau, bound to La Plata; the U. S. sloop-of-war Plymouth, bound to the same place; and the U. S. frigate Raritan, bound to the Mexican gulf. To each and all we waved our adieu, and filled away for Cape Horn. What a contrast between what lay around us, and what lay before us! We were exchanging a quiet harbor for a tumbling ocean,—zephyrs too soft to ruffle the cheek of beauty, for storms which the sturdy ship can hardly withstand,—a clime of perpetual sunshine and flowers for one of eternal ice.

Thursday, Jan. 15. We were to-day at 12 o'clock two hundred and sixty miles from our anchorage at Rio, a very good commencement of our run south. We have been looking out all day for some vessel to heave in sight, that we might throw on board her our last letter-bag, which, by a singular inadvertence, had been brought off to sea with us. It had been made up during our last night at Rio, and contained our last words of affection and remembrance; and here it was going with us towards Cape Horn, instead of our homes. This was vexatious, and required that philosophy which the heart is slow to learn. They who can write their friends every twenty-four hours, will let months perhaps roll away without penning them a sentence. But take away this facility, spread an ocean between them and their kindred, and they will look for a vessel bound home as eagerly as a condemned culprit looks for a reprieve or pardon.

FRIDAY, JAN. 16. Our wind still continues directly aft; we have all studding-sails out below and aloft. The weather is extremely warm; the thermometer ranging at 87. The night is quite as oppressive as the day, and perhaps more so, as we are then in our state-rooms. The wind-sail is a great comfort; without it the berth-deck would be almost intolerable. But we are like frogs jumping out of the sun into the frost, and then out of the frost into the sun.

Our sailors while at Rio behaved extremely well. They were constantly passing between the ship and the shore, and frequently without an officer in charge of the boat, and yet but one or two instances of intoxication occurred; only one deserted, and he was so worthless a creature that no efforts were made to recover him. We all felt quite relieved when it was known that he had run; our only fear was, that he would relent and come back. Captain Du Pont might have said to him with some propriety, "I shall punish you, not for running away, for that was relieving us of a bad man, but for coming back." Our Rio runaway did not, however, return; if this was the result of an unwillingness to ask further our charity and forbearance, he is certainly entitled to some praise.

SATURDAY, JAN. 17. The weather still continues close and sultry. The sky is filled with a dull haze, the sea is smooth, the breeze very light and directly aft, where it has been for the last eight-and-forty hours, and yet we have sailed between 12 o'clock yesterday and the same hour to-day 105 miles. Four knots the hour is slow sailing by the clock, but in the aggregate for the day extends over a wide space of water. You would think so, were you doomed to swim it, though you might have three months to do it in. No man should complain of a horse or a ship that carries him faster than he can carry himself.

Besides, why should we be in haste to reach our port? We are out here on a great ocean, exempt from all the troubles and perplexities of the shore. Realms may be revolutionized, capitals shaken, dynasties overthrown, and we feel and know it not. We are as secure as Mahomet's coffin, swinging high and serene above the careering sirocco. If the world wearies you, if its frivolities sicken or its crimes overwhelm you, proceed to sea, get out on the broad ocean, and hold communion with the stars and the free billows. Here you are not a slave to custom, you are not trammelled by party, you have not to coin your cheek to smiles. The ocean exacts no such homage; but impresses on her children a portion of her own grandeur and strength.

SUNDAY, JAN. 18. We have had divine service on a very unquiet deck. The fall of the barometer through the first watch, last night, indicated a change in the weather. It came, during the mid-watch, in the shape of a strong blow from the southeast. This is the first pampero that we have encountered, and if the rest are like this, the fewer we have of them the better. They knock you off your course, raise a tumbling sea, and then leave you like a culprit escaping from the scene of his outrage.

We have passed the Brazilian island of St. Catharine, unable to gratify our curiosity by any stay there. This small island has many attractions; its fruits are unrivalled; its scenery is wild and picturesque; its inhabitants are mild and amiable. The climate, though warm, is so modified by a sea-breeze that the heat is never oppressive. The birds of this island are remarkable for the sweetness and brilliancy of their music. The fertility of the soil is seen in the rich verdure which waves in a mass of living green over its steeps and glens. Could Eden have taken its departure from the east in the shape of an island, I should think it had anchored itself here under the name of St. Catharine.

> "How sweetly does the moonbeam smile
> To-night upon yon leafy isle!
> Oft, in my fancy's wanderings,
> I've wished that little isle had wings,
> And we, within its fairy bowers,
> Were wafted off to seas unknown,
> Where not a pulse should beat but ours,
> And we might live, love, die alone—
> Far from the cruel and the cold—
> Where the bright eyes of angels only
> Should come around us, to behold
> A paradise so pure and lonely."

Monday, Jan. 19th. The wind is still out of the south and in our teeth. It has taken up its stand there like the indignant angel heading off Balaam's ass. This reminds me of an anecdote not more out of place here than the graceless animal that introduces it. A man who stammered to such a degree that he was under the necessity, when journeying, to have an interpreter with him, encountered on the road a clergyman, mounted on rather a sorry-looking horse. Before the parties met, the stammerer told his interpreter that he was going to pro-pro-pose to the par-par-parson a certain question, and then explained, in his broken dialect, what the question was.

As the clergyman came up, the stammerer saluted him with "Good morning, Mr. par-par-parson: can you tell me wha-wha-wha"—Here the interpreter came in to his relief, and, with a satirical leer in his look, told the parson that his companion wished to ask him—what made Balaam's ass speak. The clergyman instantly replied, "Why, Balaam was a stammerer, and his ass spake for him." This is not the only instance in which a wicked wag, attempting an impudent witticism upon a simple-hearted man, has fallen into his own snare. Wisdom is justified of her children.

But I forget the ship and our destination. The last we might well forget till the wind hauls. Nothing conduces more to resignation than losing sight of your objects. We are always in the greatest fever nearest our goal. Youth may indeed pursue interests which can be reached only in age; but enthusiasm and anticipation overleap this gulf of years, leaving action and reality to come along afterwards. Love lights its lamp long before it reaches its shrine; so long, indeed, that it often goes out on the road; and when once quenched, there is no Promethean spark that can rekindle it. But what have lamps and love, or ladies either, to do with our getting to Cape Horn?

Tuesday, Jan. 20. The wind has hauled to the west at last, and we are now laying our course. But such a change in the temperature! our thermometer fell fifteen degrees in almost as many minutes, and remains there like a broken-down politician. A day or two since, and we were panting with heat even in our thinnest dress; now we are in winter apparel, and cold at that. Our crew are barking all over the ship. It is a little singular that the two animals which withstand these changes of climate the best, are man and the hog. I always had some regard for this last animal till he was introduced into Congress to help out a metaphor of party animosity; since that, I have seen him roasted without compunction. Every thing is known by the uses to which it is put.

We have had for some time past a shot in one of our spar-deck guns, which we found it impossible at Rio to dislodge, to make room for firing a salute. Every other expedient having failed, it was decided to-day to fire it off. The danger lay in the gun's bursting. It was trained to one of the forward ports, the crew ordered below, and a slow match applied to it. It went off, and the ball with it, into the infinity of space, harming nothing save the air through which it passed, and which closed up again as suddenly as Europe restored itself to its old landmarks after the battle of Waterloo. This was a tragedy running foul of a counterplot in the very last scene. It was a triumphant wave just sweeping the shore, and then suddenly thrown back by a rock to whence it came.

"Thanks for that lesson: it will teach
To after warriors more
Than high philosophy can preach,
And vainly preached before."

WEDNESDAY, JAN. 21st. We met this morning with an irreparable loss in the death of our coon. He took passage on board our frigate at Norfolk. The great presidential election having just closed, and there being no further occasion for his distinguished services, till another campaign should open, he determined to spend a portion of the intervening time in studying the habits and customs of coons in other lands.

He had been extremely occupied at Rio with the objects of his mission, and probably neglected those precautions observed by coons in a torrid zone. He was seized with a malady beyond the sagacity of the profession, and which suddenly unrove his life line. This evening he was silently consigned to the deep, by the boatswain's mate, who committed a great breach of propriety in not piping him over. But he probably thought that one who had been so honored in his life could dispense with ceremony at his death. My Ariel, however, who loved the coon, and will long lament his loss, has penned the following:

12

ELEGY ON THE COON.

Thou meek and melancholy moon!
Smile sweetly on yon curling wave,
For 'neath its foam our gentle coon
Is in his grave.

No more he'll leave his woodland hole
To frolic with the fox,
Or meet the Whiggies, cheek by jowl,
At ballot-box:

No more will stir the Locos' bile
By his provoking pranks—
To think that he, who lead their file,
Should quit their ranks.

In grand processions he stood out,
High o'er the gaping crowd,
As if to him arose that shout,
Full thunder loud.

He knew to chasten his desires,
To curb all selfish wishes,
And left to those who worked the wires
The loaves and fishes.

The flowing waves will softly wreath
A chaplet on his breast,
The sighing winds a requiem breathe
Above his rest.

We are to-day nearly past the broad mouth of the Plata. The wind for the last twenty-four hours has been extremely light, but we have made about a hundred miles on our course. At this rate we shall soon be beyond the reach of the pampero. This wind gives no admonition; it springs upon you like a serpent from the brake, striking with its fang before it springs its rattle. This is foul play, but we must put up with it, or make ourselves ridiculous over a wayward element.

THURSDAY, JAN. 22d. We caught our first shark this morning. The rogue had been following in the wake of our ship for some hours. The sailors baited a large hook with a piece of pork, and let it trail by a long line from the stern. The shark nabbed it, and finding himself caught, attempted to break the line by his vigorous plunge, but it was too strong for him. He was soon brought on deck, cut up, and on the fire broiling for dinner. The sailors ate him with that savage glee which often attends an act of retributive justice. But for eating him, they felt quite sure he would in the end eat some of them. The way to *finish* an adversary is to eat him up. He will then give you no further trouble save in the digestion. Anthropophagy is greatly abused. It is much more innocent to devour a man's body than his character; yet the latter is done every day; while even a vague rumor of the former will fill a whole community with consternation. But what has this to do with getting to Cape Horn?

Friday, Jan. 23d. Fresh meat at this rate will soon cease to be a dainty with us. One of our crew harpooned a huge porpoise this morning. He shared the fate of the shark, on coals and the gridiron. He makes very good eating; rather dry, as the Irishman said—picking the bones of an owl, which he had shot for a grouse.

We went to general quarters this afternoon; all fire and lights having been first extinguished. The crew went through with the evolutions of an engagement with an enthusiasm that would not dishonor the reality. On these exercises depends in a great measure the efficiency of a ship when the crisis comes. But there is one feature of the arrangement not quite to my liking. I am stationed at the capstan to take notes of the action; very cool business when balls are flying around you like hail! If there is any fighting to be done I wish to do my part of it, but not with a goose-quill. That weapon does very well when there are no cutlasses, powder, and shot about, but it is not quite the thing with which to protect your own deck or board the enemy. It is said the chaplain of the Chesapeake, who wielded a cutlass instead of a goose-quill, gave the commander of the Shannon, as he attempted to board, the wound of which he ultimately died: so much

For one whose courage cut him loose
From weapons furnished by a goose.

Saturday, Jan. 24. We were to-day at 12 o'clock full half way from Rio to Cape Horn. The wind is on our starboard quarter, the sea smooth, and we are slipping along six and seven knots the hour. The atmosphere has that smoky appearance which is characteristic of our clime when the autumn has set in. An albatros has been circling around our ship to-day. He is a large white bird approaching the swan in size, but with shorter neck and longer wings.

Last night, on the eve of the mid-watch, the drum rolled all hands out of their hammocks. We sprung to the deck, and went to general quarters. The guns were cast loose, and we went through with the evolutions of a night engagement. Hardly a loud word was heard, though the manœuvring of our ship, and the management of her batteries, would have signalized us in the battle of the Nile. If we are to have a fight, we shall know how to go at it, whether it come at noon or midnight. What would have surprised a stranger most, was the quickness with which every one appeared on deck, when the call was beat. From the first tap of the drum not more than three minutes elapsed before the last hammock was stowed, and its roused occupant was ready for action. The marine officer, who occupies the state-room adjoining mine, must have jumped into his clothes without the time to draw them on:

Ere you could open well your eye,
He stood in arms prepared to die.

Sunday, Jan. 25. We have had no service today, in consequence of a cold which I had taken, and which rendered speaking extremely difficult. Our wind still holds, without having veered scarcely a point, and is now carrying us onward ten knots the hour.

We had last night a splendid exhibition of aquatic fireworks. The night was perfectly dark, and the sea smooth; and you might see a thousand living rockets shooting off in all directions from our ship, and, running through countless configurations, return to her, leaving their track still bright with inextinguishable flame. Then they would start again, whirling through every possible gyration, till the whole ocean around seemed medallioned with fire. The fact was, we had run into an immense shoal of porpoises and small fish. The sea being filled at the same time with animalculæ, which emit a bright phosphoric light when the water is agitated, the chase of the porpoises after these small fish created the beautiful phenomena described. The light was so strong that you could see the fish with the utmost distinctness. They lit their own path, like a skyrocket in a dark night. Our ship left the track of its keel in flame for half a mile. I have witnessed the illumination of St. Peter's and the castle of Michael Angelo at Rome, and heard the shout of the vast multitudes as the splendors broke over the dark cope of night; but no pyrotechnic displays ever got up by human skill, could rival the exhibitions of nature around our ship. Give me a phosphoric sea and a shoal of porpoises for fireworks: out on man and his vanity; he is outdone, even with the thunders of the Vatican at his command, by the ocean hog!

Monday, Jan. 26. We have been engaged to-day in stumping our top-gallant-masts, and striking below some six of our spar-deck guns. The gales often encountered off Cape Horn render these precautions expedient on board a man-of-war. She is not like a merchantman, with the great bulk and weight of her cargo down in the hold; her heavy batteries, the strong decks which support them, her lofty masts, solid spars, and immense field of canvas, are all above water-mark. She feels, therefore, more than her mercantile sister, the strength of the wind, and rolls more fearfully to its force.

It is seldom indeed that a man-of-war is lost. But her safety lies in her precautions,—in the fact that she has not the same motive for carrying sail as a merchant-ship rushing to a market,—and in the great amount of living force which she can throw upon her yards in any sudden emergency. Her crew is necessarily sufficient not only for managing her sails, but for working her batteries, and can at a moment be summoned to this duty or that, as the occasion requires. In this lies her safety in storms and her strength in battle.

Tuesday, Jan. 27. We were at twelve o'clock to-day within six hundred miles of the Cape. We had a ten-knot breeze, and the prospect of a fine run, when a black thunder-storm careered into the sky directly ahead. We had only time to shorten sail before it was upon us. It swept past, throwing back its forked lightning. I regretted its departure about as much as I should that of a savage disappearing in the thicket, and throwing behind the sheen of his tomahawk.

But one evil the storm has wrought us: it has destroyed our good wind, and left us to look out for another, like a widow for a second husband. No lady should marry a second time. If her first husband was a good one, she should cherish his memory; if bad, he should serve as a beacon. Gentlemen may marry again; for they were once allowed as many wives as they wished, and it would be a pity if under any circumstances they couldn't have one. But somehow the ladies outdo us entirely in these second marriages, and in most other things which require tact and management. But what has this to do with getting to Cape Horn?

A large number of black whales are plunging about our ship. They have a long heavy motion, and move over a swell like a lubberly Dutch merchantman. How the lazy rascals ever secure their food is unaccountable. I should suppose every thing would drift out of their way. They move in Indian file, and their uneven backs, rippling above the water, so closely resemble the bumps of the sea-serpent, that I began to suspect we had got into the neighborhood of Nahant, or that the commanders of her fishing-smacks had lost forever their great marine fiction:

"Our army swore terribly in Flanders."

WEDNESDAY, JAN. 28. Our good wind, which the thunder-squall knocked down last evening, has not yet recovered itself. It occasionally sends out a breath, but it comes faintly, as from some dying thing. I fear we shall have to part with it. Let its grave be in the clouds, and let the softest sunlight rest upon it. May the thunder which has killed it be compelled to roll its funeral dirge.

Our thermometer has stood to-day at 60. The sky at the zenith has been brilliant, but on the horizon full of mist. The refraction of the sun's rays in the latter, has the effect to lift the distant line of the sea into a circular wall. We seem to float in the centre of a magnificent basin, the rim of which soars into the circumambient line of the sky. It is an amphitheatre of waters, and as daylight darkens over it, the stars hang in the blue dome their lamps of gushing light. No human architecture can rival its beauty and grandeur. The Coliseum, which exhausted the genius and wealth of Rome, dwindles into a cock-pit at its side. Nations might be seated here as spectators, and the navies of the world float in the arena. How nature pours contempt on the vanity of man wherever she encounters it! From the fathomless depths of the rolling ocean to the dew-drop that trembles on the thorn, she sends out her challenge, and covers the presumptuous competitor with humiliation. She is the mirror of her Maker, and images forth his power; and chiefly thou, great ocean, ever rolling, ever free and full of strength!

> "Time writes no wrinkles on thine azure brow;
> Such as creation's dawn beheld, thou rollest now."

THURSDAY, JAN. 29. We discovered this morning, on our weather bow, a small white cloud, skimming along the undulating line of the horizon. Its shape, its whiteness, in contrast with the dark background of the sky, and its horizontal movement, all gave its appearance a singularity that arrested our attention. When first seen, it was going east, but it soon tacked, and stood west. It was distinctly visible, as it rose on the crest of a long sweeping wave, and then seemed lost behind its tumbling foam—

"A speck, a mist, a shape, I wist!
And still it near'd and near'd:
As if it dodged a water sprite,
It plunged and tack'd and veer'd."

But it proved to be no water sprite—no phantom-ship, but a good and substantial whaler, of New Bedford, bound home after a successful cruise. Right glad were we to fall in with her on this frozen realm of waters. We saluted her with "Hail Columbia!" She sent a boat alongside, and her mate came on board. She had just doubled Cape Horn, where she fell in with several vessels waiting for a change of the wind. She had been out eighteen months, and was in good condition. In half an hour our letter-bag was ready, the mate took it on board, and she filled away. She is again but a speck on the slope of the ocean, and is now beneath its blue verge.

Friday, Jan. 29. Our wind, which the thunder-storm had crushed, has at last sprung up again with renewed vigor, like truth overpowered for a time by falsehood. As if to make up for its temporary overthrow, it is now overdoing the business. We have been obliged to take in our topgallant-sails, and fetch a reef in our topsails. We are now between the

Falkland islands and the Patagonian coast, some three hundred miles from the Cape. We are heading, close-hauled, for the Strait Le Mair. The sea is pretty rough, but we are tumbling over it at the rate of nine knots the hour. The air is cold and searching, sleet and hail are on our deck. What a transition from the melting rays of Rio! A leap from a lightning cloud into an iceberg!

The wind has hauled, and we are now heading in for the Patagonians. We shall find them, says one of our mess, who has been among them, not a diminutive race, as is generally represented, but tall, well formed, and possessing great muscular power. They live in huts, which resemble gipsy tents, are clad in skins, and subsist on seals, guanacoes, and birds. The women dress like the men, plait their long hair, but wear no ornament in the ear or nose. They have all a bronze complexion, smooth skin, and one accredited evidence of nobility, small hands and feet. The men are fond of the chase, and are dexterous in the use of the lance and bow. The women are attached to their children, but are kept in vassalage to the other sex. Their religion is that of nature, and its spirit partakes of the wild and dreary elements which prevail around them. Let those who prefer the savage state embark for Patagonia,

And rid themselves of ills and ails
With every meal they make on snails.

SATURDAY, JAN. 31. We gave up the Patagonians as soon as the wind permitted, and are steering again for the Strait Le Mair. The wind is fitful and uncertain, and the air cold enough to make you snap your fingers; but the sky, which through the morning was overhung with clouds, now throws its blue and brilliant lake on the eye.

The Falkland Islands lie on our larboard quarter, and serve as huge ice-breakers to the coast. Nothing can be imagined more terrible and sublime than the rush of a steep iceberg against these towering masses of rock. The tumult and roar of an Austerlitz or Marengo might pass unheeded. So much does nature outdo man, even when he rouses in flames and blood.

The Falkland Islands serve one important purpose in the economy of the nautical world. They are a resting-place between two great confluent oceans. Here ships in want of water can find it bubbling up as freshly as if it had never felt the chain of winter. Wild cattle are leaping among its rocks free and unfettered as goats among Alpine crags. Wild geese and ducks swarm in the bays; snipe are so tame, you can knock them over with your gun if you have not skill to shoot them, a circumstance that would suit me. The eggs of the penguin, albatros, and gull, as they return from the sea to rear a new generation, cover acres, as thick as hailstones; while the tea-plant, unlike its delicate Chinese sister, blooms out amid eternal frost.

Sunday, Feb. 1. Lat. 53° 56′ s., long. 64° 49′ w. We are now within forty miles of Staten Land, that huge barrier-rock of the American continent, around which raves the Antarctic sea. It is the very throne of Eolus, the centre of storms which never slumber. One of them struck us a few hours since, and carried away our fore-topsail. It was an old sail, and we bent another in its place, which will prove true to its trust. We have sent down our top-gallant yards, and set our try-sails. Sleet and hail are falling, and the night has closed over us in starless gloom.

Against the night-storm, you who dwell on the land can close your shutters, and retire in safety to repose. That storm summons the sailor from his hammock to the yards. There, on that giddy elevation, with his masts sweeping from sea to sea, the tempest roaring through his shrouds, the thunder bursting overhead, the waves howling beneath, and the quick lightning scorching the eyeballs that meet its glare, the poor sailor attempts to reef sail. One false balance, one parting of that life-line, and he is precipitated into the rushing sea. A shriek is heard; but who in such a night of tumult and terror can save? A bubbling groan ascends: the billows close over their victim, and he sinks to his deep watery bier. His poor mother will long wait and watch for the return of her orphan boy; and his infant sister, unacquainted with death, will still speak his name in gladness. But they will see his face no more! He has gone to that dim bourne—

> From which nor wave, nor sail, nor mariner
> Have e'er returned, nor one fond, farewell word
> Traversed the waters back.

MONDAY, FEB. 2. As we were close-hauled, with Staten Land on our lee-bow, we carried during the night only sail enough to steady the ship. But as day began to glimmer, we shook a reef or two out of our topsails, and set our courses. The sun came up with a cold beam out of an horizon of heavy haze. Light clouds, in the southwest, began to shoot up into the zenith, and were followed by a fierce blow, accompanied with dashes of sleet and hail. Our courses were hauled up, and we were soon under close-reefed topsails, main spencer, and fore-staysail.

2 o'clock, P. M. The indications of a still severer blow are gathering around us. The scud drives over the sky with lightning speed, throwing out here and there its wild black flukes. The sea is running high, and our ship is plunging into it like a mad leviathan. We have bent our storm-sails for the worst that may come. Among small matters, my books, in a heavy roll of the ship, have just fetched away,

and lie in every possible position in my state-room. I have more literature under my feet than I shall ever have in my head.

7 o'clock, P. M. The sun has just burst through the heavy clouds that hang on the horizon, and thrown into light a bark on our weather-quarter. She is visible only as she comes over the combing summit of a mountain wave, and is then lost in the hollow of the sea. So long indeed she disappears, you half believe she is gone forever, when up she comes, hanging upon the plunging verge of another wave. The sun has set, and night is on the deep.

TUESDAY, FEB. 3. Lat. by alt. near noon, 55° 17′ S. Long. by dead reckoning, 61° 32′ W. Distance from Staten Land, 85 miles, bearing N. W. by W. ½ W. (true) heading W. by S., and making no better than W. N. W., allowing two points variation, and one for the heave of the sea. Such is our position, such our prospect for doubling Cape Horn: a head wind, a high sea, and dashes of rain and hail. Still we take matters very quietly. Our dead-lights are in, our hatches hooded, and our ship under close-reefed top-sails. When the wind has blown its blow out, where it now is, we expect it will change its quarters like a spendthrift without cash or credit left.

We looked out this morning for the little bark thrown into vision last evening by a gush of sunset light. But she is now nowhere to be seen. She relieved for the moment our sense of utter dreariness, and will again if she comes within the dark line of our vision. It is not good for man to be alone; and this is as true of a ship at sea as of Adam in Eden. There is only one exhibition of social solitude so dreary as that of a single ship at sea, and that is the condition of an old bachelor.

A large number of the albatros and stormy petrel have been following us for hours to pick up the crumbs which the cooks of the different messes throw over. The albatros gets all the larger bits; the little petrel darts about under its overshadowing wings, and looks up for permission like an infant to its mother's eyes. The night has closed over us; not a star looks out through the thick mass of clouds above, and only the combing billow flashes through the darkness beneath.

Night, and storm, and darkness, and the ocean,
Heaving 'gainst their strength its sullen motion.

WEDNESDAY, FEB. 4. Our gale which had held out three days broke down last night in the midwatch, but the fragments of its strength have had sufficient calcitrating force to prevent our making any perceptible progress to-day. We are this evening within a few miles of where we were at the last sunset, and the wind, which comes in occasional puffs, is still in our teeth. This is doubling Cape Horn.

There is no mistake about this cape. It has shoved itself out here for no idle or mistaken purpose. It always has, and always will, exact homage from seamen. It may now and then, from some whim, allow a ship to pass without these tokens of fealty, just as the pope may permit a subject to come into his presence without kissing his great toe. But then it may put the very next ship into a quarantine from which she would be glad to escape into a Spanish lazaretto.

Our little bark is again in sight, hovering like an unquiet cloud on the horizon. She bears up with right good heart against the winds. Steady, my little ocean friend! Keep up thy indomitable courage; thou shalt yet weather this cape of ice and thunder. To-day we harpooned a cape porpoise. It differs widely from those found in other zones; is more lithe and slender; seems formed for speed, and has beautiful black and white stripes running from head to tail; the flesh is less dry, and the liver might almost tempt a pisciverous epicure.

Thursday, Feb. 5. At 4 o'clock p. m., lat. 56° 27′ s., long. 61° 57 w. In the last fifty-two hours we have made but a little more than one degree of latitude, and less than half a degree of longitude. It will take us a long time at this rate to get around Cape Horn.

The wind during the morning came in cold gusty puffs from the south. At noon the whole southern horizon seemed tumbling up in black jagged masses into the sky. This was a signal for reefing, which none could mistake. But the men had hardly got into the tops before the storm was upon us. It came charged with hail and sleet, and lasted some three hours. The masses of cloud then broke asunder, and through their rift the sun-light streamed like a torrent from a forest-covered steep.

Two enormous whales have been plunging about us to-day. Their huge backs as they crossed the hollow of the sea might have been mistaken for a reef of rocks. They blow like a locomotive puffing off steam. Every puff sends up a shower of spray which may be seen at a great distance, and which guides the Nantucketite with his glittering harpoon. But who would trust his vessel in such a sea as this with a dead whale at her side? I should as soon think of lashing to an iceberg.

8 o'clock, P. M. The cold sun has just set; and our barometer has fallen to 29.44—lower than it has been since we left Norfolk. It has never yet deceived us, and if true now, we shall have a stormy night. But let it come—

> The earth will on its glowing axle roll
> Though billows howl and tempests shake the pole.

Friday, Feb. 6. Our barometer vaticinated correctly last evening. The storm which it predicted came punctually as an executioner to his condemned culprit. It lasted through the greater part of the night, and left us with a heavy head-sea. Going on deck this morning I found it extremely difficult to preserve my balance, and brought up in the scuppers, though I have been on sea-legs between fifteen and twenty years.

A long line was floated astern this morning, with hook and bait, for an albatros. Several of these noble birds were sailing in our wake. One of them took the hook, and as he was drawn slowly towards the ship his female companion followed close at his side. When lifted in she looked up with an expression of anxiety and bereavement that would not dishonor the wife of his captor in a reverse of circumstances. We found in his shape some resemblance to the wild-goose, but much larger in head and body, and with a longer wing. The hook had not injured him, and though his wings, which measured twelve feet between their tips, were pinioned, he walked the deck with a proud defiant air. His large eye flashed with indignation and menace. His beak was armed with a strong hook like that of the falcon, his plumage was white as the driven snow, and the down on his neck soft as moonlight melting over the verge of an evening cloud.

He was captured by one of our passengers, who now proposed to kill him for the sake of his wings. But the sailors, who always associate something sacred with this bird, interfered. They predicted nothing but head winds, storms, and misfortunes if he should be killed; and unlocking his wings, gave him a toss over the ship's side into his own wild element. His consort, who had followed the ship closely during his captivity, received him with outstretched wings. She sailed around him as he lighted, and in her caressing joy, threw her soft neck now over this wing and now over that. In a few moments they were cradled side by side, and he was telling her, I doubt not, of the savage beings he had been among, and of his narrow escape.

Live on ye bright-eyed pair; the deep
Is yours, each crested wave shall keep
Its vigils o'er your cradled sleep.

SATURDAY, FEB. 7. We have made but very little progress during the last two days. A slant of wind has occasionally favored us, but with the counter-current, it has been about as much as we could do to hold our own. What we gain when the wind hauls we are sure to lose when it returns to its old position. It is in our teeth, and has been there, with brief variations, for the last six days. Unless it changes we may box about her till doomsday.

Out on Cape Horn! Had it shoved itself between Pandemonium and Paradise, Milton would never have expected Lucifer to weather it. He would have sent him across the Isthmus of Panama. There ought to be a ship-canal there; not for demons, but for men. If Cheops could build himself a tomb which the rays of the new-risen sun should greet before they touched the lyre of Memnon; if Brunell could arch a pathway under the Thames for the multitudes of London, with navies on its bosom; and if Whitney can run a railroad from the Atlantic board to Oregon through the Rocky Mountains, surely the civilized powers of Europe, and those of America combined, can cut a canal across the Isthmus of Panama. I only wish all who oppose the project were obliged to double Cape Horn; they would give in before they got round, if not, a jackass might take lessons from their obstinacy.

I have swept, with the telescope, the whole horizon to find our little attendant bark, but not a vestige of her is to be seen. We parted with her two days since at nightfall. But she is still, I doubt not, afloat, and will again loom to light. Courage, my little fellow; you may outdo us yet—

"The race is not—to be got
By him what swiftest runs,
Nor is the battell—to the peopell
What's got the longest guns."

CHAPTER V.

PASSAGE FROM CAPE HORN TO VALPARAISO.

GALE.—HABITS OF THE ALBATROS AND PENGUIN.—THE SEA OFF CAPE HORN.—SLEET AND HAIL.—FAREWELL TO THE CAPE.—DIRECTIONS FOR DOUBLING THE CAPE.—GALE IN THE PACIFIC.—APPEARANCE OF THE STARS.—A RAINBOW.—DIVINE SERVICE.—THE RAZOR AT SEA.—THE LITTLE BARK.—PLUM PUDDING AND TRIPE.—THE CORDILLERAS.—ARRIVAL AT VALPARAISO.

Amid the storm, an iceberg's form
Came tumbling through the ocean,
So like the cape in hue and shape
Our crew, who watched its motion,
While rounding-to beneath our lee,
Declared the Cape had put to sea.

SUNDAY, FEB. 8. The severity of the weather and the heave of the sea prevent our holding divine service to-day. May each heart silently erect within itself an altar on which to offer the oblations of contrition, gratitude, and faith. Religion is a mission from Heaven to the heart of man; and when taken away from that heart, and shrined in stately temples and sumptuous altars, it loses its vitality and power. No floating censer or pealing organ can have the moral efficacy of that still small voice of the Deity, which speaks in the whispers of the human conscience.

The gale which we have had for several days veered last night, and brought the heave of the sea under our quarter. It was enough to make our ship roll her masts out of her. Every thing not secured by strong lashings fetched away. Even the shot were thrown from the combings of our main hatch. As for repose in our berths, the Countess of Nottingham had as much of it under the death-shakings of her indignant queen,—till that last sleep overtook her which grief and rage reach not. I write this with my inkstand fastened down, my chair and table secured to the deck, and my paper presenting a plane at every heave of the sea steep enough, if it were covered with snow, to tempt the sledge of the truant.

7 o'clock, P. M. Our barometer is now down to 28.44, and is still falling. The gale has become truly terrific; the sea and sky seem rushing together. We can only carry our storm try-sails; and even their strength is tested to the last thread. The whole ocean is white with foam, which falls in cataracts from the crests of soaring waves. It is terrible and sublime to watch one of these huge combers heaving up within the horizon, and rolling mast high upon you. Niagara gazed at from the boiling abyss, is its only parallel. The hail is driving upon our deck, the sea breaking over our bows, and a starless night closing in. Yet a spirit of cheerfulness and alacrity in duty animates all. Captain Du Pont, with his thorough experience and sound judgment, leaves the deck only to return to it again. Our first

lieutenant is exercising that vigilance which never fails him through the ship, and our watch-officers meet the emergency with great firmness. But our trust is in Him who can say to the chainless wave, hitherto shalt thou come, and no further, and here shall thy proud strength be stayed.

Monday, Feb. 9. The gale still continues with unmitigated force. Our ship has a good character for steadiness, but last night she plunged and rolled like a leviathan in his death-throes. At every heave of the sea she rolled her lee guns under. The water which was forced through her ports lay on her gun-deck ankle deep, and rolled in sheets over the combings of her hatches. Her lee scuppers could not be opened to carry it off; and in opening her weather ones there was great danger of admitting a torrent to let out a rivulet.

In the mid-watch my library, secretary, mirror, and washstand, fetched away. The books and looking-glass rushed together into my cot. I was half asleep, and thought for the moment our guns were tumbling below. In extricating myself I cut my hands with the fragments of the mirror. I felt for my clothes, and found them on the floor, covered with the wreck of my wash-bowl and pitcher, and well drenched. I hauled on a few articles and groped out to the gun-deck to get a light. The watch on deck had just been relieved and were crowding below, covered with sleet, stiff with cold, and wading through water ankle deep to reach their hammocks; there to turn in and sleep in these drenched frozen garments. What are my petty griefs compared with this? I got my light, and dividing my berth with my books, shivered mirror, manuscripts, inkstand, razors, chessmen, and broken flasks of casash, turned in—abundantly satisfied with the romance of sea-life.

Tuesday, Feb. 10. Lat. 57° 34′ s., long. 61° 32′ w. We are very near where we were a week ago. Seven days of the roughest sea-service and in *statu quo!* Our progress resembles that of Ichabod's courtship, who being asked, after seven years of devoted attentions, how he got along in the business, replied that now and then he thought he had a little encouragement, and should feel quite sure of it were it not for the rebuffs.

The gale broke down last evening. The remnant of its force hauled round to the south and enabled us to lay our course, but a heavy head-sea has prevented our carrying sail. By the time the sea goes down, and we have shaken a few reefs out of our topsails, it may whirl back, and then we shall have to fight the battle over again, as the whigs said when President Tyler suddenly took up his old democratic position. But *nil desperandum,* the whigs will in time come into power, and we shall in time double Cape Horn. But the Cape and the democracy are both hard to weather.

Our little bark is once more in sight. She has survived the gale, and is now, with good heart, struggling forward to double the Cape. Our stormy petrels still follow us. They are ever on the wing, close to our stern, to pick up the crumbs which are thrown overboard. Capt. King, of the British navy, states that having caught one of these birds and fastened a piece of ribbon to it, to designate it, he ascertained that it followed his ship over five thousand miles. A lesson to all good wives with wayward husbands.

Wednesday, Feb. 11. The wind, as we predicted, has gone back to its old quarter, like a wolf to his jungle. We have only been able to hold our own. Sunset leaves us where the flushing day found us.

We have the albatros still about us, but we have missed the penguin. The habits of these birds are peculiar, especially when they get up their annual rookery. They select for this purpose, as one informs me who has been among them, a plot of smooth ground, covering two or three acres, and opening on the sea. From this they remove the sharp pebbles, piling them on each side into a miniature stone-fence. The ground is then plotted off into little squares, with paths intersecting each other at right angles. In each corner of the square a penguin scoops out a nest; while the albatros takes, by common consent, the centre, raises a small mound and constructs a nest on the top, so that each albatros has four penguins around him. The paths, which resemble gravelled walks, are used for promenading and exercise, except the broad one, which runs around the whole encampment, and where sentries are constantly patrolling. These sentries give the alarm at the approach of danger, and are relieved at regular intervals. The watch is kept up night and day, and is always under the command of the albatros.

When the eggs have been laid, the strictest vigilance is exercised by the albatros to prevent the penguin from stealing them; for the penguin lays but one egg, and, as if ashamed of making all this ado for the sake of that one, tries to get another from the nest of the albatros. But the latter has no idea of gratifying the domestic ambition of its neighbor in that way. There is of course little need among them of a foundling hospital.

The eggs are never left or exposed to a breath of cold air during incubation. The male bird, who has been at sea seeking his repast, returns and takes the place of his faithful consort. He always allows her the most favorable hours out of the twenty-four in which to secure her food, and often brings it to her, especially when the infant progeny requires her more delicate maternal attentions. He never ill-treats his mate, or goes off at the dead of night serenading other birds. He may have indeed his little domestic troubles, but he overcomes them by kindness and affection. His partner always greets him, on returning from his brief excursions at sea, with the liveliest expressions of gladness. Ye who prate of incompatibilities, and fly to a legislature for an act of separation if a little jar occurs at your hearth, look at these birds, and if there be shame or compunction in ye, go find your divorced mates and resolve not to be outdone in forbearance and attachment by an albatros.

When the little ones get sufficiently strong to endure a change of element, the penguins and albatros break up their encampment, and young and old take to the sea, that great harvest-field where the reapers of earth and air, under a beneficent Providence, gather their food. But what have penguins to do with our getting round Cape Horn?

THURSDAY, FEB. 12. The lion-wind still roars from its old lair. That lair lies directly in our path. If we attempt to escape it on the right, the breakers of Cape Horn lift their thunder; if we try to avoid it on the left, tumbling icebergs present their steep fronts. So here we are, hemmed in like the hero of Marengo, amid the black battlements and keen hail of Russia's capital and clime. Patience, thou meekest virtue in man, still pour on us thy soft, submissive light.

10 o'clock, P. M. The wind went down with the sun, leaving only the long, low undulations of the sea. The moon is forth, placid as if this were no region of storms. The stars, without an obscuring veil, blaze in the deep blue vault of heaven. A flood of diamond light melts down through the depths of air, and pours itself in radiant softness on the sea. There it lies unbroken and still, save where the sleeping ocean gently heaves, like one who should breathe in his shroud. Such a night as this in the region of Cape Horn! It is as if a nightingale were to pour its liquid melody through the interludes of the forest-shaking storm.

But our anxiety is to know where, amid this serenity of the sea, the wind will next wake up—where the slumbering storm will first howl on the waste. The rising sun will not find us in that repose on which he shed his parting glance.

> A change will come, like that the sculptor throws
> In lines of life, on marble's cold repose.

FRIDAY, FEB. 13. In the night, our old frigate beginning to stir herself complainingly, like one troubled with bad dreams, I asked the officer of the deck, as he came below from the mid-watch, about the wind. "In gusts from the northwest," was the reply. From the northwest! then we are laying our course—that will do; and I relapsed back again into slumber, and dreamed we had rounded Cape Horn. I saw it sheer astern, storming like a savage at the escape of his intended victim.

The wind favored us during the morning, and we shot ahead with high hopes of success. But by noon it began to haul round towards the south, and in an hour or two more reached its old quarter, the southwest. It is now blowing a gale, and we have all sails furled except our close-reefed main-top and storm try-sails. The sea is running high, and the huge combers, shaking the foam from their crests, are rushing down upon us like a host of cavalry frothing at the bit. The sun is sinking in cold dim light, and seems to abandon the ocean to the lashing tempest.

Such is the life of the sailor: one hour is full of sunshine, the next of storms. He lives between hope and disappointment: they alternate through his whole existence. Nothing but the most indomitable resolution could endure the vicissitudes of his lot. He is cheerful when others would despond, and triumphs when others would despair. He elicits sparks of joy from his hard lot, as you strike flashes of fire from flint. Ye who sigh over the tales of fictitious bereavement, bestow one glance on this real tragedy of life. Here are woes which no illusion paints,—a death-knell rung by no unseen hands.

SATURDAY, FEB. 14. The passenger who caught the first albatros, and which was liberated by the crew, caught another the day following and killed it to get its wings. It would probably have been rescued by the sailors had they been aware of the cruel intention of its captor. They associate a sacredness with this noble bird which invests it with the privileges of a charmed life, and regard a violation of this sanctity as an outrage, which will be followed by disastrous consequences. Dark ominous looks fell on their faces when the wild whisper went round among them that the beautiful albatros had been killed. We had been for several days in thick foul weather—

"At length did cross this albatros;
Through the fog it came;
As if it had been a Christian soul,
We hailed it in God's name.

"And a good north wind sprung up behind;
The albatros did follow,
And every day for food, or play,
Came to the mariner's hollo.

"And he has done a hellish thing,
And it will work us woe;
For all averr'd, he had killed the bird
That made the breeze to blow."

"And it will work us woe"—and so it has proved, for we have had ever since head winds, gales, and storms. These, in the simple creed of the sailor, are the penalties through which expiation is to be made for the crime of having killed the albatros.

SUNDAY, FEB. 15. Lat. 58° 39′ S., long. 68° 41′ W. We are at last some forty-five miles west of Cape Horn, and about one hundred and sixty south of it. This position we have gained in spite of the elements, by taking prompt advantage of those slight variations which will occur in winds of remarkable constancy: still we are not round the cape; for the wind is dead ahead, and is blowing almost a gale. We are on our larboard tack, close hauled, and shall be obliged this evening to wear ship and stand off to the southeast, where the heave of the sea alone, if the gale continues, will soon throw us back into the meridian of the cape. Such is life at sea; gaining, losing, persevering, and finally triumphing.

8 o'clock, P. M. The cutting gale still continues. The sun has set in gloomy grandeur. As he plunged below the horizon, a flood of flame flashed up through the masses of cloud which overhung his descent.

This soon vanished; and now thick darkness settles on the sea. The light of a full moon cannot struggle through it, and the brightest star glimmers on it faintly as the glow-worm on the pall of the coffined dead. Our sailors have had to-day very little of that comfort and rest which belong to the Sabbath. Though sent aloft as seldom as the condition of the ship would allow, still they have been often on the yards, with the rain and sleet driving in their faces. Nor have those on the deck fared much better. When off watch and allowed to reach the berth-deck, they have found their Bibles and tracts. May these scattered rays of heavenly light reach their hearts, and point their hopes to that shore where clouds and storms come not.

MONDAY, FEB. 16. Our southwest gale went suddenly down last night, and this morning a fresh wind rose in the northwest. We are now laying our course with a fair prospect of getting clear of Cape Horn. I have no desire of ever coming near this cape again. I would give it a berth world-wide.

Here and there a navigator, it is true, has doubled the Cape without encountering the gales which we have experienced. But his good fortune was an exception to a general rule. A man may escape death under the gallows by the breaking of the rope; but then the fifty, who come after him, will swing till dead. This cape has acquired its stormy reputation by its acts. Had nautical theory only invested it with difficulties, they would long since have been dissipated by experience. But what navigators found the Cape a century ago, their successors find it now. It is as true to its stormy character as a lion to his savage instincts. You may as well trifle with the shaking mane of the one as with the awaking tempest of the other.

A distinguished naval commander—the late Commodore Porter—who had cruised in almost every sea, inserted in his journal this significant paragraph: "The passage round Cape Horn, from the eastward, I assert, from my own experience, is the most dangerous, most difficult, and attended with more hardships than that of the same distance in any other part of the world."

TUESDAY, FEB. 17. Lat. 58° 10′ S., long. 73° 33′ W. We are at last round Cape Horn. We have left its stormy steeps astern, and are holding our course, with a stiff northwester, for more congenial climes.

FAREWELL TO CAPE HORN.

Cape of clouds, of hail and thunder,
Towering o'er a savage sea,
Let the earth's wide circuit sunder
Our departing keel and thee.

On thy scalp the keen hail dances,
  At thy base mad breakers roar,
'Neath thine eye the iceberg glances
  From its steep antarctic shore.

'Mid thy billows' wild commotion,
  In thy sea of tumbling foam,
Scaly monsters of the ocean
  Share this undisputed home.

Ships of oak, with storm-sails riven,
  From thy plunging combers reel,
Like the war-horse backward driven,
  From the serried ranks of steel.

Morn in smiles hath ne'er ascended
  O'er thy summit stark and drear;
Day and night are dimly blended
  In thy sunless atmosphere.

Cape of clouds, of hail, and thunder,
  Sinking o'er the ocean's swell,
Rallied hope and chiding wonder
  Shout to thee their stern farewell.

WEDNESDAY, FEB. 18. Our northwest wind, which we feared would fail us before we had made sufficient westing, began to awaken this afternoon apprehensions of a very different character. It suddenly rose into a gale of terrific energy. It seemed to pin the men to the shrouds as they tried to draw themselves up into the tops. Such was its roar through the rigging, you could hardly hear a man at the top of his voice six feet off. It rivalled in force the hurricane which we experienced off Tortugas, in 1831, and the sea it raised ran much higher. Our quarter-boats were in danger of being rolled under.

3 o'clock, P. M. We have had to sail under close-reefed main-top, and fore and mizen storm try-sails. It seemed almost impossible for a ship to live in such a sea as now roared and heaved around us. Each comber in its towering height, seemed to bring with it the plunging force of a Niagara. It was as if the steep side of a mountain, with torrents foaming down its crags, were thrown against you by the earthquake. Had it struck us full on the broadside it would have dashed us into fragments. But our ship, with buoyant energy, rose up steadily over it, and descended again into the abyss, to encounter another just like it. This continued till near sunset, when the gale gradually subsided, and now, at midnight, is scarcely sufficient to give us steerage way.

THURSDAY, FEB. 19. The sun came up clear, over a calm, cold sea. We waited impatiently for the wind; it came at length in broken gusts from the north, and so continued through the day. At sunset we had a dash of hail from a group of passing clouds. The troubled twilight died away into a dark, cheerless night.

In doubling Cape Horn from the Atlantic, experienced navigators, who differ in almost every other suggestion, agree in this—the expediency of keeping near the land, and especially so if the passage is made with the sun south of the equator. In this period of the year westerly winds prevail. They often rise in the northwest, yet in their sweep around the Isles of Diego Ramirez, take a westerly direction. Near the land you are within their circle, and can take advantage of every eddy to make westing, but further south you get their full force, and directly in your teeth.

Besides, there is very little danger of being driven on the cape. It is a weatherly shore. The heave of the sea is counteracted, close in, by the strength of the current, which sets with great force to the east. This current will carry a vessel off towards the Falkland Islands with the wind from the southwest and even south. And should it veer into the southeast, the reacting force of the current, close in, renders the position of your vessel comparatively safe, even when she is bound into the Atlantic. This provision of nature against being driven on the cape, is one of the few alleviations which she has thrown into the hardships of the mariner's lot.

In rounding the cape from the Pacific the summer months are the best, for then you have short nights and westerly winds. In rounding it from the

Atlantic you have a choice of evils in the different seasons. In the winter you have long nights and icebergs, but favorable winds. In the summer you have head winds, but short nights and no ice. Captain King, of the British navy, who has spent several years in the vicinity of the cape, prefers the winter months. But Basil Hall, as the result of his experience, recommends the summer season. My own opinion is, that any man who has a log-hut on land, with a corn cake at the fire, and who will consent to leave them to double Cape Horn for any purpose whatever, is a proper subject for a lunatic asylum.

Friday, Feb. 20. Lat. 59° 51′ s., long. 80° 12′ w. The wind having veered this morning into the southwest, we tacked ship and stood north. The weather through the day has had all the extremes incident to high latitudes ; an hour of bright sunshine, and then a squall. We have not had at any time since we came off the cape, a smooth sea and a steady wind. We have now the long, sweeping waves of the Pacific. They image, in their majesty, the grandeur of the ocean over which they roll. Nature never impairs the sublimity of her works by blending the trivial with the vast. The shout of her torrents fills with solemn echoes the old ancestral wood. The many-voiced waves of her oceans shake the green isles with their stately anthems.

But nature has, in this portion of her mighty domain, sources of the beautiful and sublime in the constellations which light her heavens. Each star burns out from the blue vault with the brilliancy and force of an independent sun. It has a breadth of circle and an intensity of light which opens on you like the flame from the eye of the volcano. And then there is the Southern Cross, a constellation hanging serene and beautiful over the troubled night of the grave. To it not only the Christian pilgrim turns in his path to heaven, but the weary traveller of earth seeks his late repose by its inclined beam.

"'Tis past midnight; the Cross begins to bend."

SATURDAY, FEB. 21. Our westerly winds still hold; we are braced up sharp, and steering north. But we have had to-day a strong current setting us east, and trying to drive us back again off Cape Horn. We have lost by its force one degree of the westing we had made. If it continues, and the wind remains in its present quarter, we shall be obliged ultimately to tack ship and stand off to the southwest; a gloomy, discouraging result. It is the fate of Agag after congratulating himself on his escape. But He whose steps are on the clouds, and whose pathway is in the mighty deep, will order all things right.

We had to-day, at sunset, a sudden shower. It fell from a cloud travelling east upon an upper current of air, and which carried on its front, as it passed down over the swelling arch of the ocean, a magnificent sun-bow. A moment before all had been cloud, darkness, and storm—

> " When overhead this rainbow, bursting through
> The scattering clouds, shone, spanning the dark sea,
> Resting its bright base on the quivering blue:
> And all within its arch appeared to be
> Clearer than that without, and its wide hue
> Waxed broad and waving like a banner free.
> It changed again; a heavenly chameleon,
> The airy child of vapor and the sun,
> Brought forth in purple, cradled in vermilion,
> Baptized in molten gold, and swathed in dun."

Sunday, Feb. 22. Though the sea is rough, and the roll of the ship deep, we have had divine service. Even a brief service is much better than none. It is a recognition of the sanctity of the Sabbath, and of our obligations to that Being whose guardian care is our defence.

If dependence can awaken the voice of supplication, the sailor, of all men, should be the most devout. His poor frail bark floats between life and death. A sudden tempest, a latent rock, or a spark of fire, and he sinks into a strangling grave. He may emerge, but it is only to strike his strong arms in wild despair. No drifting plank floats between him and the "pale bourne." Prepared or unprepared, he must appear at once before the dread tribunal and answer for the deeds of his erring life. He should live with these awful realities ever present to his thoughts. Like the bird of the stormy peak, his pinion should be ever ready to unfurl itself. But from *his* flight there is no return; he is off into the boundless unknown.

This is the anniversary of the birthday of Washington. Its sacredness is in harmony with his serene virtues. Too pure for corruption, too disinterested for ambition, he lived for his country and his God. The entire energies of his being were surrendered to those great interests which will quicken the hopes of man when the marble that guards his dust has crumbled. He has left an example which throws its steady light on the fetters of captive nations and into the pale recesses of kings. Millions who sit in darkness will yet hail its auroral splendors.

MONDAY, FEB. 23. To save ourselves from being carried back among the Patagonians, we have tacked ship and are standing southwest by west. This, with two points variation, and the current in our favor, will enable us to make a nearly west course. With the first material variation in the wind we shall be able to go upon our larboard tack and make a stretch up the coast.

The high sea and heavy roll of our ship made the

use of the razor this morning a delicate operation. I had strapped the instrument and laid it on my bureau, when away it went into the wash-bowl. Having fished it up and made it secure, I got out my china box of shaving-soap, but laying it down for a moment to find the brush, crash it went on the floor. Picking up the fragments, I managed to raise suds enough for the present occasion; when looking around for my razor, to my astonishment, it could nowhere be found. It had fetched away again, and brought up in one of my boots. But I had no sooner recovered it, than my candle, having caught the moving infection, rushed into my cot and scorched my pillow-case. All things being righted again, and a little fresh suds applied where the old had evaporated, I took the razor, and watching for the ship to get on an even keel, gave a clip; but it so happened the ship plunged instead of rolling, and this brought the point of the razor in contact with the extremity of the nose, where a severe cut proclaimed itself in a gush of blood. But stanching the wound, I managed at length, by a clip here, and another there, to disencumber the chin of its stubble. Such are some of the advantages for shaving at sea. Man was made perfect, but has sought out many inventions, and this of shaving at all is one of them.

TUESDAY, FEB. 24. Lat. 53° 35′ s., long. 78° 56′ w.

> "It comes resistless, and with foaming sweep,
> Upturns the whitening surface of the deep;
> In such a tempest, borne to deeds of death,
> The wild-weird sisters scour the blasted heath."

The black clouds which hovered in the western horizon last evening, hung their banners of darkness over the descending sun, as if impatient of the presence of that orb in the frightful work which they purposed. Before his level rays had left the ocean, their waiting squadrons began to rally. One black cohort after another filed into the ranks, till they presented a solid mass of impetuous strength. Thus compact, they moved down upon the plane of the trembling sea. When opening to the right and left, a tempest rushed forth, which seemingly nothing but the stable mountains could withstand.

Our ship had been put under storm-sails for the encounter; and yet, even with this precaution, she rolled down before its force like a crushed foe; while the crested waves howled over her as savages in a death-dance over their victim. It was some minutes before she could recover herself. She was overpowered, but her courage was not broken. At every pause in the storm she came up, and then plunged into it as if for life or death. The conflict closed about midnight, and our ship won another laurel for steadiness and strength. This was the most violent gale that we have experienced.

Wednesday, Feb. 25. We had this evening one of the most beautiful phenomena connected with sunset at sea. The flaming orb had been for more than an hour below the horizon, when the long, dark bank of clouds, beneath which he had disappeared, lifted, disclosing a lake of golden light, which poured its melting radiance far and wide over the sea. It seemed as a rosy morn rising out of the bosom of night.

Not a star lit the blue vault, and yet the spars and tracery of our ship became visible in the soft effulgence of the departed sun. When the beautiful of earth die, they carry their pale charms with them to the shroud; but when the brilliant orbs of the sky depart, they light their very pall with their surviving splendors. The light even of the Pleiad, lost in the infant world, still circles around her choiring sisters, who have poured for ages her sweet melodious dirge.

Our long-lost, little bark peered to light this morning on our lee-beam. We had parted with her in a storm off the Cape, and had relinquished all expectation of falling in with her again. But here she is, within three miles of us, with the American ensign flying at her peak, in answer to ours. We may yet speak her. She is, we conjecture, the Charles, which sailed from Boston on the first of November, bound to the Sandwich Islands. If she stops at Valparaiso she will probably find us there. We outsail her, though she has managed, by keeping close in, to double the Horn with us.

THURSDAY, FEB. 26. Our west wind continued through yesterday and carried us some eight knots the hour towards our port; but this morning it has veered into the north and compelled us to go upon our starboard tack. This steering due west, when our port lies due north, is reaching our destination by right angles. But there is no angle, that ever yet shaped itself in the wildest mathematical dream, which is not described by a ship at sea. The path of the boa constrictor is not further from a right line.

Our nights are beginning to lengthen as we approach the sun. Off the Cape we had only a brief dip of darkness. The day was sixteen hours, twilight three, and the night five. Our fowls lost their reckoning, and were clucking and crowing when they should have been asleep. What could be done in our country with only five hours of night? Before the élite of our city got to a party it would be daylight; and as for the rural swain, who does all his courting on Sunday night, the sun would be up before he had got half way to the all-important, yet very awkward question. He would have to begin anew each Sabbath eve, and stop where he left off before. A sailor would settle the whole business in fifteen minutes, and what is more, he would then stick to his bargain for better or worse. He never troubles a court or legislature for a divorce. If he cannot make good weather on one tack he tries another; but he never throws his mate overboard, nor scuttles his own ship. But let that pass.

Friday, Feb. 27. It is now forty-four days since we left Rio. We had a splendid run to the Cape, but since that we have wrenched every league from the elements by the hardest. We sailed two thousand miles off the Cape to make four hundred on our course. We literally beat round it. A feat that has been deemed almost impracticable. We have hardly been for an hour without a head wind and a head sea. We have the latter to-day, but a wind from the west that is driving us on in spite of it nine knots the hour.

We are rapidly reaching more genial latitudes. The transition is like that from Lapland to the Line. The severity of the cold off the cape is inexplicable. The thermometer never fell below the freezing point, and yet no amount of clothing we could put on, would keep us warm. We shivered in double flannels and over-coats; our feet, had they been chiselled from ice, could scarcely have been colder;

and all this in a temperature that would not crisp a pool of sleeping water. Hail fell, it is true, with great force and frequency, but it was from upper strata of air. The currents nearer the sea would not have congealed vapor.

It will be said we felt the cold more, coming, as we did, from a torrid clime. But the system does not cool down so rapidly. The rigors of the first northern winter are felt least by those born nearest the sun. The Italian division in the Russian campaign suffered less than any other. The Poles fell like icicles from a tree shaken by a winter storm, while the Neapolitans seemed to melt the very snows in which they bivouacked. The cold we experienced is to be ascribed to the absorption of electricity from the system by the condition of the atmosphere.

Saturday, Feb. 28. Lat. 45° 10′ s., long. 80° 24′ w. We are now making a good run towards our port. If our west wind holds we shall in a few days let go our anchors in the harbor of Valparaiso. Fresh meat, vegetables, and milk will be a luxury. Our last pig and fowl went some days since to the cook. Our potatoes still hold out, but they are not larger than bullets, and are as full of water as a tick of blood. Our hommony is in the kernel, and will not soften sufficiently for use short of a week's boiling, which is hardly practicable in a ship's economy of water.

The only fresh article of the flesh kind that comes upon our table, is salmon, which has been preserved in air-tight jars. Our bread is baked on board; by what process it is attempted to be raised I know not; but well would it be for human nature were its vanity as little puffed up. We attempted a plum-pudding to-day, but every plum was as soundly imbedded as marine fossils in primitive rocks. We have some tripe left, but I understand the leader of our band wants it for a drum-head, and our blacksmith is anxious to get it for an apron. If its aptitudes determine the disposition to be made of it, no connoisseur in gastrotomy can save it from the anvil or the drum. Well dried it would ring a good tattoo,

Or shield a Vulcan, while he shapes
The form his bolted thunder takes.

Sunday, March 1. Divine service on the spar-deck; officers and crew present; the air balmy; the broad Pacific heaving in silent majesty around, and a soft cloud, loaded with the incense of nature, soaring into the great dome of heaven. Lead me for worship—

Not to the dome, where crumbling arch and column
Attest the feebleness of mortal hand,

But to the fane, most catholic and solemn,
Which God hath planned:
To that cathedral, boundless as her wonder,
Whose quenchless lamps the sun and moon supply;
Its choir, the winds and waves; its organ, thunder;
Its dome, the sky.

Found in the sick-bay to-day a sailor, who spoke feelingly and well on the subject of religion. He is a member of the Methodist church, and carries a warm, devoted heart under his rude exterior. It is not the smoothest cloud that has in it the most of summer's balmy breath. It is a great comfort to me to find among the crew here and there one of earnest piety. His example flashes out like a star from a sky of cloud and storm. God grant these lights may be multiplied till our whole horizon shall be lit with their steady splendors.

Mrs. Ten Eyke, the wife of our consul on board, whose health has been for some time delicate, is gradually sinking. How cold the grave to one so young, to whom the earth seems so fair, and life so full of joyous pulses! O death! to thy unbreathing realm glide silently away the beautiful and the beloved.

"They hear a voice, we may not hear,
Which says they must not stay;
They see a hand we may not see,
Which beckons them away."

MONDAY, MARCH 2. We fidded our topgallant-masts; crossed our royal yards; rousted up and mounted the eight spar-deck guns, which had been struck below off the Cape; unbent our heavy topsails and courses, and bent lighter ones; holystoned our decks; scrubbed our paint-work; cleaned our brass rails; finished our new side-ladder; and repaired the whaleboat stove in the gale. A good day's work all this, and a wide stride in our preparations for port. Our band in the mean time is practising some brilliant airs, with which we expect to captivate the Chilanos. But of all the music that ever melted on mortal ear, give me

> The lay of streamlets, and the trill of birds,
> The lisp of children, and their earliest words.

The cœlebs may turn away from these earliest words, for they have a music which he understands not. There is not a string in his soul which they can touch—not a chord to vibrate as their pulses play over it. But should he wed, and a sweet miniature of life reflect his own features, lisp with his voice, and smile with his eyes, he would hang over it as the Peri over the long-sought secret that was to admit her to celestial bliss. Its faintest note would breathe a sweeter strain than ever trembled from the strings of the Orphean lyre. The earth might be full of loudest harmonies, but he would still turn his ear to that slender note of piping infancy. But let that pass.

TUESDAY, MARCH 3. Our studding-sails, which have lain undisturbed for several weeks, have been out to-day, below and aloft, to a light breeze from the south. The sea has been smooth, presenting only its long, majestic undulations. The ocean never rests. From the day morn first broke over its silent depths, it has been rolling on to the present hour. Capitals have crumbled on its shores, thrones and dynasties perished, but it still rolls on in the majesty of its unabated strength.

Our preparations for port are still going on. Our standing rigging has been tarred; our masts, yards, booms, and hull have received a fresh coat of paint. Our guns are beginning to throw back the sun-light from their polished surface. You would hardly suspect such vollied thunder could sleep in their recesses. Our cutlasses have been furbished, our boarding-pikes sharpened, and our carbines made true to their trust. We bear the olive-branch and the sword.

Our albatrosses have left us. They followed us to the verge of the summer's clime, and then, wheeling on their bold, arching wings, sped back to their wintry domain. They were our only companions off the Cape, and something like a sentiment of bereavement fell on us, as they took their departure.

The heart will doubly feel alone,
When that which served to cheer hath flown.

Wednesday, March 4. Our sick list, which ran up to forty, in consequence of the hardships and exposures off the cape, is rapidly diminishing. Commodore Stockton, who has been quite ill, is convalescent. We should regret extremely any circumstance that would deprive us of the pleasures and advantages derived from our present relations to him. Mr. G., one of our watch officers, has been for some days confined to his berth. But he is gathering strength again, and will soon be able to resume his post on the quarter-deck.

As for myself, I am a slender reed, easily bowed before the blast, but coming up again as soon as its force is spent. I entered the navy with a constitution impaired by sedentary habits, and have perhaps derived some advantage from the recreations and adventures involved in a sea-life. I have been in every variety of climate, but I doubt much if these changes have been promotive of health. My advice to invalids is, never go to sea with the expectation that ship-board is to restore you. A change of climate may be of benefit, but the passage in nine cases out of ten will begin in seasickness and end in debility. If you have a comfortable home, stay by it; if your digestion is bad, stop eating; if your nerves are deranged, bathe in cold water; if you have children, romp and frolic with them. This is much better than sucking sugar canes in Cuba, or going to Rome to kiss the pope's toe.

THURSDAY, MARCH 5. Our hawse bucklers are out, our chains bent, and we are now ready to let go our anchors; we are still seventy miles from our port, but the first breeze, which breaks the calm of the sea, will probably take us in. We are now fifty one days out from Rio, and more than half of them have been passed in storms. We have been at sea since we left the United States, one hundred and three days; and have sailed, in that time, twelve thousand two hundred and twenty miles. We have yet some twelve thousand miles more to sail before we circle round into the port where we may look for repose. Our ship is another dove over the unsubsided waters of the deluge.

Several of the stormy petrels, which joined us before we reached the Cape, are still skimming along in the wake of our keel. They follow us, as little politicians their leader, for crumbs, not of office—they are too sensible for that—but of Jack's tablecloth; and in doing this they never displace or disturb their betters. Between a stormy petrel and a little party politician I should not hesitate a moment where to place my regard. We have had about us to-day a flotilla of whales, sharks, and porpoises. Their gambols stirred the sleeping sea into foam.

They seemed to be trying their speed. The whale was quickest to the goal, but slowest in doubling it. His head is entirely too far from his tail. I commend his case to the Owenites at their next world-convention.

Friday, March 6. The light breeze which fanned us along faintly through the night, has left us in the morning-watch within twenty miles of our port. The coast on our starboard beam lies full in view, with its deep indentations, and its bold bluffs, against which the Pacific rolls its surge. Far in the background rise the stupendous steeps of the Cordilleras, throwing their shadows a hundred miles at sea. On their summit, glittering with the icy hail of centuries, the morning star furls its wing of flame. Beneath such a vision, what is man? He disappears, and his shadow, as if ashamed to linger, goes with him.

The breeze, for which we have been waiting and watching, has come. Our studding-sails, below and aloft, are out to catch its first breath. We are again moving up the coast. Fifteen miles of it are passed, but no headland appears which we can identify with those designated on the chart. Seven more, and still no evidences of a harbor. We begin to think our master, like a Millerite, has left out some figure in his reckoning.

At last we discover, upon a slight swell in the

coast, a little lighthouse, but no bay, and nothing that indicates one. Doubling this projection, we catch our first glimpse of Valparaiso, nestled among the fissures and shelves of a steep ascent of rocks. It seems one of those wild nooks in which pirates might have sought a perilous home. Taking in our studding-sails, and hauling up our courses, we have rounded to handsomely, and anchored in thirty-two fathoms.

All eyes are directed to the shipping. A French man-of-war has already saluted us; a national courtesy which we have promptly returned. But we are looking for the American flag; only one can be seen, and that is flying over a merchantman. No national vessel holds out any hope of letters from home by the Isthmus. Our disappointment is confirmed by our consul, who informs us that no dispatches have been received from the United States of a date subsequent to our departure, except a copy of the President's message, which was brought in the English mail, and which was considered quite belligerent in its tone. The news of the resignation of the Peel ministry greatly surprises us, and has in it, as we fancy, quite a little war-cloud. A national ship abroad catches every premonition of hostilities as quickly as a barometer the approach of a storm.

So, here we are at last in front of Valparaiso, with a continent and an ocean between us and our homes;

another ocean still to be traversed, and to roll us yet wider asunder; and then this war-cloud on the horizon! But there is one separation, one which awaits us all, still wider than this—the chasm of the grave. Over that no signals extend, and no messenger-bird hath winged its way. I have walked in its pale light for years, hovering between the sun and a total eclipse.

> "Art is long, and Time is fleeting,
>   And our hearts, though stout and brave,
> Still, like muffled drums, are beating
>   Funeral marches to the grave."

CHAPTER VI.

SKETCHES OF VALPARAISO.

ASPECT OF THE CITY.—GROUPS ON THE QUAY.—CHILIAN HORSEMANSHIP.—THE WOMEN.—HUTS OF THE NATIVES.—AMERICAN AND ENGLISH SOCIETY.—OPERA-HOUSE.—THE TERTULIA.—MODE OF TRAVELLING.—POLICE OF THE CITY.—VISITS FROM THE SHORE.—FEUDAL SYSTEM.—THE CLERGY.—THE BIBLE IN CHILI.—THE CONFESSIONAL.—BURIAL GROUND.—THE INDIAN MOTHER.—POLITICAL CONDITION OF CHILI.—FAREWELL TO VALPARAISO.

Where Valparaiso's cliffs and flowers,
In mirrored wildness, sweep
Their shadows round the mermaid's bowers,
Our steadfast anchors sleep.

SATURDAY, MARCH 7. Valparaiso, at a first glance, instead of justifying the name it bears—the vale of Paradise—might rather be called some outpost of purgatory. Its wild crags, its scorched hills, and dark glens might well be supposed to lead to that intermediate abode of condemned spirits. You are puzzled to know why a city should be there. Without encroaching on the sea, there is hardly room enough, between the base of the steep acclivities and the surge, to set up a fisherman's hut. The harbor is but little better than an open roadstead. A norther is an admonition to all vessels to slip their cables.

Yet Valparaiso is a city, and one which, having

once seen, you will never forget. It will stand alone in your after-dreams like Jacob's ladder. Like the rounds in that airy vision, its buildings ascend, roof over roof, till they seem to topple in the sky. One violent shake of an earthquake would precipitate the whole into the sea. And yet these terrible visitations are constantly throwing out their premonitions. There is not a building whose walls have not vibrated to their force. There is not a rock on which they rest, but is of volcanic origin. The soaring peaks of the Cordilleras, which overhang them, rest on craters that may at any moment throw them heaven-high. And yet who does not sleep sound in Valparaiso? Such is peril, when it has become an old familiar acquaintance.

We landed from our boat on the jetty, which has been thrown out from the beach to prevent the necessity of debarking in the surf. The quay was alive with boatmen, cracking their jokes over their water-melons and coarse bread. A fat friar was seen straying among them, willing to shrive the most wayward for a large melon. One fellow, who looked as if he had obliquities enough to justify some effacing process, made light of the proffered shrift. He thought a green melon would pay.

Near by sat a Chilano on a stone, which swelled up from the pavement, tantalizing the strings of a guitar, while a little cloud of tobacco-smoke curled up around the high cone of his felt hat. The only accompaniment was the sharp creak of a file, with which a muleteer was sharpening the rowel of his spurs, which resembled a circular saw, except that the teeth were much longer.

Here a beggar, who had lost a leg, hobbled up to us, wearing around his neck a label, showing that he had the permission of the police to solicit alms on Tuesdays and Saturdays. Poor fellow! if his limb was lost in a good cause, he ought to be allowed to solicit charity when he can get it. And if it was lost even in a scuffle, it would not be in my heart to deny him a penny. What a world is this in which we dwell! How is it filled with paupers, spurs, tobacco, guitars, water-melons, and absolving monks; all jangling and jargoning along together to dusty death! What an incongruous mass the grave covers!

SUNDAY, MARCH 8. Divine service on board; a large attendance of Americans from the shore. Subject of the discourse—cause and criminality of indecision in matters of religion. The state religion of Chili is the Roman Catholic. Protestant forms of worship are tolerated, but in a private way. The erection of churches for the purpose is not permitted. A hall may be used, if it has no symbols of consecration. Think of that, my dear Papal brothers in the

United States, kneeling in your sumptuous cathedrals, while your vesper-bells summon from their lofty steeples the faithful to prayer. And you talk to us Protestants about toleration! Why, there is more toleration in my Uncle Toby's teapot than can be found in the whole Papal See.

Before you assey the ballot-box again, because the Bible, without note or comment, is permitted in our public schools, look abroad and see what privileges you extend to Protestants. In those countries where your religion and laws are all paramount, you do not tolerate the consecration of the humblest chapel; and as for a steeple and bell, they would not stand long enough to knell their own ruin. And yet you talk of toleration, and lecture the whole world on Christian charity! The language of forbearance and fraternal love melts from your lips softly as dew on the flowers of Hermon. One would think, from your professions, Protestants must have a perfect elysium in your lands. But somehow it strangely happens that they are disqualified for holding any office of civil trust; and are denied even a consecrated place of worship. They are fortunate if allowed the sanctity of a grave.

In Chili, intolerance flows purely from the mandates of the Papal hierarchy. Legislators, as a body, are well disposed, but they cannot carry their liberal measures without putting the stability of their civil institutions in peril. An act of religious toleration would be followed by ecclesiastical denunciations and appeals to the passions of the mass, which would result in revolution and blood. Come here, my bishop of New York, with your smooth doctrines about the rights of conscience, and talk a little to your brother bishops in this quarter. If these doctrines are good when proclaimed to American Protestants, let us see how they will sound in the ears of Chilian Catholics. Do a few leagues of salt water destroy their force and propriety? Do they cease to be orthodox the moment they leave a Protestant shore and enter a Papal domain?

Come, my dear bishop, set down here in Chili with me, and let us talk together a little. You tell us the rights of the human conscience are sacred. What rights of conscience have Protestants in Chili—or even in Rome? You go there once in three years to report in person to the holy Father, you see Protestants filing off on the Sabbath through a narrow, dirty street, to a little, obscure chapel, without steeple or bell, where they may worship, if they won't speak above a whisper. And then you return to New York and talk to its corporation about the sacred rights of conscience! Your toleration, my dear bishop, is much like the Yankee hunter's division of game with his Indian companion—all turkey on one side and all buzzard on the other.

Monday, March 9. I encountered, in my rambles to-day, a specimen of Chilian horsemanship. The costume of the rider was in wild harmony with his occupation. His hat rose in a high cone, like that of a whirling dervish in Turkey. His poncho, resembling a large shawl, fell in careless folds around his person. His gaiters rose to the knee; his heels were armed with a huge pair of silver-mounted spurs, while a brace of pistols peered from the holster of his saddle-bow. He was mounted on a powerful animal,

impatient of the bit, and sure of foot as the mountain roe. The strong muscles betrayed their swelling lines in his limbs; the dilating nostril was full of panting force, while his arching neck seemed clothed with thunder. He was such a steed as you would hoose for that last decisive charge, in which a Waterloo is to be won or lost.

His rider knew him well and gave him the rein; on he dashed, over hill and vale, with the speed of the wind. Now shaking the topling crags with his iron hoof, now plunging down the steep ravine, now leaping, with frightful force, the sudden chasm; never missing his foothold, never throwing his rider. Both were safe where the neck of neither seemed worth a farthing. I have seen the Tartar ride at Constantinople, and witnessed, with silent admiration, the Grand Sultan's horsemanship, but he is outdone by the Chilano.

A company of circus-riders, from Europe, came here a few years since to astonish the Chilians. But they soon found they had brought their ware to a wrong market. The Chilanos took the business out of their hands; and so far outdid them that they suddenly disappeared, and have not been heard of in these parts since. It was like a buffalo entering a herd of deer to astonish them with his fleetness, or like a bull attempting a race with one of Baldwin's locomotives.

The Chilian women betray their Spanish blood. It is seen in their stately forms, their firm elastic step, their nut-brown complexion, their large black eyes, and their earnestness of manner, which is full of silent, significant force. They wear their hair in two plaits, which are sometimes coiled into a turban and interlaced with flowers, and at others flows from a slight fillet, quite down to the heel. They use no stays; the tide of nature ebbs and flows without constraint. The rich shawl which covers the neck and shoulders, neglects at times its occupation, and the silk stocking forgets now and then that it has taken the veil.

They are fond of attentions, and will much sooner excuse a liberty, which flows from admiration, than a neglect, which results from indifference; still they are not considered as very exacting. What they want is the homage of the heart. Civility that has no soul in it, they consider a mockery. Love is consequently with them a passion. As daughters, they are wild and thoughtless; as mothers, fond of their children and attached to their homes. The most sober flower will often blossom from the bud that has danced the most lightly in the sunbeam.

Tuesday, March 10. I encountered to-day in the environs of Valparaiso, a long string of donkeys, laden with vegetables and fruit from Quilota, some forty miles distant. The little hardy fellows were plodding along in single file, covered up under their huge panniers, and turning this way or that to the cry of their driver, who brought up the rear. I never could encounter one of these creatures without a sentiment of pity and even respect. He seems as one doomed to drudgery, merely because nature has wronged him in making him up. And then his patience—it is a model. He has long ears it is true, but then he never, like those who consider themselves his betters, tries to conceal them. He is an honest ass!

The markets of Valparaiso are supplied from valleys in the interior. The grounds in the immediate neighborhood are, for many months in the year, parched up with drouth. Large tracts of land, well suited to the harrow, are herbless from want of means to irrigate them. Springs have been hunted, and rocks bored almost half-way to the earth's centre, but in vain. Even the monks have tried their miraculous charms, but nature's great Nile obeys no such incantations. Their fleece, unlike that of Gideon, remained dry. No snow falls on these vallies, and no rain, except in the three winter months. The earth becomes baked and broken into deep fissures. When the winds are abroad the dust is driven over it in clouds thick enough to bury a Gipsy encampment.

The huts of the native peasantry are built of reeds, plastered with mud and thatched with straw. They have seldom more than one room, and are generally without a floor. Here the inmates sit, sleep, and work in wigwam-life. They seldom look beyond their present wants. Their industry ebbs or flows as plenty or penury prevail. Out of these murky cabins beauty sometimes emerges in a combination of charms that might stir the chisel of a Praxiteles.

The females are generally pictures of health and animation. Their diet is coarse bread and fruit. They know nothing of the luxuries of the table, and seem to care as little. They are fond of music and dancing, and throw an energy into their motions which would astonish even a Shaker. The quadrille has not sufficient action in it. They prefer the fandango. The old are grouped around the broad circle in which the young couple spring to the vibrations of the guitar or violin. The short dress of the female, and the prurient motions of both, are at war with all our sentiments of propriety. Still, unless nature libel herself, the mothers who witness these exhibitions in their daughters, must be influenced more by a false taste than a lubricity of disposition. This is as true of savage as civilized life—of the Chilian mother as the Roman matron. Nature has thrown her most beautiful iris in a mother's look over the wave which flows from the depths of a daughter's unsullied soul.

Wednesday, March 11. The features of Valparaiso, which strike the stranger with the greatest force, are perhaps the elegant articles of ornament which are presented in the fancy shops. They seem as much out of place here as a jewel in a swine's snout. And yet they are not out of place; for higher forms of fashionable life are seldom encountered. Those little cottages, which gleam from the toppling crags, are garnished with furniture on which the Parisian artist has exhausted his skill. From the balcony rolls out upon the wind the most exquisite music of harp and voice. Such strains from amid such a savage scene! It is like Proserpine, crossing the gloomy Styx, crowned with the flowers of paradise.

The English and Americans here are singularly free from those rivalries and jealousies, which are the besetting sin of foreign residents. They flow together with a congeniality of spirit, which is the source of a thousand pleasures to them as well as the stranger. Their society is the all-redeeming charm of Valparaiso. Their hospitality is open as the day, and warm as their soft clime. You forget in their company the rude rocks and barren hills around you. The earth without may be covered with brambles, but you feel for the time in a sort of Eden whose flowers have escaped the primal malediction. I do not wonder that this is the favorite port with the officers of the Pacific squadron. They always leave it with regret, and cherish for it the most affectionate remembrance.

Who would expect to find among these wild cliffs an opera house, vying, in the elegance of its decorations and the richness of its music, with some of the most liberally endowed establishments in Europe? yet such is the fact. Of its merits I speak from the representations of others, as I have not myself been within its precincts. I declined going, not from an apprehension of moral taint, conducted as the opera is here, but from motives of expediency. I would not indulge even in an innocent amusement, that had assumed a doubtful shape in the imaginations of others. But still I would not be a slave to mere whims, which have no reasonableness and force. I admire an enlightened, sober, independence of opinion and action.

I believe the opera, if introduced thoroughly into the United States, if performed in suitable edifices, and under suitable restrictions, would promote, indirectly at least, the cause of morals and good taste. It would attract to it a thousand young men, who now spend their evenings in grog-shops and at gaming-tables. The opera has its evils, but what human institution has not. If every thing is to be denounced which is not an unmixed good, then every thing emanating from man must go by the board. People will have amusements, it is a law of their social being, and it is your duty as a friend to virtue to look out and encourage the most innocent. You may deride this counsel and persevere in trying to put human nature into a straight jacket; but you will never succeed, and if you could, you would find that jacket any thing but a garment of righteousness.

THURSDAY, MARCH 12. I accompanied last evening several of my wardroom companions to a Chilian tertulia. A broad flight of stairs took us to a large and brilliantly lighted saloon, where we were met by the lady of the mansion who gave us her hand, and welcomed us to Valparaiso. It would have been a little embarrassing to encounter the flash of so many eyes, but for the ease and tact of our accomplished hostess. Instead of taking us around the saloon and introducing us, amid a general suspension of conversation, to the company, which would have embarrassed all parties, she went to talking with us, and in a few minutes managed to introduce us to several ladies, as unceremoniously as if there had been no design in it. This artless tact continued till we were introduced to every lady and gentleman present.

All were at ease and full of talk, though some of us had but a limited range of Spanish at our command. But a great deal of conversation may be made out of a few words, when the heart is glad. The ladies never corrected the wrong word, and affected to understand it just as well as if it had been the right one. Some of them attempted English with the amiable purpose, no doubt, of relieving our blunders by making as many of their own.

"'Tis pleasing to be schooled in a strange tongue
By female lips and eyes * * *
They smile so when one's right, and when one's wrong
They smile still more."

I asked one of the ladies if she would gratify us with a piece of music; she instantly took my arm to the piano, beckoned her sister to her side, and gave us a duett which called back my recollections of poor Malibran. What melodies were quenched for ever when that sweet singer died. Her strain still lingers in the hearts of thousands, but where is she! As a bird from its bower, as a rainbow from its cloud, she has passed away. Spring will call back its little minstrels, and the summer sun rebuild its airy arch. But she, who charmed the world, will come back no more. Her melodious lips are sealed in silence, and the shadow of death is on her eyelids.

'Leaves have their time to fall,
And flowers to wither at the north-wind's breath,
And stars to set—but all,
Thou hast all seasons for thine own, O death!"

But to return to the tertulia. The costume of the ladies differed but little from what you meet with at evening parties in the United States. The hair, which betrayed great care in its arrangement, was ornamented with natural flowers. The dress, generally of a light airy material, had short sleeves, rather low in the neck, with a short, full skirt. The reason assigned for this is, that the wearer may be less embarrassed in dancing, but, perhaps, the pride of a well-turned ankle is an additional motive. The gentlemen were more sedate than the ladies, but their conversation had not half the versatility. At twelve o'clock the tertulia broke up. The lady of the house gave us her hand at parting with a *beuna noche.*

Friday, March 13. Went on shore to-day to take a ride. This has to be done either on the saddle, or in a vehicle resembling our chaise, but of much ruder construction. The latter is preferred for long distances. One horse trots within the shafts, another at his left, on which the postillion is mounted, while half a dozen others accompany the vehicle to act as relays. If these give out, the lasso is resorted to, and some half-wild horse, who a few moments before snuffed the wind in freedom, is within the traces. The postillion seldom troubles himself with the question whether the animal has ever been thoroughly broken to the harness. The wilder, the more speed, and therefore all the better for his purpose. He is master of his business, and seemingly of every thing in nature that can conduce to its success. His driving is like that of Jehu. You expect every moment the old quill-wheel, in which you are embarked, will fly into a thousand pieces. But like the hurdle of the doomed, it still holds together, hurrying you, if not to the gallows, to the grave.

If you take to the saddle you will probably find your stirrups of wood, resembling in shape and size the large beetle with which a New-England farmer splits his rails. Their weight is seemingly relieved by grotesque carving; in the side is a sharp excavation, sufficiently deep to admit one-third of the foot. The saddle is made of raw hide, and a frame which an Indian's hatchet might have shaped. It rises up before and behind like a well-horned half-moon. The bridle has one recommendation, a tremendous bit. But with all this you are on a horse, wild as he may be, that is sure of foot. You can no more get a stumble out of him, were you so disposed, than Lucifer could a defection from duty out of Abdiel, or a whig a bank-vote out of a democrat.

The police of Valparaiso, which once seldom protected the innocent, or punished the guilty, is now unrivalled in efficiency. Its vigilance reaches your person and property through every hour of the day and night. You are safe even in spite of your own negligence. If, for instance, you leave your shop with the window unbolted, you will find the next morning a padlock on it, and one which you cannot remove without paying a fine of three dollars. If you dine out, tarry late at the wine, get tipsy, and can't find your way home, a watchman picks you up, puts you into a chaise, finds out by some means where you live, takes you to your door, and delivers you to your waiting wife, with the good-humored remark that you are a little indisposed. What a capital arrangement for those who have more wine than wit in them!

If you wake up in the night, find one of your family sick, and want a physician, you have only to hand his name to the watchman near your door, who passes it to another, and he to another still, till it reaches its destination, and you soon have the physician at your side. His prescription must perhaps be taken to an apothecary; it is handed to the watch, passed on, and in a few minutes back comes the medicament required. What bachelor might not venture to get married in Valparaiso?

SATURDAY, MARCH 14. The governor of Valparaiso, with his suite, visited our ship this morning. He is a man of some sixty years of age, with no very brilliant qualities, but possesses sound sense. He expressed himself delighted with our frigate, examined every part of her, and received, as he went over her side, the salute due to his rank.

Our ship has been the constant scene of visits from the Chilians. A party has just left us who came all the way from Santiago. They make themselves quite at home on our decks. When the band strikes up, they call for a waltz, or fandango, and commence dancing with just as much freedom as if they were on their own village green, beneath the light of the moon. On leaving they urge us to come and see them, promising us horses to ride, music, and the smiles of a thousand glad eyes. Their invitations are full of sincerity and heart; and for my own part I would much sooner avail myself of them, than the august condescension which should open to me the palace of a king.

The inequalities of the feudal system, introduced from old Spain, still survive in Chili. The lands are owned by the privileged few, and their succession secured by the right of entail. An effort was made a few years since to break up this system, and distribute the lands among the heirs, without reference to any advantages of primogeniture. But the great number of illegitimate children, who came in and urged their claims, rendered the measure a dangerous experiment. It was waived for the time; but unless republicanism here be a farce, it will come back again with augmented force. Freedom and equality are twin-born: they breathe the same air, and share the same destiny. Besides, there is no good reason why a natural child should not share in his father's estates. It is a hard case, indeed, if he must be made a beggar, merely because his parents have made him a child of sin. Let those who thus err pay the penalty. They have planted the tree, and now let them partake its fruit,—apples of Sodom though they be.

The elective franchise involves no property qualification in Chili. All go to the ballot-box; but few, however, deposite thoroughly independent votes. One portion is overawed by the will of their landlords, another by the will of their priests. The ecclesiastics have every thing at issue in the stability of the existing order of things. A revolution would result in a triumph of the Liberals, and a suppression of all monastic institutions. Even the connection of the church with the state could not long survive. The papal hierarchy would have to provide for its maintenance through voluntary contributions.

The ecclesiastics therefore exert all the influence which their position gives them, to uphold the present government. They look to each man's vote, and follow it with a blessing or malediction, which throws its ominous shadow beyond this life. This ecclesiastical power is the most fearful feature in the present condition of the Chilians. Instead of being a wall of defence, it is a wide magazine, laid under its foundations, with a train reaching to Rome. One spark from the Vatican, and Chili sinks in flame and blood!

SUNDAY, MARCH 15. We had to-day at our service a very large attendance from the shore. The weather was remarkably fine; the awning was spread, and we assembled on the spar-deck. After prayers, we sung a hymn in Hamburg, with the band for an orchestra. The sermon turned on the condition of the soul out of Christ: its guilt, its wretchedness, its ruin. Plain and practical sermons are the only ones that do much good. When a preacher forgets the simplicity and meekness of his office, and throws himself, though in a blaze of eloquence, between his hearers and the Cross, he is in a miserably false position. He may win perishing laurels to his fame, but not immortal souls to Christ.

The clergy in Chili exert, through the confessional, an influence which reaches the most private transactions of life. Every communicant is required to confess at least once a year. A refusal to do it is followed by the severest pains and penalties which the church can inflict. Some two years since, a daughter of one of the most prominent members of the legislature of Chili was grossly insulted at the confessional. She told her mother, who, in grief and consternation, related the circumstance to her father. He excused her from going again to the confessional. The year rolled round, and she was summoned to a compliance; the father peremptorily refused his assent. Three of the inferior officers of the church were dispatched to bring her by force. Her father planted himself, armed, on the door-sill of his house, and told them if they entered it would be at their peril. They retired and reported their ill-success to their superior. The next Sabbath she was publicly excommunicated, and her candle at the altar blown out, to signify that her hope of heaven was extinguished.

The father, indignant at the attempt to undermine the virtue of his daughter, and the cruel injustice done her in the act of excommunication, introduced a bill into the national legislature for abolishing entirely the confessional. It produced the most intense excitement; the pulpits of Chili rang with denunciation; the archbishop dispatched a messenger to Rome for the Pope's anathema. Many husbands and fathers, whose wives and daughters had been insulted at the confessional, and who from motives of prudence had remained silent, now began to speak out. But a repugnance to innovation in ecclesiastical affairs, and the combined influence of the clergy prevailed, and the contemplated law was defeated. But it still survives in the breast of its projector, and will yet speak out in thunder-tones.

Instead of attacking the confessional, the domestic evils which it inflicts would perhaps be more thoroughly remedied by abolishing the coerced celibacy of the clergy. This is the prime source of those immoralities which have sapped virtue and overthrown the peace of families. Its abolition would contribute alike to the virtue of the ecclesiastic, and the safety of the communicant. The best-informed writers on Chili, those whose observation has been the most thorough, agree in the fact that many of the clergy live in a state of the most shameful profligacy. These disclosures force upon you the painful conviction, that their illegitimate offspring are found in every circle in the community, and fill every grade of ecclesiastical preferment. Abolish, then, the forced celibacy of the clergy. Blot out at once and forever this apology for crime. Human nature is sufficiently slippery even when it has no excuse for its lapses. In saying this, I intend no sectarian reproach. I would not confide to any religious persuasion the consequences of a forced law of celibacy. Our safety lies not only in an upright conscience, but in freedom from temptation.

Monday, March 16. I have been passing an agreeable evening in the family of Mr. Hobson, our former consul at this port. The amenity and intelligence of Mrs. H. lend an unfailing charm to her conversation. Her daughters have been educated with great care, and are adorned with many intellectual and social accomplishments. It is singular what encounters will occur in one's travels. I met here a lady whom I last saw in the Naval Asylum at Philadelphia, and who had come out there to hear one of my poor sermons. This was a year since. She is now here, and the wife of one of the most enterprising merchants in Valparaiso.

I dined to-day with William Ward, Esq., an American gentleman, who is the senior partner in one of the largest mercantile houses here. His ample mansion and costly furniture are in keeping with the taste and liberality displayed at his table. I met there Mr. Barton, another American gentleman, who is engaged in surveying the route of a contemplated railroad between Valparaiso and Santiago. I passed the morning with the Rev. Mr. Trumbull, from the United States. He is out here under the patronage of the Foreign Evangelical Society. His labors as yet have been confined mostly to seamen; but he has every prospect of having within a short time a congregation on land. Mr. Dorr, our consul, has, with a praiseworthy spirit, interested himself in the objects of his mission; and other Americans have pledged their aid. Such are the stars of hope which are yet to throw their rays through the extremities of Chili.

I visited this afternoon the Protestant burial-ground, which occupies a portion of one of the hills which overlook our anchorage. The situation has been selected with good judgment, and the ground evinces taste and propriety in the arrangement. Here rest many sailors far away from their native shores. A humble slab, erected by their messmates, gives you their names and that of the ship to which they were attached; and sometimes a nautical epitaph, like the following:

> "Here lies the rigging, spars, and hull
> Of sailing-master David Mull."

This to a landsman seems trifling with our poor mortality; not so to the sailor. His technicalities have with him a meaning and a force which, in his judgment, more than sanction their use on the most grave and melancholy occasions. He would pray in this dialect even were life's taper flickering in the socket, or his soul trembling on the verge of despair.

In the Catholic burial-ground, which adjoins the Protestant, stands the beautiful monument of Portales. The genius of History is recording his glorious deeds, Grief lamenting his early doom, and Hope pointing to a fruition in the skies. Near this monument I encountered a youthful mother in weeds, leading her little orphan boy. She carried a bunch of flowers in her hand, and as she came near a new-made grave, kneeled down at its head, and planted them there. Her child kissed them, but when she attempted it her silent tears fell fast on their tender leaves. A bird lit on the tree, which cast its shadows on the grave, and poured a wild sweet strain as if to wean the mourner from her grief; but she heeded it not. Her child turned and listened; her eye fell on his; she heard the bird. Nature triumphs over bereavements through those we love and who still survive.

TUESDAY, MARCH 17. The Indian mother still adheres to the primitive method of carrying her child. Instead of supporting it in her arms, with the un healthful inclination of person which a burden there will always induce, she tosses it on her back, into the bunt of her shawl, and walks off erect as the Indian's tree, which stood up so straight it leaned backward.

When hunger overtakes it she will feel a slight pull on one of the long braids in which her hair falls over its form; and when she takes it out of this travelling cradle to nurse it, there is something new and fresh in its first look: true, it has not been out of her sight for more than an hour, but this with a mother is a long time. But her heart is now running over with happiness,

So deep and vital is the joy
That thrills a mother's breast,
Clasping her infant, blue-eyed boy
From out his cradled rest.

Many attempts have been made to introduce the Bible into Chili. Our countryman, Mr. Wheelwright, who now has a flourishing school in Valparaiso, succeeded in distributing a number of copies in the Spanish language among the people of Quillota. But the priests forbade their being read, and doomed them to the flames. They were brought out and burnt in presence of the assembled multitude. They were without note or comment, and left the sectarian bigotry, that decreed the sacrilegious act, without an apology. What would my venerable friend, Bishop Hughes, say were the Protestants of New York to collect his Douay Bibles and burn them in the Park? Would that, my dear Bishop, be freedom of conscience?

The population of Chili is estimated at about a million and a half. Her commerce is steadily on the increase. Her silver and copper mines richly repay the labor bestowed in working them. Her southern plains yield an abundance of the finest wheat. Her people in the mass are hardy, frugal, and ardent lovers of freedom. The course of education, under her new constitution, is receiving fresh impulses, and gradually emerging into popular favor and national importance. Her public debt amounts to about ten millions of dollars, which is owned mostly in England. Her military establishment, which has burdened her treasury, and sometimes perilled her peace, is melting away under her civil institutions.

In breaking the Spanish yoke, and establishing her independence, she has had to pass through a fiery ordeal. The virtues that could achieve so much, will yet win farther triumphs. No nation or state ever rose at once from vassalage and ignorance to freedom and intelligence. She may emerge into disorder, but that will be more tolerable than the despotism from which she has escaped. To meet the consequences of a revolution, to restore order where it has been broken up, to consolidate the elements of national existence, and settle them on a new and permanent basis, requires all the time which this republic has enjoyed since she proclaimed her independence. There is nothing in the present condition of Chili which should fill the advocates of free institutions with distrust. She has clouds on her sky, but most of them are skeletons from which the storm has long since passed.

But I have no space for a disquisition on Chili. A

labored essay is beyond the scope and purpose of this diary. I have only time to wave my adieu to

VALPARAISO.

Sweet Valparaiso—fare thee well!
  Thy steep romantic shore,
And toppling crags, where wildly dwell
  The echoes, which thy billows pour
As o'er the rocks their anthems swell—
  Shall greet my pilgrim steps no more.
When they whose tread is on thy steep,
  Have down to death's dim chambers gone,
Where harp and lute in silence sleep,
  Thy sweet sea-dirge will still roll on.

CHAPTER VII.

PASSAGE FROM VALPARAISO TO CALLAO.

FLARE UP OF THE PACIFIC.—SONGS OF SEAMEN.—SAILORS ON SHORE.—LOSS OF THE SAMSON OF OUR SHIP.—THE SETTING SUN AT SEA.—OUR ASTOR-HOUSE SAILOR.—THE MAD POET OF THE CREW.—LAND HO!—ASPECT OF CALLAO.—APPEARANCE OF THE NATIVES.—THE BURIAL ISLE.

" Our pennant glitters in the breeze,
Our home is on the sea:
Where wind may blow, or billow flow,
No limits to the free:
No limits to the free, my boys,
Let wind and wave waft on,
The boundless world of waters is,
My merry men, our own."

WEDNESDAY, MARCH 18. We tripped our anchors this morning and stood out to sea from the bay of Valparaiso. While getting under way, a boat from the British ship Daphne came alongside with dispatches for Admiral Seymour, in command of the Collingwood, on the coast of California. No sooner were these received, and orders given to make sail, than three other boats were seen starting from the shore at the top of their speed. Our ship was hove to till they came up. Two of them had communications to merchants in Callao. The third had in her two of our runaway sailors, who had been picked up by the police, and whom we were very sorry to see again ; for they were notoriously the two most worthless fellows on board. But we were not, it seems, to get rid of them in this way. So true is it that a bad penny always comes back.

Thursday, March 19. Before coming into the Pacific, our imaginations were filled with dreams of its majestic tranquillity. But if the exhibition it made of itself last night be a fair specimen of its character, it is a living libel on its own name. It flared up like an enraged maniac, and stove in our cabin windows, which even Cape Horn had spared. Its rage seemed wholly unprovoked ; for the sky was almost free of clouds, and even the few which did darken its face, moved on lazily as those in which the winds have fallen asleep. The moon looked down on the uproar in perfect calmness. Her light fell on the crest of the wave, soft as dew on the death-foam of the savage.

One of our boys ran away at Valparaiso. He had but just recovered from the effects of a fall down the main-hatch. He probably thought the best method of escaping the chances of another fall, would be to give the hatch the widest berth possible. But the poor lad will find worse hatches on land than he ever yet stumbled through at sea. Here he broke only a limb, but there he may break his peace of conscience, and his hope of heaven. But sailors are of all beings in the world the most thoughtless. The monitions of the future are lost in the impulses of the present. They have been known, for some temporary gratification, to run from a ship with two years pay due them, and to forfeit the whole by that act of folly. This running commences in rum and ends in ruin.

FRIDAY, MARCH 20. We have the wind directly aft. Our fore studding-sails are out like the wings of a bird on the breast of a gale. We have run within the last two days four hundred and forty miles. This is good sailing considering we have six months' provision on board, and lie consequently too deep for the greatest speed. The air is balmy, and the songs of our sailors, at sunset, rose exultingly into its blue depths. A sailor always sings with heart. His music rolls out like a dashing stream from its mountain source. It is never gay; it always has a deep vein of melancholy. If a few more lively notes mingle with the strain, they come only at intervals, like flakes of moonlight between the cypress shadows which mantle the marbles of the dead.

He is a gay being when he gets upon shore; but he is then no longer on his own element. Give him a day's liberty, and he will commit more follies than he would in six months at sea. If he charters a hack, he will ride out on the box with the driver and make the hold, as he terms the interior, welcome to any one who may be disposed to use it. If he hires a horse, he will ride him at his utmost speed, though he knows no more than you do where he shall bring up. He goes to church on the Sabbath, and if no one offers him a seat, brings in a huge billet of wood, or a stone, and moors ship in the middle of the aisle. He sits there grave as a deacon, never once nods during the sermon, and when the contribution box comes along for sending missionaries to the heathen, drops in the last dollar which his fiddler has left him.

Saturday, March 21. We lost at Valparaiso the Samson of our ship. He was from Bremen, and of German extraction. He stood seven feet in his stockings. His arm was as large as the leg of an ordinary man. He could carry a water tank, which any two others among the crew could only lift. He went with the rest upon shore on liberty, fell in with a few of his countrymen, drank too freely, and stayed beyond his time.

He would have returned on board, but he shrunk from the disgrace of corporal punishment. He had the finest sensibilities, and looked upon a blow, inflicted in the shape of a chastisement, as a brand of indelible infamy. To escape this he had no resource, as he supposed, but to conceal himself till after our ship should sail. Every effort was made to recover him, but without success. His conduct had been unexceptionable. He had never fallen under censure. His fidelity to duty had won the regard and confidence of all. His loss was the more regretted as it flowed from a misapprehension on his part. He would not have been punished had he returned on board. His next liberty day might have been withheld, and that would have been all.

He would have been a tower of strength in an engagement. He could have wielded a sky-sail yard as a boarding-pike. But in the centre of all these giant energies gushed a fountain warm and fresh as that in the heart of a child. He carried with him his mother's picture, and hung over it with that fondness which absence cannot wean or age chill. Keep that picture, thou noble tar! all is not lost while the love of that remains.

Sunday, March 22. The sky covered with a soft haze, the air balmy, our ship moving four and five knots; divine service at 11 o'clock. The subject of the discourse, the power of evil habit; the progress of crime traced; its incipient insignificance, its tremendous results; the stealing an apple leading to highway robbery; an irreverent word paving the way to profaneness; a play of chance for amusement leading to the hazards of the gaming table; the social glass ending at last in delirium and death.

But a future state revealing the more full effects of an evil habit. Here the traces of guilt dimly apparent on the man, there deep and indelible on his soul; here an outcast from the community, there an outcast from heaven; here suffering the loss of a transient temporal good, there an immortality of bliss. God grant these admonitions may arrest some poor sailor in his career of folly and ruin.

Monday, March 23. The wind has been faint and directly aft through the day; still we have made a hundred miles in the last twenty-four hours. We have just had a splendid sunset. The whole western horizon was a sea of cloud and flame.

The setting sun is beautiful at sea,
And throws a richer splendor on the eye
Than when on land beheld; the cause may be
A brighter, bolder amplitude of sky.
And then the fathomless immensity
Of waters, and the twilight clouds, which lie
Along the west, and which at sea appear
As islands in a golden atmosphere.

But then there follows this resplendent sight
An hour of deeper beauty to the shore;
The glowing west has darkened into night,
The stars are out, and from their cisterns pour
On tree and tower a flood of mellow light,
Through which the crags in sheeted silver soar;
While caverned cliffs the billows' dirge prolong,
And roll it back a murmuring tide of song.

And this is rapture—thus alone to stray
  Along the moon-lit shore, and hear each wave
Repeat its dying anthem round the bay,
  Or rush exulting down some sparry cave
With death-defiant roar; though on its way,
  With all its swelling peans, to the grave.
And then 'tis hushed again, except the song
Of breaking billows, which the cliffs prolong.

Oh, you may talk of banquetings and balls—
  Of wit and merriment at masquerade—
Of revels held in old baronial halls—
  Or music murmured in the serenade:
Give me the lay of distant waterfalls,
  The song of May birds in the forest shade,
And that deep anthem, which the choiring waves
Of ocean roll from her melodious caves.

Tuesday, March 24. What ups and downs there are on board a man-of-war! The young Englishman who left the elegancies of the Astor House, and shipped as a common sailor on board our frigate, continued to win upon the friendship of the crew. He was hail fellow well met with the whole. He was always at his post, and prompt and cheerful in duty. No weather ever sent him below, when it was his watch on deck. He struck out so strongly, that he soon gained a position aloft, and had his eye on being captain of the maintop.

But on reaching Valparaiso his *nom de guerre* took flight. He was recognised as the son of a wealthy broker in Manchester, England ; and the important intelligence had just reached here that his uncle, recently deceased, had left him twenty thousand pounds. The correctness of this intelligence was ascertained from sources which left no doubt ; and still he hesitated about applying for his discharge, and declared he had never been so happy as since he turned sailor. He brought on board a letter of credit on a large banking-house in New York, but had never availed himself of it. He at last yielded to the importunities of his friends at Valparaiso, and applied for his discharge, which Captain Du Pont, with the sanction of our commodore, ordered to be made out. He shook hands with his shipmates, wished them stiff breezes and snug harbors, and in his tarpaulin and roundabout, left his station on the main-yard for a London coach.

Wednesday, March 25. We have among our crew a youth who is touched with insanity. The hallucination takes every variety of shape, and every degree of force. A few days since he fancied that he had but one friend on board, and wanted a lantern at noon, with which to look him up. To-day his conviction has been that he shall not see the sun rise again ? As the glorious orb went down, he stationed himself on the steps of the accommodation-ladder to take his farewell look. There was as much poetry in his fine wild features as in the tragical idea that had brought him there. He poured his mournful adieu to the sun in the lines of Manfred, which seemed more his own than the guilty misanthrope's who uttered them :

> "Thou material God!
> And representative of the Unknown—
> Who chose thee for his shadow. Thou chief star!
> Sire of the seasons! monarch of the climes,
> And those who dwell in them! for near or far,
> Our inborn spirits have a tint of thee,
> Even as our outward aspects;—thou dost rise
> And set in glory. Fare thee well!
> I ne'er shall see thee more. As my first glance
> Of love and wonder was for thee, then take
> My latest look: thou wilt not beam on one
> To whom the gifts of life and warmth have been
> Of a more fatal nature. He is gone!"

THURSDAY, MARCH 26. We discovered a sail this afternoon on our starboard-bow, and stood down for her. As our noble ship, with her heavy batteries frowning death, neared her, she run up the American ensign at her peak. We captured her in mimic war. She proved to be the Balæna, a whale-ship, or, as our sailors term it, a spouter, from New Bedford. She had been out five months. She had two men at her main, two at her fore, and one at her mizen top, looking out for whales. Success to them. I would as soon seek a tree-top in a thunder-storm. The mimic fight took place after she had shown her colors, and was gone through with merely to accustom our men to some of the evolutions of a real engagement.

Our crew is composed in too great a proportion of young men. They have not that solidity and strength of muscle which our heavy guns require. But they are very active, and would pour themselves, as boarders, in a living tide on the enemy. Our best crews are those enlisted after war has been declared. Thousands who now seek our civil marine, would in that event rush to our armed decks.

The Balæna must have been christened by some lady of New Bedford who has a touch of Latinity about her. The name, it is true, signifies a whale, but no vulgar vandal spouter, but an elegant Roman balæna—such as might have danced on the harp-strings of a Lucretius, or streamed in the insignia of Cleopatra's barge, as it rocked on the amber waves of Cydnus, and threw back the sun's rays from its decks of burnished gold. Give me that lady who can throw a classic charm around a whale-ship. A cabbage in her hands would soon take the colors and perfume of the rose.

Friday, March 27. Our slumbers were broken this morning by the cry of land ho! from the watch in the fore-top. We had been under shortened sail through the night for fear of shooting too far ahead.

But we made an excellent landfall. As day glimmered, the barren isle of San Lorenzo loomed into the light on our starboard bow. It was sufficiently near to throw its jagged outline full on the eye.

The sea breeze soon sprung up, when we made sail, and doubling the northern extremity of San Lorenzo, the harbor of Callao opened upon us. We moved up its ample expanse with our topgallant sails set, and came to in handsome style with our starboard anchor. We were welcomed by clouds of gulls and pelicans, which floated around our ship and cast the sea into shadow. Had they possessed anthropophagous propensities, we might have felt some solicitude for our personal safety.

Our sails were hardly clued down when our vice-consul, Mr. Johnson, came on board. Our first inquiry was for letters from home. Deep was our disappointment when told there were none. Almost six months from the United States and not a single mail yet,—not even a straggling letter! Think of that, ye who cannot leave your homes for a week without a letter each day. We may have children born without knowing it, and find them, on our return, some three years old. It is no wonder they timidly stare at their strange fathers, and take refuge in their mothers' arms.

SATURDAY, MARCH 28. Callao falls immeasurably

short of the picture which my imagination had painted. It is a collection of low, dingy dwellings, occupying the rippling verge of a vast sand-plain. The only beings which give to it an air of life are buzzards; or here and there a fisherman hawking the trophies of his hook; or an Indian woman on a donkey, riding straddle.

We encountered on reaching the landing two immense piles of wheat, which had been shipped from Chili. Each pile must have had in it not less than twenty thousand bushels. Neither had any covering, and needed none, as it never at this season rains or snows here. Nature allows man to be as lazy as possible, and he seems to have availed himself of the privilege to the utmost extent. Even the dog which slumbers on the trottoir will sooner hazard your heel than break his dreams. The children run half naked; and the women, too indolent to hook the tops of their dresses, throw a loose shawl over their shoulders, and nurse their infants as publicly as they would take out a pocket-handkerchief.

The fort, a place of great strength in its day, has been dismantled. It had become the rallying point of the disaffected. A few revolutionists could here set the arms of the whole republic at defiance. The government, standing in greater dread of domestic than foreign foes, issued a decree for its destruction. The government must be weak indeed, which is obliged to consult its safety in the destruction of the defences of its territory.

SUNDAY, MARCH 29. We are lying in the bay of a Roman Catholic country where no place of worship is allowed to Protestants. There is not a hall or chapel within the limits of Peru where they who differ from the papal see can assemble on the Sabbath. Repeated efforts have been made to obtain permission to erect such a place, but as yet without success. The archbishop of Lima, who gets his instructions from Rome, has set his face against it, and the government is at present too weak, were it so disposed, to set his ecclesiastical authority at defiance.

It would not be amiss for some of our Catholic bishops to come here and preach up a little toleration to their brethren; and, before they go away, I wish they would pass over to the barren isle of San Lorenzo. On this bleak, herbless rock, which is frequented only by pelicans and vultures, they will find the graves of nearly all the Protestants who have died in Peru for centuries past. Not one of those who lie here could have procured himself a grave on the mainland.

But we have one resource on board ship which no proscription can reach. We carry our chapel with us on the open deck. Our capstan is a pulpit which has never been overawed. We have our worship on the Sabbath, in whatever port we may lie, without consulting the authorities on shore. Our privilege is wide as the ocean, and the shores which it laves. Would it were so with every denomination of Christians. The faggot which bigotry kindles may burn the recusant first, but is pretty sure in the end to consume those who light it.

Our forefathers were driven out of the old world by the intolerance of an arbitrary authority, attempting to enthrone itself on the human conscience. I seem to stand once more beneath the wintry trees which threw their bleak shadows on the rock where they first knelt, in their wild inhospitable home. Their memory stands apart, as a thing by itself, sacred and imperishable in the reverence and love of millions. Hail to

THE PILGRIM FATHERS.

They were men of giant soul,
Men of faith and deeds sublime;
Men whose acts will reach their goal
In the mighty depths of time.

They resigned, at God's behest,
Kindred, home, their fathers' graves—
Pilgrims o'er the ocean's crest,
Mid the thunder of its waves.

Here—where pathless forests frowned,
Wailing torrents rolled their foam,

Wolves and wild-men prowled around—
  Rose their altars and their home.

What to them were stately shrines,
  Gorgeous dome, or towering spire?
'Neath their sturdy oaks and pines
  Rose their anthems, winged with fire!

When oppression reached the coast,
  With the tyrant's purpose flushed,
They to peril's deadliest post
  For their God and country rushed.

As the steep volcano throws
  From its burning breast the rock,
They o'erthrew their columned foes,
  In the battle's fiery shock.

All that consecrates their fame,
  All that sanctifies our hearth,
All that freedom here can claim;
  In their noble minds had birth.

By their dead, on Bunker's steep!
  By their bones, in Monmouth's plains
We their faith and trust will keep,
  While their blood rolls in our veins!

Thou who heard'st the Pilgrim's prayer—
  Nerved him for the doubtful field—
Made his sacred cause thy care,
  O'er us cast thy mighty shield!

CHAPTER VIII.

SKETCHES OF LIMA.

INCIDENTS OF THE ROAD.—THE GRAND PLAZA.—SHOPS AND HOUSES.—THE SAYA Y MANTO.—AMERICAN LADY.—MIXTURE OF RACES.—DEMEANOR OF GIRLS AND BOYS.—PROCESSION ON PALM SUNDAY.—CONVENT OF THE FRANCISCANS.—DOCTORS OF LIMA.—GOOD FRIDAY.—THE LAST SUPPER.—PILATE'S COURT.—GARDEN OF GETHSEMANE.—CLOSE OF LENT.—JUBILATIONS.—CLIMATE.—AN OFFICER IN PRISON.—LAWYERS.—THE INDIAN'S EYRIE.—THE LOTTERY.—BULL-FIGHT.

In Lima's streets a stranger stood,
Who wrapp'd his thoughts about him
So close, that they who watched his mood,
But deemed the place without him.

Monday, March 30. We were off this morning at an early hour for Lima. The distance is only seven miles, and is travelled by a line of omnibuses, drawn by six horses, three abreast. Our companions were lieutenants S. and L. of the Congress, two Peruvian officers, a Spanish lady with a lapdog, a creole girl smoking a cigar, and a quadroon in white-kid slippers.

We passed on the right an obelisk surmounted by a cross, designating the spot to which the sea was thrown, in the great earthquake of 1746. A little further on we passed the neglected dwellings of Bellavista, projected as the new Callao, and built further inland, that it might escape the terrible fate of its predecessor. But fear soon yielded to the suggestions of commercial convenience, and Callao went back again to the strand of the sea.

After dragging along for nearly an hour, with our old vehicle buried to the axle in sand, we reached the halfway station, which consists of a dilapidated church and a grog-shop. In the ruined turrets of the one the martins had built their procreant nests; at the bar of the other stood a bare-headed monk, soliciting the change which the glass of toddy might leave. His large feet were protected by sandals, and his Roman nose was so red that one of the passengers got out a cigar.

Having breathed our steeds, we started again, when a fierce quarrel arose between the Spanish lady and her poodle. The little fellow had wet her pocket-handkerchief, and had his ears soundly boxed for the indiscretion. The quadroon took the part of the poodle, and the creole girl smoked on. We now passed several huge tumuli—the burial mounds of the aborigines. The heroic virtues which they entomb have perished. No Homer has swept his lyre in their giant shadows. The road, as we approached the city, presented on either side double rows of poplars, beneath which the Limanians take their twilight promenade. But at this time only a few donkeys were winding their way through them, buried up in grass, which they were taking to market. You saw only the burden; the animal was concealed under it, like a tortoise beneath its shell, or a mouse under a crow's nest.

We found at the gate a sentry posted with as much solemnity as if the old bastion could still thunder out its defiance. We rattled up a broad street into the heart of the city, where we were emptied from our crazy coach into an office surrounded by boys, who vociferously claimed the privilege of transporting our baggage. The urchins had hold of it before we could even tell them where we were going. The lady with her repentant poodle, and the creole with her cigar, went their way, and we brought up at Morin's hotel on the grand plaza. The keeper met us in the hall, welcomed us to Lima, and allotted us our apartments. Here we were then at last in the "city of kings," and in the most sumptuous hotel which its ambition and luxury could furnish. What a transition from the storms, the sleet, and whales off Cape Horn!

TUESDAY, MARCH 31. The heart of Lima is occupied by a great public square, in the centre of which stands a fountain, the showering waters of which fall into a wide marble basin. Beneath the verandas which open on this square are the fancy shops of the city, while the Cathedral towers over all in its solemn magnificence. Around the fountain, instead of marble statues, you find donkeys, waiting to have the tanks, which are swung across their little pack-saddles, filled with water. As soon as this has been done, off they start on their destination, without leader or rein. For these two kegs of water the owner gets a real, or twelve and a half cents. Thus is Lima supplied with water ; when it might be conducted by pipes through every street of the city.

In the shops, which line three sides of the grand square, are found almost all the elegant products of art and mechanical ingenuity. The long colonnades which protect them from the sun, are paved with smooth pebbles, and are sufficiently wide for several persons to walk abreast. Here you encounter, at all hours of the day, the indolent and the active, the grave and the gay of Lima. A more motley crowd in color and costume cannot well be conceived. The language of almost every nation on the globe throws its peculiar accents on the ear. The poorest have on them generally some article of luxury or refinement. The Spanish lady is seen in her *saya y manto;* the mestizoe in her gayly-figured shawl, and the quadroon in her white-kid slippers.

WEDNESDAY, APRIL 1. Since the great earthquake of 1746, the houses in Lima have generally been confined to one story. A few families of wealth, who consulted their pride more than their personal safety, have run their dwellings a little higher. The walls are uniformly of sun-baked brick, and the roofs flat. The more pretending houses have an open court between the heavy gate and the main building. The front of the dwelling, with its fresco paintings, and gilded window-frames, glimmering through the evergreens which fill the court, has a fine effect; every thing looks inviting and cool, well suited to the climate—but a dash of snow would ruin its attractions.

Almost every house betrays the Moorish origin of its architecture in its veranda. This appendage resembles a long, capacious bird-cage, fastened to the wall; it is composed of lattice-work, and is painted green. Here the inmates can observe the passing crowd without being themselves seen. But all the buildings in Lima have about them the evidences of decay. Many of the mansions of the rich have passed into the hands of foreign merchants, and are used as counting-houses; while others have been converted into hotels and restaurants. Many families of distinction, after the revolution, returned to Spain; and not a few of those who remain are slowly exhausting the remnants of their once splendid fortunes. A Spaniard with the most diluted drop of noble blood in his veins, will about as soon starve as work. He regards labor as a degradation.

THURSDAY, APRIL 2. The novelty in costume, which first strikes the stranger in Lima, is the *saya y manto* of the ladies. At a distance this dress looks like two petticoats; the one hanging down where all petticoats should hang, and the other drawn

up over the head, as if lifted by a little whirlwind in mischief. But the lower garment proves to be a rich silk skirt, so plaited and arranged as to betray the swelling outline of the person and fall in wooing drapery around the limbs, while the upper one combines the advantages of the hood and mantle. It is fastened at the bottom within the band of the skirt, and falls over this cincture in a flowing wreath; while the top is gathered over the head and face, and so held by the hand within as to expose but one eye.

The disguise is complete; no husband could recognise his own wife in such a dress.

The apology attempted for this dress is, that it enables a lady to go out in the morning, to mass or shopping, before she has made her toilet. The objections to it lie in the facilities which it lends to purposes of a very different character. It veils a love intrigue from all but the guilty. The jealous care of the husband, and the sleepless vigilance of the duenna, are alike baffled by its impenetrable folds. With the young it often paves the way to ruin and a life of crime. No virtuous community would tolerate its presence for a moment. It has been relinquished by some of the better families in Lima, and was once put under the ban of a legislative statute; but it still survives, and is still in extensive use. The Evil One, could such a thing be, might drop tears over its fall.

How the heart turns from such a picture as this, to that of one whose breathing features throw at this moment their unveiled sweetness on my eye. Born in other climes, she blooms here in all her native modesty and grace. There is an air about her, a delicacy, and a heart that speak the truthfulness of her nature, and her freedom from those affectations which vanity and a false taste induce. My Ariel, who loves these qualities in woman, has thrown into a few simple stanzas a faint outline of the original.

THE AMERICAN LADY.

She moves among us, but apart
From folly's empty din;
The smile that lights her silent heart
Flows from a fount within.

The incense of the flatterer's tongue,
Which each in turn may share,
She lightly deems as bubbles flung
Upon the empty air.

And when a flash of anger's force
Would light resentment's flame,
She only pities more the source
From which the menace came.

There's not a throb which sorrow brings,
Or sigh of the oppress'd,
But pours its pulses o'er the strings
Which tremble in her breast.

There's not a smile which hope bestows,
Or light in memory's dream,
But o'er her changing aspect throws
Its warm reflected beam.

Her bright thoughts greet us as the rays
Of some sweet star at even,
Seen o'er the twilight's misty haze,
Climbing the verge of heaven.

Friday, April 3. Slavery is near its extinction in Peru. No one can be born a slave under its new constitution, and the introduction of slaves from other provinces or states is prohibited under penalties which involve a loss of citizenship for life. Any slave can obtain his freedom for a few hundred dollars, or by taking refuge among the Indians who inhabit the glens of the Cordilleras. It is unlawful for any master to strike his slaves. If they misbehave, he can increase their task, but cannot inflict corporal chastisement.

Nothing puzzles the stranger here so much as the singular mixture of races. The Spaniard, the Indian, and the African run together like the hues of the dying dolphin. It is impossible to tell where one color ceases and the other begins. Even in the same family, complexions frequently differ wide enough to embrace both extremes. The African in other countries can be traced; but here, after a few generations, he becomes so bleached by the climate that you lose sight of his origin. Even his hair, that almost infallible indication, straightens out into the texture of the European's. Add to this the results of intermarriage, and you may well be in doubt where to class him.

Some of the best-looking females in Lima are of this description. They resemble in hue and form the Circassian, and would be regarded at Constantinople as extremely beautiful. They are soft and engaging in their manners, amiable in their dispositions, excel in music, and are often married to gentlemen of distinction and wealth.

Saturday, April 4. The college boys in Lima look like little military captains. They strut about in cocked hats and laced coats; the sword only is wanting. The last thing with which you would associate them would be a severe ancient classic. You would as soon look for Greek among the matadores at a bull-fight. Peru will produce no Porson while these cocked hats and gilt buttons continue in vogue among the boys.

But all the little boys belonging to families of note are dressed here like gentlemen. Your first impression would be, that you had arrived among a race of Lilliputians. But a closer observation shows you that these little well-dressed gentlemen are infantines, let loose from their nurses' arms. They are but little more than knee-high; but wear, with singular gravity, their black beaver hats and long-tailed coats.

The same holds true of the little miss of eight and

nine. Her hair, of singular length for that of a child, instead of falling in ringlets or plaits, is done up with a comb like that of her mother's. Her silk dress, with its close bodice, depends gravely to the instep; her mantilla falls down her shoulders with the precision of that of a nun; while her hands and arms are adjusted with the utmost composure. Her whole air is that of a lady over whom some thirty years have passed, and she expects you to address her in the same respectful terms. She is the pocket-edition of a precise spinster.

Sunday, April 5. This being Palm Sunday, all Lima turned out to witness a procession intended to convey an idea of the last entrance of our Saviour into Jerusalem. On a platform, borne forward on the shoulders of six stout men, stood a donkey, on which a wax figure was mounted, while the staging was strewn with leaves of the palm. As it passed, hosannas broke from the lips of the spectators.

On the staging which followed this, stood the Virgin, in glowing wax. She wore a sparkling diadem, and a robe of purple velvet, gorgeously inwoven with gold, and flowing off into a magnificent train, supported by angels. As she passed, the crowd fell on their knees and whispered their Ave Marias, while the swinging censers of the priests sent up their curling cloud of homage.

The third and last staging supported a tree, high in the limbs of which clung a little wax cherub, intended to represent Zaccheus. He was looking down with an expression quite removed from one of reverential curiosity. The children shouted, and it was as much as their mothers could do to hush them into silence. Thus passed this religious pageant; when the crowd broke up in much the same humor with which they would leave their seats at a theatre. Were the historic symbols of our religion intended to amuse mankind, this spectacle might possibly answer its purpose. But here the awful reality so overpowers the representation, that it cannot leave in the imagination even the solemnity of a religious delusion.

MONDAY, APRIL 6. We visited to-day the Franciscan church and convent. They cover seven acres of ground, and combine a degree of architectural grandeur and cloisteral luxury singularly at variance with the mendicant virtues of the fraternity to which they belong. The church, indeed, is one of the most sumptuous in Lima, and showers its rich gilding upon you from pavement to dome. In its niches, and over its altars repose statues, on which art has bestowed the highest expressions of its ambition.

In one of the altars we recognised St. Benedict, holding a black infant Saviour in his arms. The existence of this representation has been denied by a distinguished prelate of the Roman Catholic church in the United States, but of its truth I have the testimony of my own eyes. The idea originated, undoubtedly, in a wish to conciliate the African. Rome becomes all things to all men, and I hope for the purpose of saving some.

The convent has four hundred cloisters, which open on stately corridors that circle around central courts, where fountains play among evergreens, fruits, and flowers. Who would not gaze on a skull and a life-glass only an hour or two a day to enjoy such a residence as this? These gloomy emblems of our mortality might almost be forgotten in the deathless bloom of the amaranth. Give me a monk for exigencies; he can make solitude social, and convert a golgotha into a garden. He lives in affluence without a ready penny, and is sainted without an active virtue.

Tuesday, April 7. To die regularly in Lima the patient must be admonished of his approaching end by his physician, and receive extreme unction from his priest. The physician who should let his patient die without this timely warning, would receive the severest censures of the relatives of the deceased, and be required by the church to pay for masses for the repose of his soul. He is consequently faithful in this last sad office. With us the sick often die in glowing dreams of life. The pale shadow flits before their glassing eyes, but is not seen.

The medical profession here, in dignity and respect, ranks far below the pulpit, the bar, and the camp. It involves too many cares, too many vigils, too many humble offices to suit the indolence and pride of the Spaniard. It is consequently exercised mainly by those of African or Indian descent, and a thankless office they have of it. If their patient survives, it is ascribed to some miraculous intervention of the Virgin; if he dies, it is attributed to an unpardonable want of skill: so that between the imputed miracle in the one case and inevitable death in the other, he gets but little credit for his professional sagacity. His only resource in all critical cases is to call in half a dozen consulting physicians, and share with them the responsibility of the issue. I always pity a consulting physician; he must approve what has been done, though in so doing he often gives the lie to the change of treatment which he directs. But let that pass.

Wednesday, April 8. The great cathedral was crowded at an early hour this morning to witness the ceremony of the "Banner." As the organ commenced a low, mournful air, a tall priest, robed in black, took his station in front of the high altar, where he unfurled from its staff a large sombre banner.

After having waved it for a few minutes in front of the lights on the great altar—knocking over one of the candles, which I suppose went for Judas Iscariot —he faced about, and with his long train, supported by three pages, marched down, with a slow stately step, into the centre of the cathedral. Here twenty-four priests, through whose files he passed, and who were in sable robes, with dark crowns on their heads, fell flat with their faces upon the pavement. The banner continued waving over them for several minutes, while the low tones of the organ died away on the silent air. Several of these prostrate functionaries, when their eyes met each other, found it almost as difficult to preserve their gravity as Cicero's augurs.

The banner now disappeared through one of the side chapels ; the priests got up, replaced their crowns, and the spectators departed. Not a word was spoken during the whole ceremony; what it meant, is more than I can say. I made repeated inquiries of those present, but no one could give me any information beyond the fact that it belonged to Holy Week. I must, therefore, refer the reader to those better versed than myself in symbolic worship for an interpretation of the vision.

Thursday, April 9. At twelve o'clock to-day all the bells in Lima rung out a simultaneous peel, and were then sent to Rome to be blessed by the Pope. They will return again, it is understood, on Saturday, and announce their arrival from their respective steeples. Their visit to the *pontifex maximus* must of course be taken in a metaphorical, or Picwickian sense. It is a constructive journey, such as our honorable senators take at the inauguration of a new president.

As the bells left for Rome every shop in Lima was closed. No public or private vehicle was seen in any street. Even the donkeys, with their water tanks, disappeared from the city fountains. Every man, woman, and child suspended their amusements, labors, and secular cares. The dominoes lay untouched, and the cue of the billiard-table stood unmolested in its rack. Men passed each other in the streets without the customary salutations. It was as if the whole city had been suddenly struck into a speechless awe and reverence.

This was intended to portray an appropriate sense of the scenes which occurred in Jerusalem, when redeeming Love underwent the agonies of the Cross. Its significance lay in the exhibition of a seeming sympathy with the sorrows of the sufferer. It was a silent allegorical tragedy, in which each one found himself an actor. To me no other exhibition in the ceremonies of Holy Week had so much moral force. Silence often makes itself felt, when thunder passes unheeded.

FRIDAY, APRIL 10. All good Limaneans, with the president and his cabinet at their head, made last night the circuit of the principal churches. In each was a representation, in effigy, of some scene connected with the Crucifixion. In San Lorenzo was the Last Supper. The table was spread within the chancel in front of the high altar, and was loaded with the richest viands and fruits, while each plate had its bottle of wine and roll of bread. A profane epicure might have forgotten the sacredness of the symbols in the culinary skill and taste which they displayed.

In the church of San Domingo was represented the accusation before Pilate. Beneath the high altar sat the Roman governor, with his court on either hand; before them raved the accusers, while within stood in silent meekness the divine Victim. Near Pilate knelt a page, with a bowl of water in one hand, and a napkin in the other, that this arbiter of life and death might cleanse his hands of guilt. The whole scene betrayed an extravagance in attitude and emotion better suited to the drama than the solemnity of the occasion.

In the church of San Francisco the slender trees

of Gethsemane cast their still shadows over the kneeling form of the Son of God. By his side stood an angel with that cup which might not pass away. In the great Cathedral, the summit of Calvary, with the cross and the crowd, rose in solemn gloom. In San Pedro, the Roman guard, with drawn swords, kept their grim watch over the tomb. The moral effect of all these exhibitions in a Protestant community would be to impair the awful reality; and even here they appeared to inspire but a qualified reverence. The mass gazed as a curious child stops in its play to look at a picture that has momentarily caught its roving eye.

Saturday, April 11. The great band of musicians, connected with the army, passed through the principal streets of Lima last night, playing a funeral wail. The subdued strains rose through the silent air mournful as melodies from out the grave. This was intended to be significant of the anxious sorrow which watched around the tomb where Death had temporarily asserted his empire over the Prince of Life.

At an early hour this morning the church of San Augustine was filled to overflowing with the beauty of Lima. A large choir and orchestra had been brought together on the occasion. The music commenced in strains of lamentation and grief; and at last burst into expressions of the most triumphant joy. At this moment the bells in all the towers of the city, and which had been silent since Thursday, rung out an exulting peel. This was the announcement of the Resurrection! The whole assemblage fell on their knees and joined in the Hosanna which seemed to shake the pillars of the great edifice.

The whole scene was now changed. Throughout the city gladness lighted every countenance, and the gayest attire took the place of the gloomy sables. The confectionaries, the fruit-stalls, the wine-shops, the billiard-tables, were all thrown open, and were filled by crowds giddy with the excitement of the joyous transition. Mothers played with their infants; maidens twined jessamine-flowers in their locks; children fired off their crackers; cripples neglected their crutches; creditors forgot their insolvent debtors; and even the barefooted monk passed you without soliciting charity. He strode on, independent as a lord.

Sunday, April 12. The jubilation continued through the whole of last night. Evening found the living tides of the city upon the great public square. Here every species of trick and merriment, with the humor of the hour, convulsed the crowd with laughter. All distinctions and all restraints were cast aside. All classes and all colors mingled together like leaves of the forest in the whirl of the autumnal winds.

Some were fiddling, some dancing ; some singing, some shouting ; some niggling, some nudging ; some declaiming, some drinking ; some pilfering nosegays, and some picking pockets ; some making mischief, and some making love. Here a harlequin turned somersets, and there a half-naked rope-dancer figured on the suspended cord. Here a Punch and Judy played off their pugilistics, and yonder a puppy and porcupine bristled and barked. Here a broken-headed drum flapped its roll, and there a cracked guitar squeaked its discords. Here wit ruled the hour, and there rum.

Thus passed the night till the Sabbath morn threw its broad light on the scene. Thus closed Lent, and thus commenced Easter-Sunday. Thus terminated the ceremonies of Holy Week,—begun in penance and prayer, and ended in frolic and fun. That such a celebration can substantially promote the cause of piety and the proprieties of life, must surpass the belief of any one whose faith has not lifted the ceremonies of his church above the reach of human fallibility.

MONDAY, APRIL 13. The climate of Lima has no extreme variations. The mercury on Fahrenheit's scale rarely rises in summer above eighty, and rarely falls in winter below sixty-five. The prevailing temperature is about seventy-five. But there is a surprising sensitiveness in the inhabitants to these slight variations. Let a cooler current of air sweep from the Cordilleras, and you will encounter everywhere the ample cloak and heavy shawl. You hardly feel the change yourself, and think for the moment you have got among invalids.

The effect of the climate on the constitutional habits of the European, soon betrays itself in a relaxation of his energies. He loses his enterprise, enthusiasm, and flinty endurance, and sinks into that dreamy listlessness which pervades the great mass. His descendants dwindle in intellect, and are dwarfed in person. If white, his complexion becomes bronzed; if black, it is bleached into hues less sable. The climate acts like the crucible which fuses the different metals which it contains into one mass.

The climate acts with the same softening and subduing effect on the force and ferocity of animals. The dog becomes spiritless, the tiger ceases to spread dismay and terror when he leaves his lair, and the wild bull brought within the arena, has to be goaded to the combat by a system of refined cruelty and torture. No animal fights save in his own defence, and the men, if roused and forced to action, rarely pursue an enemy beyond the limits of the field where fortune has favored their arms.

TUESDAY, APRIL 14. We visited again to-day the Franciscan convent. This magnificent establishment had once some four hundred inmates, and an income suited to the easy and sumptuous style in which they lived. But in the Revolution its funds disappeared, and the monks sought an asylum elsewhere. We encountered in its vacant halls but one, and he darted out upon us seemingly to frighten away an American lady whom we had in our company. He appeared, as he flitted along the silent corridors, more like a dusky ghost than aught of flesh and blood. His long robe draped his person; his cowl half concealed his wan features; his thin hands held a crucifix; and his steps glided over the pavement noiseless as his shadow. He was here, and there; now in the faint light; now in the shadow of the wall; now in his cell; now in the chapel, and then sweeping the long, dim corridor. You saw no motion of any limb; you heard no sound; and if the glance of his eye fell on you, it was but for a moment.

"Beware! beware of the black Friar,
Who flits through these halls of stone,
For he mutters his prayer in the midnight air,
And his mass of the days that are gone.
His form you may trace, but not his face,
'Tis shadow'd by his cowl;
But his eyes may be seen from the folds between,
And they seem of a parted soul."

Wednesday, April 15. The most intolerable feature of a legal process in Peru grows out of the "law's delay." A foreigner may be imprisoned for weeks, and perhaps months, without being able to secure a hearing before the proper tribunal. If he applies to the functionary, who represents his country at this court, his case then takes a diplomatic character, and wanders back and forth, in shadowy shape, while moons wax and wane. His case is loaded with all grievances, piques, and prejudices, which have agitated the parties, who have the management of it, through a series of years. Till at last he finds it quite as difficult to get out of the diplomatic net of his minister as the clutches of Peruvian law.

Now our commodores have a very brief mode of settling these difficulties. They man their batteries and demand the release of the prisoner in twenty-four hours. He is then held amenable to the laws, which it is alleged he has offended. If innocent, he is rescued from false imprisonment; if guilty, he pays the penalty. There are here no stately forms of court etiquette, no subscriptions of having the honor to be, with high consideration, your excellency's most humble nincompoop. Instead of this a demand is made, founded in humanity and justice, and enforced by argument which the wise will not and the timid dare not resist. Such is one of the advantages of having a navy. Disband it and our citizens go to prisons and our commerce to pirates.

In the general tumult of Saturday night one of our junior officers came in conflict with an irregular detachment of the military police. Weapons were drawn; the leader of the file was disarmed by him, and several others received slight wounds, when he was overpowered by numbers, and led off to the guard-house. His liberation was promptly demanded by Capt. Du Pont, but his amenability to the laws of Peru, of course, recognised. The demand, after the responsibility of the case had been shuffled from the intendente to the prefect, and from him to the criminal judge, was complied with.

As soon as it reached the lawyers of Lima that a case of this kind had got into their courts, they gathered around the young officer like forty rival lovers for the hand of the same lady. Some proffered their services for half the usual fee; some for what he might please to give, and several said they should charge him nothing except for stationery. Some pressed their pretensions through the legitimate character of their diplomas; some through their relationship to the judge; and one quoted half the Justinian code, as evidence of his qualifications.

But they were all a little too disinterested; and it was determined to let the case go by default; and pay such damages as the court might decree. The result was that every rascal who had received a scratch, no matter from whom, on Saturday night, came in for damages. The sagacity of the judge set the claims of most of them aside; but enough succeeded to mulct our young officer in several hundred dollars, though his sword had as little to do with most of their wounds and bruises as the pen with which I write this. An offence here connected with a foreign officer, has as wide a responsibility as the magic of a Salem witch. Hardly a hen can miscarry, but the loss of her egg is traced in some way to this military Achan.

But yesterday the captain of an American merchantman was imprisoned at Callao. Commodore Stockton immediately inquired into the circumstances, which were these:—The captain had come down to the Landing to go on board his vessel, when he found his boat's crew in conflict with a party on shore. The difficulty originated with a midshipman in the Peruvian navy, who had struck one of the Americans. The captain made a resolute effort to detach his crew from the engagement, when the whole were overpowered by the military and lodged in prison.

These being the facts, Commodore Stockton called in person on the governor of the port and demanded the captain's release. His firmness, and his ability to back his demands with the guns of the Congress, had the desired effect. The captain was liberated. This was done, not to rescue the captain from just amenability, but from unjust imprisonment. When the case was examined into by the proper authorities he was acquitted of all blame: still his innocency would not have saved him from a vexatious confinement but for this resolute proceeding on the part of the Commodore.

Thursday, April 16. The Indian's eyrie, on the summit of some steep and lofty mountain, says a traveller, may be easily passed many times unnoticed by the stranger. But he will one day encounter a swift-footed Indian, closely followed by a person on a well-accoutred mule,—whose geer is all laden with silver ornaments; and the rider, who sits at his ease in a saddle of the country, with a rich pillion, wears a large brimmed hat, with a black silk cap emerging to view at the ears and temples. He has on a couple of ponchos, well decorated and fringed:—his brown stockings are of warm Vecuña wool; and the heel of his small shoe, half concealed in a clumsy, though costly wooden stirrup, is armed with a prodigiously disproportioned silver spur, with a large tinkling roller, used to keep his noble animal in mind that she is but the harbinger of death, and carries on her back the keeper of the sinner's conscience.

This minister of peace to the miserable hurries to

shrive the soul of a dying Indian, whose abode, like the falcon's, overlooks the paths of the ordinary wayfaring man; and which, when descried, seems to the sight of the observer underneath to be, indeed, the loftiest earthly point between the ground he himself stands upon, and the heaven for which, it is believed, the anxious and fluttering spirit of the dying man only waits the curate's absolution and blessing to wing its immortal flight. When all is over, when the absolving benediction has been pronounced, and death has triumphed where life took its last stand, the pale pulseless form, wrapped in its most costly vest, is dressed for burial. Wild-flowers are strewn on the dead by the Indian maiden, while the cliffs around mournfully echo back the funeral dirge. How true is human instinct to the awful mystery of the grave!

Observing an immense concourse on the grand plaza, I elbowed my way among them, and soon ascertained the cause of the rush to be the drawing of the public lottery. On an elevated ample platform were seated the judges, before whom revolved three hollow globes. The first contained the billets representing the prizes, the second the names of those who held tickets, the third the numbers of these tickets. When the globes stopped revolving, the lads stationed at each drew, through a small aperture, simultaneously, a billet. One contained the prize, another the number of the ticket, the third the name of the owner. Every heart was now in a terrible flutter till the number and name were announced; and then a shadow fell on many faces that were bright a moment before.

The largest prize was a thousand dollars; the least was a silver pitcher, or a silver *unmentionable*, belonging to chamber furniture, and which was displayed without the slightest sentiment of mirth. A more motley crowd than those whose dreams of wealth were here dashed, delusive hope never brought together. They assembled in noise and mirth, and separated in silence and sadness. Such a scene as this the grand plaza presents on the afternoon of every Wednesday. The proprietor of the lottery pays the state annually forty thousand dollars for his privilege. The tickets are one real, or twelve and a half cents each. They who cannot buy ten, twenty, or a hundred, can buy one. In this lies the secret of its success and mischief. It finds a dupe wherever it can find a fool with a penny. The venders of these lottery tickets hawk them through every street and lane, and from the stepstones of every church in Lima. The pious signature assumed by the purchaser, shows that he connects his hopes of success with the assurances of his religious faith. No one here would pit a cock without a prayer to his patron saint.

Friday, April 17. On the Sabbath which succeeded Holy Week I went to the cathedral to attend worship, and found it closed; continued on to the church of San Pedro, and found that closed; turned off to the church of San Augustin, and found that also closed. Observing the streets full of people, who were moving towards the broad bridge which crosses the Rimac, I concluded that there must be some great religious festival in that quarter, and followed on.

The crowds continued to move over the Rimac, but instead of entering any church, wound off, in solid column, through the rows of trees which shade its left bank. I at last inquired of an intelligent looking man who was walking at my elbow, to what sacred spot they were bound. When, with a look of half wonder at my ignorance, he replied, To the *corrida de toros!*—the bull-fight! I turned on my heel and threaded my way back, with some difficulty, through the crowds who were pressing onward to the savage spectacle. Among them were groups of children from the schools,—boys in gay frocks, and girls in white, with wreaths of flowers around their sunny locks, headed by their teachers. Monks with their beads, mothers with their daughters; infancy at the breast, and old age with one foot in the grave; all chattering and laughing, and jostling and shouting, and pressing on to the bull-ring, on the Sabbath!

Upon inquiry, I found that these bull-fights formerly took place on Monday, but that the Archbishop of Lima, to enable the laboring classes to attend them, had changed the day to the Sabbath. They are a horrible spectacle at best, utterly revolting to every sentiment of refinement and humanity; and the social and moral evils which they inflict would be sufficiently revolting were they confined to secular occasions, but they become doubly pernicious when they involve such an outrage on the sanctity of the Sabbath, under the sanction, too, of the highest ecclesiastical functionary in the state.

Bull-fights, as conducted here, involve very little peril and suffering except to the poor beast. His antagonists are pretty safe, or he would drive them out of the arena. It is an exhibition of craft and cowardice on one side, and courage and despair on the other. Of the two, the bull sustains much the nobler part, and would have much the larger share of my sympathy and respect. If men must fight for the amusement of their fellows, let them fight one another. If the death of one don't furnish sufficient excitement, then let the other be shot or hung, as the taste of the spectators shall suggest. But let them not catch a poor beast, torture him with fagots and fire, skulk themselves, and pick him to death with their long weapons, and then insult the intelligence of the community by calling the dastardly act an exhibition of chivalry and valor.

It is no wonder the ladies in Lima are deficient in delicacy and moral refinement, accustomed as they are from their childhood to such savage spectacles. It is but justice, however, to say, that there are some mothers here who will not permit their daughters to attend them; nor will they allow them, for this, or any other purpose, to disguise themselves in the *saya y manto.* There was one righteous man in Sodom, and there is more than one good mother even in Lima.

CHAPTER IX.

SKETCHES OF LIMA.

EDUCATION OF FEMALES.—MARRIAGES.—LAPSES FROM VIRTUE.—THE SUNSET BELL.—SILK FACTORY IN A CONVENT.—HABITS OF THE INDIANS.—THE HALF WEDLOCK.—BLIND PEDLER.—PROTESTANT YOUTH IN LIMA.—RELIGION OF THE LIMANIANS.—INTRIGUES AT COURT.—MODES OF LIVING.—THE ZAMPAS.—CHURCHES.—INDIAN DOCTORS.—FRUITS OF THE COUNTRY.—OLD SPANISH FAMILIES.—MASSES FOR THE REPOSE OF THE SOUL.

"I say in my slight way I may proceed
To play upon the surface of humanity;
I write the world, nor care if the world read,
At least for this I cannot spare its vanity."

SATURDAY, APRIL 18. A girl here at the age of ten or eleven is as far advanced in her social and matrimonial anticipations as she is with us at seventeen. She expects in her fourteenth year to sway hearts, as the moon the troubled tide. For this period she trains herself with an ambition far beyond her years; and when it arrives, she is armed with all the brilliant weapons of beauty, wit, repartee, and a lively self-possession. Her wit never wounds, her repartee never gives offence. She is thoroughly amiable in all her sallies, she means to make you think well of her, and is equally anxious that you should think well of yourself. She understands how to inspire self-complacency without any broad flattery. She is sportive, but it is with dignity; and will sooner excuse a liberty than a slight.

When this hey-day of life has been sufficiently enjoyed, she marries, not from having fallen in love, but for the sake of an establishment. If her husband devotes himself to her, she is generally faithful; but if he spends his nights in clubs, at the billiard and card table, she is apt to permit the intimacy of some one whom she ought not to love. This is rarely, if ever, followed by a domestic explosion. She feels secure of all that forbearance and silence which the most jealous regard to the peace and reputation of the family can suggest. With us, the injured party, though first himself in the fault, yet in his resentment often turns his own hearth-stone into a tomb. Guilt never fails to carry with it, in the end, its own punishment. There is a serpent in the cup of guilty pleasure, whose fang will inflict wounds on which the tears of repentant anguish will yet fall big and fast.

Sunday, April 19. There is one religious observance in Lima which reminds the traveller of the call of the muezzin from the minarets of Constantinople, when he summons the Mussulman to prayer. When the bell of the great Cathedral tolls the departing sun, every one, whether on foot, in his curricle, or on horseback, and whatever may be his speed, stops and takes off his hat. The gayest look grave, and the serious whisper a brief prayer. The shopkeeper suspends his bargain, the billiard-player lays down his cue; the gambler folds his cards and reverently rises. In a minute the bell ceases: the horseman dashes on, the cue and cards are resumed, and Heaven seems again forgotten.

Many of the simple artisans ply their trades outside their shops. You will encounter twenty or thirty shoemakers driving the awl in a single court, and as many tailors pushing the needle in another; while a third is filled by milliners, bleaching and trimming gipsy-hats for Indian girls. The Limanian lady seldom wears a bonnet; she prefers the manto; with that she can conceal her face, save the peeping eye, and pass unrecognised. The saya or skirt of this disguising dress is not the work of her own sex; it is always cut and made by the same hands which fit and seam the coats of the gentlemen. What can be expected of a nation where the men are engaged in making petticoats for the women? Enterprises of pith and moment are not achieved through the stitches of that garment. But let that pass.

MONDAY, APRIL 20. The convent of San Pedro, an extensive, costly edifice, has been converted into an establishment for raising and twisting silk. The few monks who still lingered in their cloisters, when they saw the worms slowly winding themselves up in their continuous thread, as if the sole object of life was to secure an undisturbed exit from it, concluding that two of a trade could never agree, picked up their rosaries and relics, and departed. The worms work on, and wind their silk sepulchres as industriously as if the monks who have gone had left behind them their ghastly mementoes of life's brevity.

How strangely sounds that steam-engine as it turns the twisting machinery, and throws its ceaseless echoes around among these chambers once dedicated to the spirit of silence! And the thread, as it reels itself off from the cocoon, seems as if it unwound the quiet existence of some recluse, whose life was here "rounded with a sleep." These threads are to be woven into a rich tissue, beneath which the bounding heart and glowing limb will but faintly indicate the penance and vigils which once reigned in these gloomy chambers, from which they stream to the light. Such are the strange mutations to which the enterprise of the age brings us. A convent is converted into a factory, its skulls into steam-boilers, and its beads into bobbins! It is enough to wake St. Anthony out of his sunless sleep!

A relic can no further dwindle
Than when 'tis reeled from spool or spindle.

TUESDAY, APRIL 21. I have encountered no class

of persons in Peru that have awakened the same degree of sympathy and interest as the native Indians. On them have been piled misfortunes that would have crushed a less enduring race. Their lands, their forests, and their streams have been wrenched from them through treachery and force. The mounds in which the bones of their forefathers were entombed, have been violated, and these sacred relics exposed to the gaze of a profane curiosity. These are wrongs against which his untutored nature rebels, and which he partially avenged in the frightful scenes of the Revolution. The power of Spain in Peru went down like a wreck, over which the whelming wave rushes in remorseless triumph.

The Indians on the coast, born among Europeans, have still something of that sedateness which is characteristic of their race, when reared under the influences of civilization. But those from the interior, whose cradles were swung among the stupendous steeps of the Andes, have a stern, wild force, which shows where their home has been. They look with scorn on the tricks of the toilet. They may indeed wear plumes in their dark hair, but they are from the pinions of some daring bird that has battled with the mountain storm, or whose rush has been over the cataract's plunging verge. Still, they are in a great measure free from ferocity and disguised revenge. They are magnanimous as conquerors, and patient as captives. They never lose their equanimity in good or ill fortune.

Wednesday, April 22. Flowers here play an important part in love matters. If a lady presents a gentleman with a rose in the morning, it is significant of the fact that he has not yet, at least in her imagination, passed into the yellow leaf. But if she presents it to him in the evening, there is no hope for him, unless he can rejuvenate himself. These floral gifts at the anniversary of the lady's birthday, fly about thick as Cupid's arrows. They are graceful advances when presented by gentlemen, and delicate responses when given by ladies.

The Indian girl has less reserve in her love recognitions. She sends a pretty doll on a nice little couch, covered with white jessamine flowers. This is a broader intimation than that given through the rose by the Spanish lady; but it proceeds from a heart quite as guileless and chaste. If I must confide in the purity and fidelity of either, let it be in the one who thus embodies the instincts of her sex in these mimic miniatures of life. Yet with all this seeming delicacy in an affair of the heart, the Spanish lady indulges in a latitude of speech that would quite disturb female modesty with us. Her allusions are as broad as are the exhibitions of folly and vice. She speaks of a man's mistress, or a woman's paramour, just as freely as she would of their carrier-pigeons, and with just about as little surprise or virtuous indignation. She seems to consider it neither a high crime nor a pitiable weakness; but one of those fortunes which mysteriously connect themselves with the conditions of humanity. When she weds, she will probably need the same charitable construction, and she will be pretty sure to receive it from her family and friends. They will deprecate and resent as suicidal folly, any public demonstrations of domestic disquietude. The husband, if a foreigner, is told that these are the habits of the country; if a native, he needs no such information.

Thursday, April 23. When a young female consents to become the mistress of a man here, she requires of him a certificate that he will not marry without her consent. This certificate she deposites with the Bishop of Lima, and purchases a dispensation for the irregularity involved in the compact. Should the man, from weariness or any other motive, attempt to effect a marriage arrangement with another person, without her consent, she calls at once on the bishop, who threatens the delinquent, if he perseveres, with the highest pains and penalties of the church.

He is thus reduced to the necessity of either making an adequate settlement on the person with whom he entered into the illicit arrangement, or of foregoing entirely his matrimonial purposes. The object of the bishop in this matter is to prevent a dishonored female, with perhaps three or four children, from being thrown on the world without any means of support. Whether this motive, even when its object is achieved, can justify the semi-official sanction of the compact, is another question. But this I may say, it often prevents the heartless libertine from selfishly abandoning one for whose guilt and ruin he is measurably responsible. If he don't like the conditions, then let him decline the arrangement; it is at best only a passport to guilt and sorrow.

Friday, April 24. I encountered to-day a blind pedler, of whom there are several in Lima. He carried two baskets, the one filled with elegant toys, the other with ribbons, thread, needles, and pins. He knew where to find each article, and the price which he should get for it. Even the quality of the ribbon could not deceive his delicate touch; nor could the coin which he received in exchange, palm itself off for more than its value. Heaven guide and protect thee, thou poor blind pedler! We all feel our way through this dim world in the hope of reaching a brighter and better.

There are a great many families in Lima who

have no cooking done in their houses through the year. They send out to the cook-stands which are sprinkled all over the city. They thus save the expense of extra servants and fuel. It is another mode of disguising poverty, and of avoiding the necessity of breaking up their establishments. When a Spanish family of some pretension becomes reduced, and it is necessary to sell the carriage, the coat-of-arms and every clue to its previous owner, are, as far as possible, effaced. As a last resort, the household servants are allowed to hire themselves out, and bring back a portion of their earnings to their owner. When these die, or desert, the last string in the old harp is broken. If a tone lingers still, it is so sad you would not hear it breathe again. There is something in the condition of a man who is now poor and who has seen better days, with which only the most callous levity can trifle. It was only out of Eden that Adam felt in its full force his irreparable loss.

Saturday, April 25. Foreign youth who come to Lima from Protestant countries to engage in business, often disappoint the fondest expectations of their friends. Cast adrift from the moral and religious restraints which they felt at home, and having no respect for the solemn pageantries of religion which they encounter here, they fall easy victims to the vices of the metropolis. Hardly one in ten escapes the giddy maelstrom, down which they are whirled from light and hope. Their ruin would at least be retarded were the institutions of the Protestant faith permitted here. But the Roman hierarchy, which cries aloud for freedom of conscience in the United States, here tramples it down with Bastille ferocity. If the masses in the Catholic church here are bigoted and intolerant, their spiritual superiors have made them so. The depth of the forest wakes or sleeps with the tempest that walks over it.

The frailties of the Limanian female seem not to extinguish her sympathies with distress. She is often at the couch of pain with that tender assiduity which we can hardly dissever from a virtuous life. Her watchful care is not denied to the stranger, or to those utterly incapable of rewarding it. This surviving virtue, amid the wreck of others, is to be ascribed perhaps to that forbearance which her frailties experience. With us she would be abandoned by her relatives, and delivered over by her former associates to irremediable crime and shame. The result of this is a fearful proclivity in guilt and ruin. Whether virtue is best vindicated by a denunciation which never relents, or a forbearance which tries to save, is a question which would not long hold me in suspense. No heart is wholly bad; it has some string in it that will vibrate if rightly touched. He who suffered on the cross died to *open* the door of mercy, not to shut it.

SUNDAY, APRIL 26. The religion of the Limanians is entitled to a charitable judgment. The mass of the people are not responsible for the pageantries with which it is invested. Their uninformed faith may be perplexed among shadows, but it often penetrates to the substance. Among the frivolous there are not a few with whom religion is an earnest reality. Among the skeptical, many may be found who have cast the anchor of their hopes within the veil.

We may denounce the proscriptive polity of their church, but we should not denounce them. They worship in a temple which the zeal of ages has reared to their hands. They found its doors barred to other religious persuasions, and it is requiring too much to expect that they will at once throw back its bolts. This can be realized only through the influence of that higher light which the Bible is now pouring into the recesses of every sectarian shrine. Even our own Protestant altars are now visited by rays which have long been shut out, or permitted to fall in only faint fragments. The spirit of intolerance which has pervaded our churches, has been a source of vast moral mischief. The road to heaven is covered with the footprints of thousands, who have been won to it by the accents of Christian love.

Monday, April 27. When a political intrigue explodes in Lima, the first inquiry is for the woman that sprung the mine. She is generally found to be some courtesan, whose success lies more in the power of her personal charms than her force of intellect. Her carriage in Lima and her rancho at Chorillos, sufficiently attest her means, and the honor of those favors through which she beguiles the unwary statesman into her plans and purposes.

If the plot fails, her coadjutors may atone for their political profligacy with their lives; but she lives on, and may yet ensnare the judges that doomed them. She has a tact that eludes sagacity, and a perseverance that seems to challenge obstacles. She makes her way where the maturest counsels are disconcerted, and triumphs where the most daring courage is foiled. She detects at a glance the unguarded point in the most crafty, and turns his weapons against himself. Her intrigues sometimes result in benefit to the state. The same mysterious hand, that traces in ominous characters the doom of the obnoxious or incapable minister, often executes its own sentence.

All this indicates a truth, which a thousand other facts corroborate, that the women of Lima are far in advance of the men in sagacity and force of purpose. In the frightful conflicts of the Revolution, when men's hearts failed them, they were in disguise on horseback among the troops, nerving the timid, and rallying the brave. No political party can long maintain its ascendency in Peru that has not their confidence and support. They will make it ridiculous with their raillery, or odious with their denunciation.

TUESDAY, APRIL 28. Out of Lima, the masses in Peru subsist mostly on a vegetable diet. The flour of maize, wheat, peas, beans, barley, rice, and arrowroot, are made into a soft pap, or mush, which is sweetened exceedingly with sugar or molasses. This is the great Peruvian dish called "masamora," and which is the edible staple in every family. It produces sleekness without strength, and fatness without fire. They who subsist upon it retain their flesh till they pass forty; then begin to dwindle away; at sixty they are extremely thin; and at seventy have hardly substance enough to cast a shadow.

A mother here never nurses her child when she is angry, for fear of imparting to it a choleric temperament. If unable to perform herself this agreeable maternal function, she procures a black nurse, but never an Indian. The vital tide from a red skin she feels assured will give it a fiery irascible disposition. She considers the milk of the black cow cooler than that of any other, and anticipates a mild and amiable temper in her children as she pours it into their porringers. I like this idea of not nursing a child when angry. It is another check on peevishness and passion. It would not be amiss were the superstition universal. Of all objects in the world the most painful to me is, a mother nursing and scolding at the same time. It is worse than thunder out of a soft April cloud.

Wednesday, April 29. There are in Lima two associations which are very attentive to strangers. A member of one is called a pillo, a member of the other a pillofero. The first is a genteel loafer, the second a dexterous gambler. So you have your choice between a good-humored graceless uninvited guest, and a refined cheat. The one is satisfied with your table and floating change, the other goes for your purse and its entire contents. The one plunders you through your vanity, the other through your bad fortune.

Priests here not only guard the prerogatives of their order, but the purity of their Spanish blood. A high ecclesiastic, of Indian or African descent, is not to be found in their ranks. Such a lineage would debar him the sacred functions of the altar. Those who exercise them are as jealous of the Castilian blood which flows in their veins, as an old Hidalgo furbishing his family coat-of-arms. They inculcate equality among their communicants, and make them kneel together on the same stone pavement, but they stand aloof in the immemorial privileges and dignity of their order. They have inferiors who mix with the masses: some of these are devoted men; they encounter incredible hardships in propagating their faith. Their self-denying zeal may well be a lesson to Protestants.

The most amusing being in Lima is the mestizo—the offspring of the European and Indian. His wit and humor never fail him. He will convulse you with laughter, and be himself quite sedate. It puzzles you that a bird of such dazzling plumage should fly out of the shadows of such a sombre tree. The zambo, half Indian and half African, has a broader humor. His allusions are under no restraints from sentiments of delicacy, or respect for the presence of the other sex. I have seen one of them keep a street crowd in a roar by the hour.

Zambos are generally employed as household servants. The children naturally fall into their care, and become early accustomed to the language suggested by their prurient imaginations. Love intrigues are with them a never-failing source of entertainment. Even the "peccadillos" of their parents are sometimes made a subject of mirth. The adventures of the mother are thus made known to the daughter. Her prudent counsels, after that, sound hollow indeed. It is not to be wondered at that she should turn away from the precept to imitate the example. Many families, and among them some of the first in Lima, have thus been plunged in irretrievable humiliation and grief. The cause may be, and generally is, carefully concealed. But an unseen wound may rankle as deeply as that which has no covering. The light which a mother should depend upon to guide the steps of her daughter, is that which is reflected from her own example. If shadows rest on this—if it falls only in transient flakes, seen one moment and lost the next, like the firefly's fitful beam—it will only serve the more to bewilder and betray. What the mother would have her daughters, she should be herself. It is her example, and not her precepts, that shapes their social and moral being.

Thursday, April 30. In the native Indians is found the productive industry of Peru. The products of their gardens and fields roll in a ceaseless tide into the markets of Lima. Their jewelry and ponchos, wrought with little aid from machinery, rival in elegance some of the most finished productions of art; while their sturdy arms fill with ceaseless echoes the deep silver mines of the Andes. The roads which they constructed under their Incas still run along the jagged steeps of the Cordilleras; their swinging gardens still throw their fragrance on the wind; and through their aqueducts still rolls with refreshing force the mountain stream. But many of their richest plains and glens, Spanish rule and indolence have turned into sterility.

An Indian boy from the interior, domesticated in a European family in Lima, will at first show some alacrity in duty; but when he enters the summer of youth, he flies back to his mountain home. And the Indian girl, who has little else to do than carry a mat to church, on which her mistress may kneel at mass, when the levities of childhood are passed, turns an earnest eye to the picturesque glades of the Andes. The sequestered hut, the wild fruits and flowers which bloom around it, the stream that ripples past the door, the lama-skin couch, and one by whom she can be loved and protected, float through her young dreams, and off she flies for the reality of this romantic vision. Her mistress, the next time she goes to mass, looks for her Indian girl, and begins to think

"That love in simplest hearts hath deepest sway."

FRIDAY, MAY 1. The most tender and melancholy associations here are those which crowd upon one, seated at twilight by the burial mounds of those who were once sole possessors of the soil. The yellow-leaved willows wave in the still moonlight; their whispers are in mournful unison with the dirge of the Indian, which still floats over the graves of his fathers, and melts into harmony with the voice of the cuculi, that responds in plaintive notes from the guarango grove. Every thing around you breathes of the past, and of the ruins which time and disaster have left behind.

> "Thou unrelenting Past!
> Strong are the barriers round thy dark domain,
> And fetters, sure and fast,
> Hold all that enter thy unbreathing reign.
> Far in thy realms withdrawn,
> Old empires sit in sullenness and gloom,
> And glorious ages gone,
> Lie deep within the shadow of thy womb."

The swinging hammock is the sofa of the Limanian lady. This airy couch, twined of beautiful grass, and died into the varied hues of the rainbow, swings in the cool corridor, while flowers of loveliest tint throw around it their fragrant breath. In the midst of these odors the fair one takes her siesta, while her cheek is flushed with the triumph that floats along her rosy dream. Sleep on while yet thou mayest; a morrow comes when these visions of pride and happiness will take to themselves wings and fly away. Care and sorrow will cast their shadows upon thee, and thou must walk in their gloom down to the dreamless sleep of the grave. But there are visions which will not depart; there are flowers that will never die; but they belong to the spirit-land.

SATURDAY, MAY 2. The cathedral, and indeed all the principal churches of Lima, impress you more through the magnificence of their proportions than any richness of architecture. They are generally built of a coarse freestone, stuccoed and painted. Their domes and towers rise on the distant eye, in gaudy grandeur, but betray their poverty on a closer vision. The statues which adorn them are generally coarse and frail in the material, and without taste in the execution. Over every altar is a statue of the Virgin in the hues of life. Her costume is light or dark, as the occasion is merry or sad; but the skirt of her dress always spreads to the right and left like a great fan. This depression is given it, so that the priest officiating at the altar, when he looks up, may see her benignant face.

SUNDAY, MAY 3. In the church of San Domingo is a statue, in which there is an attempt to represent, under the similitudes of the human form and countenance, the Supreme Jehovah. The idea is taken from those ancient sculptures which embody the attributes of the Olympian Jove. The analogy between those statues which Christianity has been made to sanctify, and those which she cast off with the mythology of paganism, is painfully true. We have here the Venus of the Greeks in the likeness of the blessed Virgin, and the Jupiter of the Romans in the representations of the Supreme Being. Mercury, in the character of the Angel of the Annunciation, brings tidings from heaven; and Pluto, under the thunder-scarred front of Satan, reigns over hell. The unpurified, instead of wandering on the gloomy Styx, now wander in purgatory, till some Charon, in the person of an absolving priest, ferries them over to the fields of purple light. I know the force of visible symbols, and the facility and seeming advantage of impressing man through his outward senses; but something is due to the dignity of truth and the sanctity of that spiritual revelation which God has made of himself, and above all to that fearful mandate—"Thou shalt not make to thyself any graven image, nor the likeness of any thing that is in the heaven above, or in the earth beneath, or in the water under the earth: thou shalt not bow down to them nor worship them."

MONDAY, MAY 4. The aborigines of Peru still wear a bean at the temple as a charm against disease, and still adhere to their herb doctors. These simple disciples of Esculapius, laden with their barks, balsams, roots, and herbs, traverse the steeps and glens of the Andes, descend into the plains of Chili, and the pampas of Buenos Ayres. If they seldom cure, they have the satisfaction of knowing that they never kill. But as the legitimate province of medicine is to amuse the patient, while nature cures the disease, perhaps the result of their practice will not suffer by a comparison with that of their more learned brethren. It is much wiser, in ordinary cases, to hang a bean to the temple, than to put a pill into the stomach. Nature never complains of the bean, but she is often very much puzzled to know what to do with the pill. Were the ghosts of those who have fallen victims to medicine to appear on this earth, there would be a more terrible shaking among the medical profession, than there was in the valley of Ezekiel's vision of dry bones.

Tuesday, May 5. The winds in Peru prevail for nine months in the year from the south. These cooler currents, mingling themselves with warmer airs, produce what is called the Scotch mist. It instils itself into your garments slowly, but in a continued exposure will completely saturate them. It is experienced most at night, and disappears beneath the slanting rays of the sun. Strangers are apt to disregard it; but the natives put on their ponchos.

The traveller from a northern zone finds the seasons quite reversed here. Spring opens with September. When the farmer with us is gathering in his last harvest, the seeds of the first are sown here. When the birds forsake our groves for winter quarters, they are here selecting their vernal mates.

When the flowers with us perish, they are here just opening their bright eyes to the sun. Nature never leaves herself here without a witness, nor society without its signals, as seen in this monk and Peruvian farmer.

Monk. Peruvian Farmer.

I encountered two things in the markets of Lima rather peculiar in their way. The first was a chicken quartered as if it had been a sheep or bullock, and sold in parts to suit purchasers; each part bringing the price of a whole one with us. The second was a monk carrying a little tray, with a crucifix embossed upon it, which every one was invited to kiss, and pay for the privilege what he might please to put in. One cast into it a biscuit, another a sausage, a third a potatoe; so the monk went off with quite a breakfast, and will be back assuredly to-morrow morning to have it filled again in the same way. It was the first time I ever saw the privilege of a kiss purchased with a potatoe. But a monk is seldom at a loss for an expedient.

Of all the fruits in Peru, the most esteemed is the chirimoya. It grows rather larger than our pippin, has a rough exterior, but is filled with a soft pulp, which resembles in taste our strawberries and cream. It is scooped out with a teaspoon, melts in the mouth, and gushes over the palate in a luscious tide. The tree which bears this fruit requires seventeen years before its seminal buds ripen into their precious burden.

Next comes the granadilla, the fruit of the passion flower. It resembles, in shape, size, and smoothness of texture, the egg of our domestic fowls. You break the shell, and swallow the rich mucilaginous pulp with its delicate seeds. The taste has no analogies in any other fruit. At first it seems to want character or palatable emphasis, but it wins upon you, till that which appeared a defect becomes an excellence. It is just such a fruit as the seeming sacredness of its origin would lead you to expect. It brings you back in your sensations to that fount which nursed your infant life.

Close on this follows the palta-pear, with its large central stone resembling that of the peach. This fruit, which is protected by a hard, thin rind, has the consistence of thick cream, and, with salt sprinkled on it, is used upon bread as an excellent substitute for butter. I do not wonder that the epicurean monk, in his desire to lift the flagging imaginations of his hearers to the fruitions of the better land, represents the chirimoya, the granadilla, and palta, as nodding over its crystal streams. They have that which never entered even the imagination of Mahomet, when he spread the verdant lawns and wove the ambrosial bowers of his pictured heaven.

Wednesday, May 6. The therapeutics of the Limanians are as peculiar, when applied to their tempers, as their bodies. They never drink cold water when angry, from an apprehension that it conduces to hepatic diseases. In their opinion it chills and contracts the biliary excretories, prevents a natural flow of the bile, and leads to congestion. The physician often attributes the death of his patient to this fatal indiscretion. He would sooner give an angry man alcohol, than a glass of iced-water.

The old Spanish families, who were swept away by the Revolution, resembled the Mussulman in many of their characteristic habits. They were remarkable for their commercial probity, their love of ease, their hatred of innovation, their intolerance of the slightest indignity, their pride of lineage, and their indulgence in sensual gratifications. Their dwellings were stately castles, where the indolent lounged, the gay revelled, the sad were beguiled of their sorrows, and the poor forgot their poverty. But they have passed away, save a few who remain, like the sturdy trees of a forest, which the hurricane hath swept. The few who remain are rarely engaged in any important enterprises. What capital they have is often locked up, where they forego the interest for the safety of the principal. There is one old Spaniard who has now, and has had for years, eight hundred thousand dollars packed away in the vaults of a large commercial house here. An interest of twenty per cent. would not draw it from its stronghold. Revolution and rapacity have wrecked his confidence ; and he is in this respect only one among thousands. The result is, the commerce of Peru has fallen mostly into the hands of the English and Americans. Their daring spirit will carry it on, though revolutions succeed each other strong and fast as the breaking waves of ocean. But the storm is past, and the great deep is rocking itself to rest.

The Spanish lady has but little book-knowledge, but a most observant sagacity. She has no acquirements in letters, but reads character as by intuition. She never essays an argument, and is never at a loss for a pertinent reply. She is ardent in her temperament, and yet rarely loses her equanimity. She is alive to adulation, and is never overawed by menace.

She is punctilious in all the forms of religion, and persevering in all the perils of an intrigue. Her mornings are spent with her confessor, her evenings with her lover.

Masses for the repose of the soul are inculcated by the clergy as an indispensable religious duty. They are a source of vast revenue to the curate, and often involve the relatives of the deceased in ruinous expenses. It is considered worse than cruel to leave in purgatory the soul of a relative, which might be relieved through the efficacy of the mass. The dictates of religion and nature are therefore both enlisted in securing a punctual performance of this pious obligation. It is an expensive duty, and the burden often falls where it is least able to be borne.

The poor widow, believing, as she is taught, that masses can relieve the condition of her deceased child, mitigate its sufferings, and hasten its transit from purifying flames to perfect bliss, parts with her last shilling, as well she may, and even sells her mourning weeds for this purpose. The author of "Three years in the Pacific" says :—"I saw in Pisco an Indian boy, who had been sold by the curate in one of the interior provinces, to pay for the requisite number of masses for the rest of his father's soul!" There is a company in Lima, instituted under the sanction of the archbishop, which engages, for the consideration of a real a week from any poor family, to purchase, at the death of a member of the household, a sufficient number of masses to liberate the deceased from the pains of purgatory. This company has a hundred applicants where the life-insurance corporation has one. Masses for the dead, claiming as they do to reach the condition of the departed soul, cast into insignificance every thing this side of their object, and leave nothing for a superstitious faith to desire beyond it. The human imagination cannot conceive of a more tremendous ecclesiastical engine.

THURSDAY, MAY 7. The pleasures of our visit to Lima were not a little enhanced by the arrangements and hospitalities of Commodore Stockton. He took ample apartments in the elegant hotel which opens on the grand plaza, where he had his own table and attendants. We met here not only the officers of the Congress, but the first gentlemen in Lima. These entertainments were free of ostentation, and that parade in which the heart is lost in the forms of etiquette, and were on a scale in keeping with the rank and ample means of the individual who dispensed them. They have had the effect not only to strengthen friendship among ourselves, but to win the good opinion and favor of those whose prominent position here gives them an influence over the character of our foreign relations.

The gentlemen connected with the Alsop House have also contributed largely to the pleasures of our visit here. We shall long remember in connection with this hospitable mansion the kind attention of Mr. McCall, Mr. Foster, and our worthy Consul. Their liberality, ample means, and sterling integrity are a rock on which the American name may safely repose at Lima.

The time had come for me to leave Lima, and take up my quarters again on board the Congress. I took a seat in the diligence just starting for Callao, and which was already pretty full with other passengers. But I had the advantage of not requiring a great deal of room, and so squeezed in. Opposite to me sat a fat Peruvian lady, whose huge fan, which threatened my nose as much as her broad face, was in a constant dash to create a breath of air, while her flesh shook at every jar as if it would break from its moorings. Two lap-dogs, one under either flank, pushed out their panting noses with many ineffectual attempts to extricate themselves from the heat of their smothered condition; but were rebuffed by a slap from the lady's hand, which was too fat to hurt them but for the massive rings on her fingers, in which flashed gems enough to stud a sultan's snuff-box. She wore no bonnet or broad gipsy hat to protect her from the rays of the sun, which broke through the open crevices in the roof of the diligence; and indeed she needed none, for the heavy puffs of her cigar rolled up there, and hung over her head in a thick floating cloud.

On one side of me sat an officer of the Peruvian army, in full uniform. His chapeau, tasselled, plumed, and covered with gold lace, rested on his knees, and exposed the heavy black wig, in which each hair had been made to take its particular place. His thick coat, with its massive embroidery, was buttoned, notwithstanding the heat, so close over his chest and up to the neck, that it seemed to dispute with his stock the office of supporting the chin. His pantaloons, down which flowed a broad stream of gold lace, were straightened and stretched in every thread by the short straps under the boot, which might have lifted his feet from the floor, but for the ponderous spurs which projected far behind the heel in a shaft, at the end of which rattled a roller in the shape of a circular saw. Not a smile or emotion of any kind once disturbed the fixedness of his bronzed features. He sat crank and motionless as a statue, save the bony hand which now and then gave another twist to his moustache, which curled its horns into the corners of his mouth. But for this slight motion, he might have been taken for one of those old heroes whom Egyptian art more than three thousand years ago embalmed into immortality.

On the other side of me sat a middle-aged native,

in a white fringed poncho, a large Guyaquil hat, and figured trowsers. An old-fashioned ring was conspicuous on his finger, and the remnants of a gold mounting still lingered on the top of his cane. His features were sharp and prominent; and he had a remarkable strabismus of his eyes, which seemed to be trying to look into each other across the bridge of his nose. On his knees he carried an article of chamber furniture, which, though manufactured of silver, shall be nameless here.

Having occasion to light a cigar, which required the use of both his hands to manage the flint and steel, which he carried in his pocket, he placed the *unmentionable*, without saying a word, in the lap of the passenger next him, who happened to be the captain of an American merchantman, and who as quickly thrust it back on the knees of its owner, with the ejaculation, "Carry your own teapot." The eyes of the proprietor flashed fire into each other, but not a word was said. The officer gave his moustache another twist, the fat lady fanned herself as before, but the two other lady passengers seemed to be not a little surprised at the rudeness of the American; neither of them smiled, nor seemed to perceive the least impropriety, or the slightest shade of the ludicrous in the conspicuous position which the unmentionable occupied. With us, two ladies so situated, would have jumped out of the stage, if not through the door, then through a window.

> Better at once to fly the sight,
> Than stay to perish with affright.

FRIDAY, MAY 8. We were all again on board, and watching for the appearance of the steamer from Panama. Seven months had elapsed, and we had received no intelligence from home, and could expect none now through any government mail. Indeed, our government has no mail arrangements in the Pacific. Once in two or three months a packet is dispatched to Chagres with a mail, which finds its way over the isthmus to Panama, and there goes soundly to sleep. For matter of reaching its destination, it might as well be in the moon.

Commodore Stockton had dispatched Mr. Beale and Mr. Norris to the United States, with instructions to join him by the nearest practicable route in the Pacific. The line of steamers between the West India islands and Chagres, and between Panama and Callao, had not then been completed, and it was therefore extremely doubtful whether they would attempt to reach us by this route. The probability seemed to be they would take the route by New Orleans, and across the continent to Mazatlan, and thence to California.

In the midst of these doubts, the steamer threw

her black mass within the bright line of the horizon. "There she comes!" ran in quick whispers through the ship. As she neared us, the all-absorbing question was, whether the secretary of the commodore was in her. On this depended our last and only hope of letters from home. She passed us at no great distance; but we tried in vain to discover, through our glasses, the individual for whom we were looking. No sign of such a person appeared among the few passengers who paced her deck. I went below; I had seen enough of steamers, and never desired to see another. The third cutter was called away, and directed to proceed to the steamer; but that seemed only blotting out the last ray of possibility.

In twenty minutes, an officer rushed below with the surprising intelligence that the secretary of the commodore was in the boat alongside. I was not long in reaching the deck, and could hardly credit my own eyes when I saw him come over the gangway; and still less when he placed in my hands some twenty letters from my family and friends. Our advices were within about thirty days from the United States. The commodore received a large mail; Capt. Du Pont, and nearly all the officers, got letters from home. For this intelligence, with files of papers from the press, we were indebted to the arrangement of Commodore Stockton, carried through at his private expense. We spent the greater part of the night in reading our letters and penning answers to them, as we were to sail the next day for the Sandwich Islands. These details may not be interesting to some, especially those who have not been absent from home a week without intelligence; but let more than half a year of their brief life circle round without any information, and they will appreciate the significance of such seeming trifles. The surest source of sympathy is found in an experience of the same calamity.

The Incas of Peru, who invested their imperial sway with the mandates and sanctions of a supreme theocracy, are in their graves. Their palaces and temples remain; and in these vast monuments are shrined the evidences of their departed grandeur and power. The solid blocks of porphyry which pave the great public way from Quito to Cuzco, and the table-land of Desaguadero, still invite the footsteps of the moving masses, and still roll back the sunbeams in showering gold.

The dominion of the usurper who entered this peaceful realm with the cross and chain, has at length been broken. It lies in ruins, amid penitent tokens of guilt and sorrow, around the sacred ashes of the Incas. The fiery deluge of revolution which has swept this fair land since, has also passed away. The calm hearts of two millions of freemen remain. They bend the knee to no iron despotism, no consecrated pageant of power. They have rights which they assert in the unrestricted freedom of the elective franchise. Their progress to constitutional freedom and repose has been tumultuous and wild, but they are within sight of their goal, and will reach it as assuredly as the wave of the rolling deep its destined strand.

But our anchors are up, our courses set, and we are away for other shores.

Land of the Incas, fare thee well!
  For thee my fancy twines
A rarer, richer coronel
  Than glitters in thy mines,—
A circlet where each jewel flings
A ray that blasts the hope of kings.

CHAPTER X.

PASSAGE FROM CALLAO TO HONOLULU.

DEPARTURE FROM CALLAO.—THE RUM SMUGGLER.—SUNSET.—SEA-BIRDS.—A SAILOR'S DEFENCE.—GENERAL QUARTERS.—SPIRIT RATION.—THE SAILOR AND RELIGION.—THE FLAG.—SAGACITY OF THE RAT.—THE CLOUD.—CALMS AND SHOWERS.—RELIGIOUS TRACTS.—CONSTELLATIONS.—TRADE WINDS.—CONDUCT OF THE CREW.—MOON IN THE ZENITH.—LAY SERMON.—FUNERAL.—LAND HO!

"Huzza! for Otaheite! was the cry,
As stately swept the gallant vessel by,
The breeze springs up, the lately flapping sail
Extends its arch before the growing gale."

SATURDAY, MAY 9. We rousted our anchors this afternoon from the bed in which they have slumbered for the last six weeks, and stood out to sea from the bay of Callao. The breeze freshened as the sun set, and before our mid-watch was out, only the rock of San Lorenzo was seen lifting its naked peaks into the light of the moon.

Farewell, Callao! I have seen quite enough of your destitution and dirt, your pickpockets and parrots, your fish and your fleas, your brats and your buzzards. I wonder not that nature in sore disgust sunk your progenitor from the light of the sun; and unless you reform, you may expect to share the same fate. Through your chambers the dolphins will sport;

your forsaken harps will thrill beneath the wild fingers of the mermaid, while, far above, the hoarse wave pours on the rocks your death-dirge. The sea-gull only will know the place of your rest, and only the poor pelican mourn that you are not.

Sunday, May 10. Divine service: officers and crew all present. Subject of the sermon, the temptations of the sailor. A chaplain in the navy has one advantage over his brethren on land. He has his parishioners in the most compact of all possible forms, and every one present when he officiates. In making his official visits he has not to ride around among five hundred families located at all points of the compass. He cannot stir without coming in contact with them. But he has this disadvantage; in the vicissitudes of a sea life they are extremely apt to break away from his constraining influence. They may be brought back again, but it is too often through the deepest self-inflicted humiliation.

I was called down from Lima to see a sailor who was supposed to be dying. As I came to the hammock in which he was lying, he told me he did not think he should live, and that he felt unfit to die. He made a free and frank confession of the errors of his life, and desired me to pray that he might be forgiven. I tried to lead his thoughts to the cross and to the fountain of Christ's blood. To these his contrition and solicitude quickly turned. He seemed not to doubt, in his infinite need, their full sufficiency. I prayed with him; he earnestly responded, and so did his messmates, who stood silently grouped about his hammock. Sailors well know what is involved in that awful transition which we undergo in death. They never trifle with the event itself, however heedless they may be in the indulgences which lead to it.

Monday, May 11. We have a fine, steady wind on our larboard quarter. It has carried us, with the aid of a strong current, during the last twenty-four hours, two hundred and sixty miles. This good fortune, however, cannot last. We must part with the wind as we approach the equator, and perhaps before. But sufficient to the day is the evil thereof. It is much wiser rightly to enjoy the blessings of the present, than to yield ourselves to anxieties about the contingencies of the future.

We have a beautiful sunset. The air is serene, and the blue circle of the sky rests in tranquil softness on the utmost verge of the ocean. The whole realm of waters seems cradled in its limitless sweep. The rays of the descending orb lie along the gently heaving billows in lines of level light. The clouds which o'ercanopy his couch of repose, are robed in purple and gold; while the long vistas which open through them, seem as soft avenues to the spirit-land.

"Methinks it were no pain to die,
On such an eve, when such a sky
O'ercanopies the West.
To gaze my fill on yon calm deep,
And, like an infant, fall to sleep
On earth, my mother's breast.

"There's peace and welcome in yon sea
Of endless blue tranquillity.
The clouds are living things;
I trace their veins of liquid gold,
I see them solemnly unfold
Their soft and fleecy wings.

"These be the angels that convey
Us weary children of a day—
Life's tedious journey o'er—
Where neither passions come, nor woes,
To vex the genius of repose
On Death's majestic shore."

TUESDAY, MAY 12. We have now leisure to look back as well as forward. Our crew conducted themselves remarkably well at Callao. Our boats were in constant communication with the shore, without an officer in them. And yet, during six weeks, no disturbances took place, and only one or two cases of intoxication occurred. One attempt was made by a hand in the third cutter to smuggle off a skin of rum. It was discovered by the officer who overhauled the boat as she came alongside. An effort was made to find its owner, but no one would acknowledge the ill-gotten thing. As the crew of the boat must have been cognizant of the fact, they were informed by Capt. Du Pont, that unless the name of the offender was given up, they would all be punished. They were given an hour to decide what should be done. Before its expiration three of the crew gave in the name of the smuggler; and he paid the penalty, which involved a loss of the contraband article and the infliction of a severe chastisement. We have no laws with us which are a dead letter.

Wednesday, May 13. Our wind has veered still further aft, and consequently fills fewer of our sails; but we are running before it at the rate of nine and ten knots the hour. The sky is covered with light, fleecy clouds, through which the sun's rays melt without any intensity of light. The ocean has a long, undulating swing, like that of some vast mass which has been seeking for ages to rock itself to rest, but is prevented by some invisible power that has decreed against its repose.

Thirty more of the crew to-day voluntarily relinquished their spirit-ration. They considered it a source of mischief. A sailor attached to one of our frigates was court-martialed for an attempt to break open the spirit-room. His defence before the court was ingenious, to say the least of it. The government, he said, had given him two tots of grog during the day, and a third by way of splicing the main-brace. The wardroom steward had given him, for some service he had rendered, two more, and these five had made him crazy. It was not him, he said, but the *whisky* which was in him that had made the assault on the spirit-room. And now, as the government had administered to him more than half of this whisky, the government should bear half the responsibility of the offence. He therefore prayed that one half of the lashes which this offence merited might be given to the government, and the other half he would take himself.

There is a volume of argument, in this defence, against the whisky-ration. It is a shame for the government to render a sailor half intoxicated, and then punish him for becoming wholly so. It is the *first* glass, and not the last, on which your indignation should light. This whisky-ration has done evil enough in the service; let it be consigned to perdition, where it belongs.

Thursday, May 14. The birds which followed us from the coast have returned; but several boobies, who had probably lost their reckoning, circled around our masts at sunset. As twilight deepened, they perched on our yards, and were in a few minutes sound asleep. They might have been easily captured, but sailors are not very partial to such trophies. There is something in their name which they do not like, and which seems to react on the valor of the captor. Give them a tiger, and they will storm his jungle with only such weapons as they can pick up on the way. But a booby, that can harm no one, and whose stupidity seems to have suggested his name, is allowed to go unmolested. The weakest man in the community has generally the fewest detractors, while an intellectual giant will always have a pack at his heels. There is more honor in striking *at* a lion, than there is in killing a monkey.

FRIDAY, MAY 15. The sick sailor whom I came down from Lima to see, has passed the crisis of his disease, and may recover. He fluttered for some time between life and death. The vital flame seemed to come and go as a thing apart from him. But now its ray is more bright and steady. He is an orphan, without father or mother; but has a sister, to whom he is much attached. The idea of being permitted to see her again, is almost too much for his exhausted state. If you would get at the true character of the sailor, you must visit him in his sickness. His better feelings then gush out over the asperities of his lot, like a spring from amid the tangled shrubs of the wildwood.

SATURDAY, MAY 16. We went to general quarters

this morning at three bells, and exercised the guns. Those on the main-deck are so heavy, they require a prodigious outlay of strength to work them. Any irregularity in the application of the force frustrates all dexterity of movement; each man must forego all individual volition, independent action, and become a part of the mechanism which is to be tasked to the utmost as a whole; and yet he must have all that enthusiasm which is felt in freedom from constraint, and when the strong impulses of the soul throw themselves off in resistless action. It is much easier to slash away gallantly with the sabre, than to train quickly and accurately on the enemy a forty-four-pounder. This requires self-possession, and indomitable firmness. Sailors have no retreat. They must conquer, die, or surrender. The last they would seldom do, were it not forced upon them by the laws of humanity. They would sooner die, as boarders, on the deck of the enemy, than survive, as captives, over their own keel.

Sunday, May 17. Divine service: subject of the sermon, the influence of religion on a man's intellectual character. The object of the speaker was to show that religion aids mental development,—that while it strikes down pride, it imparts true dignity. Nothing can be more absurd than the idea, that religion impairs strength of character. It invests even the timid with a firmness and force which stand undismayed amid dungeons, racks, and flaming stakes.

To possess the religious character seems to the sailor such a vast stride in advance of his ordinary habits, that he is extremely diffident in preferring his humble claims. He will pray when peril presses, for he thinks a wicked man may do that, but he connects a worthy profession of personal piety with a degree of sanctity hardly compatible with the infirmities of his nature. He has rarely enjoyed the advantages of a religious education; no moral training has gradually introduced him to the sanctities of the Christian life. The utmost that he feels himself fit to do is, like the poor publican, to smite upon his breast, and exclaim, "God be merciful to me a sinner!" But to take his place among those whose piety is to guide and animate others, is to him as if a lost star were to spring out of the depths of darkness, and take its station among the burning constellations of heaven. When therefore he does avow his religious faith and hopes, it is generally with him no halfway measure; no decent compromise between conscience and inclination. He takes with him his all for this world and the next.

MONDAY, MAY 18. The phrase "fickle as the wind" is not applicable to the trades of the Pacific. The wind before which we are running has hardly veered a point for the last week. I commend its steadiness to those politicians who find it necessary every few months to define their position.

We have had about our ship this afternoon several sea-birds, to which sailors have given the name of boatswains. They have a long feather in their tail; which streams behind them like the train of a duchess at court. But it answers a much wiser purpose, for instead of embarrassing motion, it acts as a rudder, and steadies the bird in navigating the aerial currents. Nature never bestows any useless appendages. These are the achievements of human vanity; and sorry achievements they are. They even enter the grave, and mock with their tinsel its awful reality.

Tuesday, May 19. We have had through the day a soft, hazy atmosphere. At sunset these light, floating vapors gathered themselves into more substantial clouds, and promised a shower. But after hanging on the horizon for a time, they seemed to sink below its rim. The moon came up late; her soft light fell on the sea, but the wings of the clouds, if touched by the effulgence, were invisible. The wind, though of sufficient force to carry us on some eight knots, scarcely agitated the breast of the ocean. It seemed as something intended to move over its level plain and not to disturb its depths. It was like a shadow gliding over the tops of a vast sleeping forest.

WEDNESDAY, MAY 20. Our gun-carriages, with their black paint on a white ground, could never be made to look neat for any length of time. The white was perpetually working itself through its sable covering, like an inborn levity of heart through an assumed gravity of demeanor. Our captain and first lieutenant, who have an acknowledged taste in every thing that belongs to the appearance of a man-of-war, ordered the carriages thoroughly scraped of every particle of paint. A dark stain was then given to the wood, through which the grain shows itself in its native strength. Over this a thin varnish of spirit and oil was spread, imparting to the wood a beautiful polish, and blending itself with its texture. The battery of a frigate, especially as you come upon her gun-deck, is that which first strikes the eye. Like the pulpit of a church, if forlorn in its appearance, elegance elsewhere will not retrieve the error. A rough pulpit may have thunder in it, but the thunder don't lie in its roughness.

THURSDAY, MAY 21. One of our quarter-masters has just finished a new and splendid flag, which we shall display at the islands. How profound the love and reverence of the sailor for his flag! He connects with it, as it streams in freedom and light on the wind, a thousand glorious memories. It points to crimson waves where his comrades of the deck have triumphed or sunk overpowered to their rest. He holds the deepest crime to be that of treason to its obligations and sacred hopes. He would surrender it only to the King of kings.

The last words of the late Commodore Hull were addressed to the stern majesty of Death.

"I STRIKE MY FLAG."

I strike not to a sceptred king—
  A man of mortal breath—
A weak, imperious, fickle thing;
  I strike to thee, O Death!

I strike that flag which in the fight
  The trust of millions hailed,
The flag which threw its meteor light
  Where England's lion quailed.

I strike to thee, whose mandates fall
  Alike on king and slave,
Whose livery is the shroud and pall,
  And palace-court the grave.

Thy captives crowd the caverned earth,
  They fill the rolling sea,
From court and camp, the wave and hearth,
  All, all have bowed to thee.

But thou, stern Death, must yet resign
  Thy sceptre o'er this dust;
The Power that makes the mortal thine,
  Will yet remand his trust.

His signal trump shall pierce this ear
  Beneath the grave's cold clod—
This form, these features reappear
  In life before their God.

FRIDAY, MAY 22. I was sitting at a late hour last evening on the gun-deck to catch the breeze, which came freshly through the larboard ports, when a large, sleek, long-tailed rat, with a slow, aristocratic step, approached the combings of the hatch, which he mounted, and then deliberately descended into the steerage among the junior officers. What his errand was there, I know not; but there was a dignity and self-possession in his demeanor which was admirable. He seemed as one conscious of his rights, and not at all disposed to waive them. I have always felt some regard for a rat since my cruise in the Constellation. We were fitting for sea at Norfolk, and taking in water and provisions; a plank was resting on the sill of one of the ports which communicated with the wharf. On a bright moonlight evening, we discovered two rats on the plank coming into the ship. The foremost was leading the other by a straw, one end of which each held in his mouth. We managed to capture them both, and found, to our surprise, the one led by the other was stone-blind. His faithful friend was trying to get him on board, where he would have comfortable quarters during a three years' cruise. We felt no disposition to kill either, and landed them on the wharf. How many there are in this world to whom the fidelity of that rat readeth a lesson!

Saturday, May 23. We have now been out fourteen days from Callao, and have sailed two thousand eight hundred miles, making an average of two hundred miles a day. Not a squall, nor a threatening cloud, have we encountered; nor have we once furled our royals, or taken in our studding-sails. The wind has been, with scarce a point's variation, dead aft; and has maintained an equanimity which the most serene philosophical temper can scarcely hope to rival. Contentment, cheerfulness, and alacrity have been everywhere visible among the crew. Not an offence has been committed which has received or merited punishment. Such is our condition in the midst of the Pacific—under the influence of its balmy airs—and under a discipline in which justice and humanity are admirably blended. We have yet to sail some twenty-eight hundred miles before we make our port. The distance between Callao and the Sandwich Islands is about twice as great as that between New York and Liverpool. Yet we all remember the time when a man bound to Liverpool, or London, took leave of his friends with a sadness and solemnity, which augured a dismal doubt of his return.

SUNDAY, MAY 24. Though we are near the Equator, where the weather is apt to be variable, yet we have had a delightful day, a brilliant sky, a smooth sea, and a mild aft wind. We had divine service at six bells. The subject of the discourse was, the example of the primitive Christians,—their faith, their zeal, their constancy, their sufferings, their triumphs. They are a cloud of witnesses who have gone before us to heaven, but they have left their footprints on the shores of time. The example of their faith and constancy remains for our imitation.

Every man, however humble his sphere, may be, and ought to be, in his own life a preacher of righteousness. A religious example, wherever found, is invested with a prodigious moral power. Such an example is within the reach of every one on the decks of a man-of-war; and there is no situation where its effects would be more certain. We are as responsible for the good which we can do, as the evil which we have done. The man who had one talent was condemned, not because he had only one talent, but because he hid that talent in the earth.

MONDAY, MAY 25. We crossed the Equator last night in our first watch, at longitude one hundred and twenty west. We crossed it first on our way to Rio de Janeiro; since that we have sailed through one hundred and twenty degrees of latitude, and almost as many degrees of temperature. At Rio we were melted down with the heat; off Cape Horn our fingers were stiffened with the cold; and now the most grateful gift in the world would be a glass of ice-water. Such extremes of temperature are the more felt in the exposures inseparable from a sea-life. We have on board ship no forests into which we can rush from the heat; no glowing grates, around which we can gather from the cold. We must take the elements, whatever they may be, in their full force. They shatter the constitution; and sink a grave in the sailor's path, over which he rarely passes to a green old age.

Tuesday, May 26. Clouds hung in thick masses on the eastern horizon this morning. They had not that jagged outline, which in other seas indicates a severe blow. They loomed up lazily, as if they knew not themselves for what purpose their dark forms had been shoved between us and the splendors of the breaking day. We supposed they were charged with showers, and watched their motions with some interest. But the higher they ascended, the thinner they became, till at last they gradually melted away, and left only the soft over-arching sky. But they may gather themselves another morn, each take a distinct shape, and utter its satirical soliloquy, like the cloud of Shelley:—

I am the daughter of earth and water,
    And the nursling of the sky;
I pass through the pores of the ocean and shores;
    I change, but I cannot die.
For after the rain, when with never a stain,
    The pavilion of heaven is bare,
And the winds and the sunbeams, with their convex gleams,
    Build up the blue dome of air,
I silently laugh at my own cenotaph,
    And out of the caverns of rain,
Like a child from the womb, like a ghost from the tomb,
    I arise and unbuild it again.

WEDNESDAY, MAY 27. We have been becalmed all day between the northeast and northwest trades. The ocean has slumbered around us with scarce a ripple. A large shark was seen hanging around our ship through the morning. A strong hook, attached to a rope and baited with a pound or two of pork, was drifted astern. He nabbed it as a famishing politician an office. He was a monster in strength as well as size, and made the sea foam with his struggles to break away. It required four or five sailors to draw him in; and when on deck he cleared a pretty broad circle by his ferocious sweep. But he was soon overmastered, deprived of his head and tail by the axe, and cut up into pieces accommodated to the sailors' culinary apparatus. Many, as they ate him, derived their keenest relish from their inherited antipathy to his species.

Thursday, May 28. We have had through the day scarce a breath of wind; the thermometer has ranged at 85; the heat below has been quite insupportable. The sun set through a thick, stagnant atmosphere; our sails hung motionless, save an occasional flap against the mast, given them by the sluggish swing of the ship. This continued till six bells of the first watch, when the rain fell in a perfect deluge. The water formed an instant lake between the bulwarks of the spar-deck, fell through the hatches, and flooded us below. It was some minutes before the hatches could be hooded; and when they were, our last breath of fresh air was shut out. We continued in this situation through the night. The sun rose into a dim, murky haze, in which his beams were quenched long before they reached our position.

Friday, May 29. The most gorgeous sunsets I have ever witnessed at sea have been near the equator. We have just been watching one from the deck; all eyes were fastened upon its magnificent phases. The whole west appeared at first as if it had lost its steep wall, and seemed to stretch away like a limitless prairie in conflagration. It changed and presented itself as a wild, picturesque landscape; mountain forests were on fire, throwing their lurid flames upon the rushing torrents, and into the deep ravines, and upon the sleeping lakes. It changed again, and poured its splendors upon the bastions, domes, and turrets of a vast city. Princely palaces, columned temples, and monumental pyramids, soared into a crimson atmosphere. A rushing wind swept the aerial structures, and over their gigantic ruins rolled an ocean of flame. If this be sunset, what will that conflagration be which will at last wrap the world!

SATURDAY, MAY 30. We have been in a calm the greater part of the day. The mirror of the ocean has been broken only by the plunges of a huge whale. He rose at times within a few fathoms of our ship, blowing the brine almost into the faces of our crew. They would, if permitted, have retaliated with their harpoons; though the result would have been only the loss of their weapons, for the monster would have carried them off with as much ease as Samson the bodkins of Delilah. He tumbled around us for several hours, as if measuring his size and strength with that of our frigate. At last, with one great heave, made as if in pride and scorn, he plunged and disappeared. Long life to him. I like his independent bearing.

One of our seamen got tipsy to-day, and raised a disturbance on the berth-deck. How he managed to get a double dose from the grog-tub is not known. And yet he alleges his liquor came from that nuisance which the law has sanctioned. I have taken some pains, during the long period that I have been in the navy, to ascertain the causes of the offences which have called for punishment; and from these inquiries I am clearly of the opinion, that these offences, in nine cases out of ten, are connected with ardent spirits; and are committed, in almost every case, by those who draw the whisky-ration provided by the government. I am clear in the conviction, that any statutes intended to restrain or punish intoxication in a national ship, must be without moral force so long as our legislation panders to this appetite in the sailor. The government presents itself before the seaman with a cup of whisky in one hand and a cat-o'-nine tails in the other. Here, my good fellow, drink this; but if you drink any more, then look out for these cats. It is amazing that such a flagrant violation of every principle of justice and humanity should escape the reprobation and even oblique animadversion of the department, and be left to the remonstrances of those who hold no official relation to the navy.

Sunday, May 31. Ill health has disqualified me for performing service to-day. Indeed it would have been difficult had I been well, as the rain has been falling in frequent and copious showers, attended by squalls, which have obliged us to take in our lighter sails about as soon as they were set. I gave tracts to the crew who called for them, and nearly all applied. Every chaplain should supply himself with a good store of these silent preachers. They help him on in his good work. They will be read by seamen when more labored efforts would be neglected. Many a sailor owes his conversion to the modest tract. They have poured a steady light around his dying hammock which had else been wrapped in darkness. The brightest triumphs of religion are found nearest the grave. Its last great triumph will be over death itself.

There has been for some weeks past a growing seriousness among our sailors. The indications are too obvious to be mistaken. Two or three of them I have reason to believe have experienced religion. They meet every night and pray for the conversion of others. This little cloud may yet extend itself, and its drops may fall in a copious shower. Let us have confidence in the power of God's grace.

MONDAY, JUNE 1. The northern constellations which have been lost to us for several months, now that we have recrossed the equator, begin to emerge into vision. They come back like old, tried friends, whose fidelity time cannot chill or distance impair. Man may change, but nature never. The same look of love which she cast upon our cradles she will cast upon our graves. The same exulting streams, whose melodies charmed our childhood, will at last roll among the echoing hills our loud requiem; while the gentle dews steep with tears the flowers which spring shall sprinkle around our place of rest. But yonder streams upon us again the constellations of our youth.

> "The northern team,
> And great Orion's more refulgent beam,
> To which, around the axle of the sky,
> The Bear, revolving, turns his golden eye."

TUESDAY, JUNE 2. The northwest trades brought us on briskly till within a few degrees of that point where we crossed the equator. We there fell into calms, light baffling winds, and tremendous falls of rain. We were several days working our way through these to the seventh degree, north latitude, where we took the northeast trades, and we are now running ten and eleven knots the hour. These trades blow obliquely to the equator, and prevail with a surprising regularity and force. A ship bound to the Sandwich Islands, as we are, should make the shortest cut across the variables. When the northwest trades leave her, in consequence of her proximity to the line, she should take advantage of every puff of wind to make northing, till she gains the northeast trades. She may run a little further, it is true, by this course, but she more than makes it up by her ultimate speed; and she escapes, by the shortest route, the extremely disagreeable weather which prevails near the equator.

WEDNESDAY, JUNE 3. A large flying-fish flew this evening into the cabin, through one of the side ports. It was rather a difficult achievement, as we were running ten knots. The little fellow had been attracted by the light, and flew at it, as the mullet in our southern streams leap at night into the lighted canoes of the negroes. Our flying-fish made a bad exchange, not out of the frying-pan into the fire, it is true, but out of the water into the frying-pan. But then he was dazzled, captivated by a floating light, gave chase, and came to ruin. It is ever thus with man; his life is an eager chase after some false light, some ignis fatuus of his imagination, which leads him on till at last he drops into his grave and disappears forever.

THURSDAY, JUNE 4. We have the chart used by the frigate United States in her passage from Callao to Honolulu, on which her route is designated, and the distance which she ran each day dotted down. Up to the equator, we ran neck and neck with her. In the variables she got ahead of us; but we have now left her some three hundred miles astern. We have been making an average of two hundred and forty miles a day, without motion enough to shake a dew-drop from its level leaf. We have not had, except for a few days near the equator, occasion to take in our top-gallant studding-sails. The thermometer has stood pretty steady at about seventy-five, and the air is pure and bracing. If we reach our port on Monday next, which we have now a fair prospect of doing, we shall have made our passage from Callao in twenty-nine days; one of the very shortest passages on record. Five thousand four hundred miles in twenty-nine days! That will do.

FRIDAY, JUNE 5. We have the moon again directly in the zenith; she hangs there like a resplendent orb in the centre of a magnificent dome. The stars gleam out with timid auxiliary light; while soft clouds float with incense from earth's thousand altars. The dome, beneath which the turbaned representative of the Prophet kneels, and that which bends in grandeur over the supplicating form of the papal hierarch, are poor when compared with this. The walls of St. Sophia will crumble, and the pillars of St. Peter's give way, but nature's great dome will still stand, brilliant and undecaying, as when it echoed the song of the morning stars over the birth of our planet; and it will stand the same,

> "Till wrapp'd in flames the realms of ether glow,
> And heaven's last thunder shakes the world below."

SATURDAY, JUNE 6. We have in the sick-bay a sailor, James Mills, who must die. He may survive a few days longer, and must then go. He is in the prime of life, and a few months ago ranked among the most athletic on our decks. He is now but the shadow of the past, and hovers dimly on the verge of life. The night of that narrow house is not all dark to him; some rays of light reach it from the Cross. These are now all that can cheer him; they are all that can cheer the descending footsteps of the proudest monarch. Into death's domain the honors and friendships of earth cannot enter; they leave their possessor in the hour of his utmost need. But there is One whose love will remain with the meek, when these depart; One whose smile will kindle up a morn even in the night of the grave.

SUNDAY, JUNE 7. Commodore Stockton, who has always taken an interest in our religious exercises, having occasion to speak to the crew to-day, I induced him to extend his remarks to topics more sacred than those which lay within his original purpose. He spoke of the Bible as that crowning revelation which God has made of himself to man, of its elevating influences on the human soul, of the priceless counsels which it conveys, and the immortal hopes which it awakens. He contrasted the gloomy condition of those tribes and nations which were without it with that of those where its steady light shone, and found in this contrast a vindication of its divinity, which none could gainsay or resist. He commended its habitual study to the officers and crew as our only infallible rule of duty, as our only safe-guiding light in the mental and moral twilight of our being here. He rebuked the idea that religion was out of its element among sailors, and told them that of all classes of men they were the one that most needed its restraining influences and glorious promises, and denounced as insane a disposition to trifle with its precepts. He commended the good conduct of the crew on the Sabbath, and expressed the earnest hope, that they would continue, in the event of probable separation from them, the same respectful and earnest regard for the duties of religion.

Such remarks as these, coming from the commander of a ship or squadron, will do more to sustain a chaplain in the discharge of his difficult duties than any privileges which can be conferred upon him through the provisions of law. They honor the heart from which they flow, and their influence will be felt in the moral well-being of hundreds, when that heart shall have ceased to beat. The tree you have planted will grow, and its fruit come to maturity, though you see it not.

MONDAY, JUNE 8. At seven bells of our forenoon watch the call of the boatswain, "All hands to bury the dead!" rolled its hoarse, deep tones through the ship. The remains of the deceased—wrapped in that hammock from which he had often sprung as his night-watch came round—was borne by his mess-mates up the main-hatch, and around the capstan, to the slow measures of the dead march, played by the band. In the starboard waist, and on a plank, one end of which rested on the sill of an open port, the relic reposed, till in the funeral service the words were announced, "We commit this body to the deep;" —the inner end of the plank was then lifted, and the hammocked dead, with a hoarse, rumbling sound, glided down to his deep floating grave. Thus passed poor Mills from our midst in the morning of his days, with broken purposes and blighted hopes. Though the wave rolls over his form, and none can point to the place of his rest, his humble virtues still survive in the recollections of those who knew him.

"The departed! the departed!
They visit us in dreams,
And glide above our memories
Like shadows over streams.
The good, the brave, the beautiful,
How dreamless is their sleep,
Where rolls the dirge-like music
Of the ever-tossing deep!"

Tuesday, June 9. Last evening, while it was yet some three hours to sunset, the cry of "Land ho!" rang from mast-head. It was the island of Hawaii boldly breaking the line of the horizon over our larboard bow. We were now near our port, but not sufficiently near to reach our anchorage by daylight. We were running ten knots, and orders were given to take in sail, that we might not shoot too far ahead.

Night, and the hour of slumber came on, and our dreams were filled with the flowers and fruit of sunny isles. Day broke over the steeps of Oahu, and threw its light into the port of Honolulu. Here at last we let go our anchors, and once more clewed up our sails. We had made one of the shortest passages on record from Callao. We had run for the last seven days an average of two hundred and thirty-five miles. We had sailed about six thousand miles, and had hardly disturbed a royal or studding-sail, and the sea had been smooth as the slumbering surface of an inland lake. Give me the Pacific and the trade winds. You have here a quiet ocean, a steady breeze, and an even temperature. In the Atlantic you are in squalls or calms; in the one you plunge about, and in the other you sleep.

Here we are to part with our passengers, Mr. Ten Eyk, our commissioner to the Sandwich Islands, with his lady, children, and Miss J——; and with Judge

Turrell, our consul to these islands, with his lady, children, and Mr. H. They have been with us since we sailed from Norfolk. Their society has helped to relieve the monotony of a sea life. They have manifested no impatience at our delays, and have cheerfully conformed, in all respects, to the usages of a man-of-war. The consequence has been, an uninterrupted harmony between them and the officers, and an interchange of all those civilities on which the happiness of our social condition depends. They are to be landed under the salute to which their rank entitles them. They carry with them our esteem and our best wishes. May a kind Providence be their guardian and friend.

"Farewell! a word that may be and hath been,
A sound that makes us linger—yet, farewell!"

CHAPTER XI.

SKETCHES OF HONOLULU.

BAY OF HONOLULU.—KANACKA FUNERAL.—THE MISSIONARIES.—HUTS AND HABITS OF THE NATIVES.—TARO-PLANT.—ROAST DOG.—SCHOOL OF THE YOUNG CHIEFS.—RIDE IN THE COUNTRY.—THE MAUSOLEUM.—COCOANUT-TREE.—CANOES.—HEATHEN TEMPLE.—KING'S CHAPEL.—RIDE TO EWA.—FATHER BISHOP.—HIS SABLE FLOCK.

WEDNESDAY, JUNE 10. The bay of Honolulu is only a bend in the shore. About a mile from the strand, a coral reef emerges, over which the rollers pour their perpetual surge. Through this reef, nature has left a narrow passage, which admits smaller vessels, but a ship of our depth is obliged to anchor outside, and nearly two miles distant from the shore.

The right extremity of the bay, as you enter it, is guarded by the steep cone of an exhausted volcano, which has taken the less terrific name of Diamond Hill. The left is defended by a bold bluff, which shoulders its way, with savage ferocity, into the roaring sea. The town of Honolulu stretches along the interval, while close in the background soars the wild crater of another extinguished volcano, under the bewildering name of the Punch-Bowl. The steeps beyond are broken into deep ravines, which wind off in rich verdure into the heart of the island.

On its mountain crags the boldest eagle might build; in its glens the callow cygnet slumber.

While I was inquiring for a good hotel, the Rev. Mr. Damon, seamen's chaplain at this port, came on board, and invited me to take quarters with him, an invitation which I cheerfully accepted. Months of boxing about at sea give a charm to the land-berth, which only they can fully appreciate who slumber over keels. On landing, my trunk was claimed by some twenty boys and porters. In the general strife I gave it to the one who appeared to need a shilling the most. His fellows took their disappointment in good humor. A short walk brought me to the domicile of my friend, where an agreeable lady welcomed me in.

Thursday, June 11. I had only seated myself in my new abode, when Mr. Damon invited me to accompany him to a funeral. The deceased was a foreigner, of some popularity among the natives, who attended his remains in large numbers to his grave. They were all on foot, moving in silent, but tumultuous order. There was no solemnity in their motions, but a subdued air in their faces. Some were helping along those who were bowed with the infirmities of age, and others were carrying piping infants in their arms, lashed to their backs.

The burial-ground is a mile, or more, from the

town, on a slight elevation, fenced in and shaded with native trees. Here the procession halted, and gathered in dark, silent masses around a new-dug grave. The coffin was lowered; a few words of appropriate admonition addressed to those around; a prayer offered; the earth returned to its place; a slight mound raised; flowers and sprigs of evergreen cast upon it, and the crowd wound their way back in the same silent disorder in which they came. Here was no pomp, no trappings of grief, but that simple homage of the heart, which bespeaks a sentiment of bereavement and respect. Let others have, if they will, a funeral pageant, but give me rather that flower which grief gathers and affection plants, or that tear which trembles in the eye of the untutored child of nature.

Before the missionaries introduced a change of customs, the natives were in the habit of expressing their grief, at the death of a favorite chief, by knocking out two or more of their front teeth. The strength of their attachment was evinced by the extent of this dental devastation, which sometimes involved the destruction of every tooth. This is the reason that so few of the older inhabitants have their teeth entire. The missionaries substituted for this act of self-inflicted violence, the innocent tokens of bereavement, and that tribute of respect which is conveyed in casting on the grave a sprig of evergreen, as a type of the soul's immortality. Humanity and religion always go hand in hand.

Friday, June 12. The morning has been passed in receiving calls from the missionaries. They are plain in their apparel, easy in their manners, and intelligent in their conversation. They have none of that rigid solemnity, which a sectarian puts on, who would throw his religion into his looks; and yet they are free of that lightness and triviality which are incompatible with a high and earnest purpose. They have cheerfulness without levity, and sobriety without sternness. They are far from being men of one idea; their mental horizon is broad. They have impressed their genius upon all the social habits and civil institutions of the islanders among whom they dwell. Indeed, all that exists here, upon which the eye of the Christian philanthropist can dwell with complacency, has risen from a weltering tide of barbarism, through their agency, as the islands themselves have emerged from the ocean through the action of the volcano.

Saturday, June 13. The huts of the natives dot with a cheerful aspect the broad plain on which Honolulu stands, and stretch away into the green gorges of the mountains. They resemble in the distance ricks of hay, and you half persuade yourself that you have arrived in a community of thrifty farmers. This impression almost flashes into conviction, when you see herds of cattle reposing in the valleys, and goats bounding among the cliffs. But the rush of children from the interior of these hay-stacks, and their prattle and laughter among the vines which trail their porches, soon dispel the illusion. You find them human habitations, and possessing, in many instances, an air of surprising neatness and comfort.

True, you find in them no chairs, tables, or ordinary cooking utensils; nor do the habits of the inmates render these articles necessary. But you find thick mats, on which they sleep and sit, as Adam and Eve did on the leaves which the autumnal wind shook from their bowers. They need no fireplaces, no glowing grate, or crackling hearth,—a broad, bright sun, wheeling up in splendor out of a quiet ocean, reigns monarch of the seasons, and tempers the air aright. Their apparel extends but little beyond the simplest requirements of the nursery. It is a garment seemingly thrown on for the sake of modesty, as drapery is sometimes attached to a statue. But the proportions still swell in their roundness and strength on the eye. It was with no little difficulty the missionaries could persuade them to assume even this scanty garment. It seemed to them a superfluity, suggested neither by the characteristics of the climate, nor sentiments of delicacy. They would have gone without it as readily to a church as to a carousal. Such is habit impressed on a people by the force of barbaric ages.

Near each cot you encounter an oven, not obtruded on your eye as if to mock your hunger, but modestly sunk in the earth. The cavity is lined with stones, in which a fire is kindled ; when sufficiently heated, the embers are removed, a few taro-leaves thrown in, and on this the taro itself and meat. The whole is then covered over with taro-leaves and earth. The meat thus preserves its juices, and has an advantage in this respect over all modern inventions. This primitive process of cooking is called the lua.

The most esteemed roaster, that undergoes the lua, is one of the canine species. It is a dog resembling the larger-sized poodle, with smooth hair and soft flesh. It is nursed at the breast of the women, and never allowed to eat animal food. It is baked entire, like the pig, and is said to taste very much like that little grunter. This is considered the most choice dish which an epicurean chief can present to his distinguished guests. I was earnestly invited to partake of one, but the little fellow's once cheerful bark, his wagging tail in token of recognition, his love of children, his participation in their sports, his gratitude and unsuspecting confidence, were all too warm in my imagination to permit the deed. I would never take life for the sake of animal food, and least of all the life of one that is

"The first to welcome, foremost to defend."

In another hut which we entered, we found the mother and her children seated around a large calabash, which contained poi. This is the dish on which the natives mostly subsist. It is made of the root of the taro plant, which resembles in shape the large beet. A plat of low ground is thrown up into little hills like a potatoe-patch, and water let in sufficient to fill the furrows. In these hills the taro grows, shaded only by its own luxuriant leaves. At maturity, which it reaches in a few months, the men and women dash into it, and, with the water ankle-deep, commence pulling. The bottoms, which are intended for consumption, are conveyed to the earth-oven; being baked, they are then pounded, and water added till the mass assumes the consistency of paste. In this state it undergoes a partial fermentation, and is then in prime order for eating. It is conveyed to the mouth by the two forefingers, which are dipped into it, and to which it adheres in a pendulous globule, which a slight shake detaches.

This was the dish to which the mother invited us, and which it seemed almost discourteous to decline. Her little daughter exclaiming, "Mili, mili—good," coaxed me to let her drop a globule of it from her small fingers into my mouth. Down it dropped, and down it went, leaving only a sour taste. I tried to keep up a look of relish, but the effort must have betrayed itself. This was the last time I attempted poi. On this the natives live, and their physical developments sufficiently attest its nutritious properties. Some of them, who are exempted by their means from labor, attain a giant stature. They become extremely fat, and roll along as if bone and muscle were hardly equal to the task of locomotion. What think ye of that, ye carnivorous tribe, who judge of a man's bulk by the amount of roast beef which he consumes! The Hawaiian outdoes ye on paste!

SUNDAY, JUNE 14. I have exchanged to-day with Mr. Damon; he taking the capstan of the Congress, and I the pulpit of the mariners' chapel. The audience both morning and evening has been large, leaving hardly a vacant seat. It is composed of foreign residents and sailors in port. The music, led by a seraphine, would have been creditable in any place. I could hardly persuade myself that I was in an island of the Pacific, where but a few years since the homage of man rose only in howls to a pagan idol.

The attendance at this chapel is the best evidence of the success with which Mr. Damon performs the duties assigned him by the American Seamen's Friend Society. But his sphere of activity is not confined to these walls; it extends to the moral wants of the different ships entering the harbor, and embraces also the management of a periodical devoted to seamen. This publication was eagerly sought by our crew. To sustain it a subscription was proposed, which was headed by a liberal donation from Commodore Stockton, Captain Du Pont, and the officers.

MONDAY, JUNE 15. There are two large churches for the natives in Honolulu. The services in these are conducted in the native language by the Rev. Mr. Armstrong and the Rev. Mr. Smith, both intelligent and devoted missionaries. These men and all their brethren occupy a difficult position in these islands. It is made so, less by the fickleness of the natives than the interference of foreigners. The very men who, coming as they do from civilized and Christian lands, should be the first to countenance and sustain them, are those from whom they experience the most opposition. It seems impossible to avoid their cavils. If the missionaries devote themselves exclusively to their spiritual duties, the complaint is, that the temporal interests of the community are neglected. If they interest themselves in the encouragement of agriculture and the mechanic arts, the cry is, that they are interfering in secular matters which do not belong to them. Between these two rocks no ship can pass without having her copper raked off on one side or the other.

The truth is, the missionaries are pursuing the only plan which can produce decisive and satisfactory results. They are inculcating the precepts and obligations of the Bible on all classes, and educating the young. Their schools embrace hundreds of native children, who will themselves become teachers. In one of these schools, which is under the superintendence of Mr. and Mrs. Cook, I found the children of the high chiefs, and among them the heir-apparent. They spoke the English language with entire freedom, and wrote it with surprising accuracy. Their acquirements, in all the branches of a useful education, would have done credit to youth of the same age in any country. In mental arithmetic, I have never seen them surpassed. They multiplied five decimals by five, named at random, and gave the result, with perfect accuracy, in less time than any one could possibly have reached it on a slate. We now adjourned with the scholars to the parlor, where Mrs. Cook placed one of the misses at the piano, while another took the guitar, and they all struck into a melody that might have gratified a more fastidious taste than ours.

Now these are the children of the chiefs—their

sons, and their daughters; those whose intelligence and influence are to shape the destinies of these islands. If this is not beginning at the right end of the business, I should like to have some one tell us where the right end is.

Tuesday, June 16. My kanacka brought me his horse this afternoon punctual at the hour. This horse, a noble animal, is all his capital. I give him a dollar a day for the use; can have him at any and all hours, though I seldom ride but once. This is enough, unless the showers hold up more than they have; for they now fall as easily as a hasty word from a heated heart; or a blow from the ferule of a vexed pedagogue; or a yellow leaf from the twig of a blighted tree; or a false smile from the eyes of a cunning coquette; or a hollow nut from the teeth of a squirrel; or a silver eel from the hand of a fisherman; or any thing else, which escapes very easily from its confinement.

My fair companion being firmly in her saddle, we started, at an easy canter, over the plain, which stretches away from the eastern section of the town. We passed on the right the royal mausoleum, lifting its sombre roof over the coffins of barbaric kings. Before Christianity, with her silent rites, reached these islands, the death of a monarch or sachem was followed by a wail that poured itself over hill and vale, in a roaring tide. Then followed a scene of promiscuous licentiousness, from which the orbs of heaven might have withdrawn their light. Over these obscene orgies Christianity has spread her influences, and the dead now go quietly to their rest, and the living lay it to heart.

Further on, we passed through a cocoanut-grove. This singular tree shoots up some fifty feet, without seeming to know for what purpose; it then suddenly branches out, and is so eager in this spreading business that it seems to lose its soaring ambition; and there it stands, like a naked shaft, with its umbrella-shaped top. Its broad leaves hang down as if to conceal its blushes. It is naked as sin driven from its last subterfuge. It fain would reconcile you to its deformity by its milk; but this is as insipid as its own look is foolish. This tree, with a half-naked kanacka climbing its shaft, is the most effective picture of poverty with which I have ever met. It is, if possible, worse than a monkey on the sign-post of a groggery, beckoning to his fellow-topers to come in. But the decoy, in this case, wiser than the dupe, never drinks.

We passed near the shore a large number of canoes, in which the natives were engaged in fishing. They keep them pointed towards the sea, and one person vigorously at work with the paddles, so that the rollers, which set in here with great force, may not heave them high and dry on the beach. They show great skill in the management of these treacherous canoes. A novice would upset one before he was well in. They are often themselves capsized, but it costs them only a ducking; the canoe is instantly righted, and they are back again in its hollow. As for the water, it is almost as much their element as that of the fish for which they angle. They can dive from ten to fifteen fathoms, and bring up shells; or swim many miles without apparent fatigue. There is a native woman, now living in Honolulu, who, being wrecked at sea, swam twenty miles to the shore of a neighboring island. Her husband, of feebler constitution, gave out; she buoyed him up, swimming with him till they had come in sight of the shore, when he sank overpowered. Still she clung to him, and brought the lifeless form to the beach. Give me a kanacka wife in a gale.

Winding around a bay which circles up, with a rippling verge, into the mainland, we arrived at the blackened ruins of a celebrated heathen temple. The rude foundations only remain; the superstructure has been swept away with the savage rites which it enshrined. The smoke of human victims here appeased the violated tabu, and the putrid exhalations of decaying beasts cancelled the turpitude of human guilt. But Revelation has poured its clear light into its dark recesses. The sorcerer has fled, the victim been unbound, and the guilty have gone to that mercy-seat where penitence never pleads in vain.

High over these fearful ruins soars the steep crater of an extinguished volcano, to which a capricious fancy has given the appellation of Diamond Hill. It still stands in all the stern ruggedness which its adamantine features assumed, when, ages since, its burning torrents of lava stiffened into rock. It is now the beacon of the mariner; the first that greets his glance, and the last that fades upon his eye. Against its base the broad Pacific heaves its swelling strength; but it will stand unshaken till the pillars of nature's vast fabric fall.

We passed, on our return, the king's chapel, a spacious edifice, of one hundred and fifty-four feet by seventy-eight. It is reared of coral rock, hewn into uniform blocks, and impresses you with its architectural sobriety and strength. The interior of its high walls is relieved by a substantial gallery, while the ample area of its floor presents to the eye, in the form of seats, the varied means and ingenuity of their occupants. The pulpit is the same which once gravely dignified the central church in New Haven, Conn., but which a more fastidious taste recently set aside. It answers its sacred design very well here. Sinners are converted under its droppings just as readily as if the marbles of Carrara gleamed from its panels. The truth of God falls with the same power in the sumptuous shrine of the prince and the wigwam of the savage. The towers of the triple crown, and the tent of the Arab, tremble alike beneath its force.

The sun had set before we reached our home. The bustle through many of the streets had subsided; but the loud words and laughter of the crowd that had gathered to witness the approach of a strange sail, came floating on the wind. The hour of ten is announced by a gun from the fort,—a signal for the keepers of pulperias and places of amusement to close their doors. The king himself, if abroad, though engaged in a game of chess, would forego the triumph of a checkmate, and return to his palace. He aims, in this particular at least, to maintain a wholesome regulation through the influence of his own example. Prouder potentates may laugh at this punctilio of his Hawaiian majesty, but were they to imitate it, their thrones would be quite as safe and their subjects quite as virtuous. A good example is like a guinea, which shines just as bright, however deep and dark the mine from which it came. Our wisest lessons often come from our inferiors, as the choicest fruit is frequently found on the humblest shrub. The condor may dwell in the lofty steeps of the mountain, but it is to the modest thrush or meadow-lark that we turn for a gush of music.

Wednesday, June 17. Mr. Damon and myself took horses this morning for Ewa, lying in a valley, which opens on the sea, and distant some twelve miles. Our horses were in fine spirits, and started off at a hand-gallop, across the broad lagoon, which skirts the western extremity of the town. Over this fertile interval swell many round knolls, crowned with kanacka huts, and surrounded with thrifty taro patches. Ascending the spur of a mountain range, a deep, green valley opened on the right, through which a winding rivulet babbled, and where herds were seen cropping the grass, or ruminating in the shade. From its bosom rose the walls of a spacious enclosure, into which the cattle, horses, and sheep are driven at night,—to protect them, as one would suppose, from ravenous beasts; but there are none in the island: the object is to keep them from straying off among the mountains, and becoming too wild for domestic purposes; for every thing here runs instinctively to wildness.

Further on, we passed upon the left a lofty rock, over the steep stern face of which a convolvulus had spread its verdure, throwing out its green leaves and delicate blossoms, like smiles on the face of a hypochondriac. Here we met a native driving two large pigs to market, and carrying a third lashed to his back. I expected to hear a squeal at least from his living knapsack; but the mouth had been tied up, leaving only room through the nostril for air. When the pig is to be killed, no knife is drawn, no blood taken; but this cord around the nose is tightened till respiration ceases, and death ensues. Rather a hard end awaits the poor pig, whether it come by knife or cord; and yet no other animal, in his last struggles, has so little sympathy. That he is uncomely, is most true, but he did not select his own shape; and true it is, that his habits are not quite neat, but he has been turned out of doors, and left to shirk and shack for himself. It was not his fault that the devil once got into him, and run him down a steep ledge into the sea. The devil leads his betters to a much worse place. I see not therefore why all feeling should be denied the pig in death. But let that pass.

Proceeding on, we soon reached the precipice which overhangs the deep ravine, through which the Pearl river holds its exulting course. Here we might have stopped; but our horses, which well understand these difficult paths, and are as sure of foot as the chamois, wound down the steep, and hurried, with clattering hoof, over the bridge which spans the rushing stream; and then swept up the opposite elevation at the top of their speed. Ewa now broke on the eye, swelling from a wide verdant plain, embowered in shade, and looking out on the sea. A winding path, which obeyed the curve of the shore, took us into the heart of the little village, where we alighted at the door of our venerable host, the Rev. Mr. Bishop.

This devoted missionary was at the time with his sable flock in the church, where he meets them once a week, independent of the Sabbath. They look up to him with feelings which only goodness can merit and reverence inspire; and well may they pay him these tokens of love and respect. He has been long with them, restraining their wild propensities, training them to habits of industry, and leading them to the path of immortal life. This is with him a labor of love. The stipend allowed him by our Board of Foreign Missions is all spent in maintaining schools and destitute places of worship. He lives on the proceeds of a dairy, which his good wife manages. If this be not Christian benevolence, will some opponent of the missionary enterprise tell me what is.

The house of Father Bishop, as he is familiarly called, is a plain, one-story building, with a rude porch running around it, covered with the vines of the creeping-grape. It stands in the midst of fruit and shade trees, which throw their shadows to the verge of a garden, where the varied plants of a tropical clime are in luxuriant bloom. Yet every thing seemed as free of display and mechanical arrangement as if its growth had been spontaneous. The family consisted of Mrs. B., two sprightly native children, whose mother had recently died, and a kanacka domestic. At two o'clock we sat down to dinner, which consisted of mullet, presented our host by a native chief, and a turkey of his own raising. Then came figs and milk, with the fruits of his garden. All presenting a pleasing specimen of pastoral life.

After a siesta, to which the climate here inclines one, we rambled over the parsonage, among the neat huts of the natives, and, at about two hours to sunset, took our departure. We soon fell in with a herd of cattle, which two or three noisy kanackas on horseback were driving to their enclosure for the night. When a beast attempted to break away, one of these started in pursuit; and instead of heading off the animal, brought him up with the lasso, which he threw, with surprising dexterity, over his horns. In one of the narrow runnels which crosses the last lagoon, we found a horse, which had missed his step on the two logs which compose the bridge. The channel was only broad enough to let in the length of the horse, and on each bank stood a kanacka, the one hold of the bridle, the other hold of the tail, trying to lift the animal out. We told one of them to jump in and turn the head of the horse up stream, and the other to drop the tail and take his whip. These orders obeyed, the animal gave a spring, and was soon out of his difficulties.

We reached home before dark: we had rode

twenty-four miles on a road running over steep ledges, across deep ravines, and around toppling crags: I was bruised and fatigued, and determined to try, before retiring to rest, the bath and the "lomi-lomi." The latter is a kind of shampooing much resorted to here to relieve fatigue. A kanacka who understood it was at hand, and, on my coming out of the bath, commenced his kneading process. He used me much as a baker would a lump of dough. He worked me into this shape, then into that, then into no shape at all. My limbs became flat, or round, or neither, at his will. My muscles were all relaxed, and my joints seemed to have lost a sense of location. He put me back into the shape in which I came from nature's mould, and I sunk to sleep softly as an infant in its cradle. Ye who take to anodynes and inebriating potations to relieve a sense of pain, restlessness, or fatigue, try the lomi-lomi.

CHAPTER XII.

SKETCHES OF HONOLULU.

THE KING AND COURT.—AMERICAN COMMISSIONER.—ROYAL RESIDENCE.—THE SALT LAKE.—SURF SPORTS OF THE NATIVES.—GALA DAY.—THE WOMEN ON HORSEBACK.—SAILOR'S EQUESTRIANISM.—THE OLD MAN AND THE CHILDREN AT PLAY.—ADDRESS OF COM. STOCKTON.—CAPT. LA PLACE.—HIS JESUITS AND BRANDY.—LORD GEORGE PAULET.

THURSDAY, JUNE 18. To-day, at twelve, the officers of the Congress, and Captain Harrison, of the schooner Shark, assembled at Commodore Stockton's rooms, and proceeded in a body to the royal palace. The object was the installation of Mr. Ten Eyk in his new functions as United States Commissioner at this court. We were received, on our arrival, by a small guard posted at the palace, and conducted into a spacious central hall. From this we were ushered into a large saloon, rather plainly furnished, but light and airy. In front of us stood the king, with the heir-apparent and high chiefs on the right, and his cabinet on the left.

Ex-commissioner Brown advised his majesty of his recall, and introduced his successor, Mr. Ten Eyk, who presented to the king an autograph letter from the President of the United States, which he accompanied with some appropriate remarks. These were followed by a brief address from Commodore Stockton, in which he expressed the earnest hope that uninterrupted amity might prevail between the two countries. He assured the king of the lively interest felt in the United States for the successful issue of all his majesty's plans and purposes for the benefit of his people, and pledged the cordial support of our government in any aggressive emergencies, which might threaten the tranquillity and integrity of his realm.

To each of these addresses the king made a brief and pertinent reply. Not having sufficient confidence in his English, he spoke in the native language,—his minister of finance, Mr. Judd, acting as interpreter. There was no parade, or affectation of court phraseology in what he said. His language was remarkable for its directness and simplicity. His reply concluded with these words: "Commodore, I thank you for your visit to our islands; your words will long be remembered; may you be happy." The king is about thirty-four years of age, of a stout frame, dark complexion, and with good humor, rather than strength of intellect, betrayed in his features. He wore a blue military uniform, with gold epaulettes and sword. The prince and chiefs were without any badge of distinction, except a star worn on the breast. Their costume was all in the European style. The cabinet, consisting of the minister of finance, the minister of foreign affairs, the minister of instruction, and the attorney-general, all of whom, except the second, are Americans, were in plain garb. You see more parade at Rome in five minutes, when the Pope steps from the Vatican into St. Peter's, or a red-stockinged cardinal enters his carriage, than you would here in six months.

The king confides the affairs of government very much to his ministers. Succeeding to power at an early age, without a political education, or established principles of action, his policy would be inconsistent and wavering, but for the steady influence of those around him. He evinces his moderation in foregoing the dictates of an arbitrary will, and consulting the judgments of those whose intelligence and experience have given them a broader scope of vision. The foreigners who have settled in his island, and who seek to undermine the influence of his counsellors, are the most subtle and dangerous enemies with which he has to contend. Their selfish and mischievous dispositions are masked under professions of friendship. They talk of changes for the the better, but they aim at revolution. They are willing to run the hazard of the great political earthquake, for the chance of being hove into stations of emolument and power. But if the present social fabric falls, they will be buried in its ruins; and there they may lie, sepulchred under the horrors of a betrayed people, and the execrations of the civilized world.

Preparations are making for the erection of a royal residence, which shall be in keeping with the progress of the arts in these islands. The mansion at present occupied by the king, is the property of one of his chiefs. It is built of coral; a graceful portico adorns the front, and the whole is surmounted by an elegant belvidere. The grounds are ample, tastefully laid out, and shaded by beautiful forest trees. No splendid coach dashes through its avenues; no train of servile retainers lounge in its shades; no throng of parasites disturb its domestic quietude and social ease.

The amusements of the king are with the bow and arrow, in his bowling-alley, and at his billiard-table. In these pastimes he is cheek-by-jowl with his chiefs, and any well-bred gentleman. He was inclined in his youth to habits of dissipation; and often drained, at the expense of his dignity, the inebriating bowl. But he is now at the head of a national temperance society. He is perhaps the only monarch, civilized or savage, who has abjured, in his own example, all intoxicating drinks. Go, ye potentates of prouder thrones, and take a lesson of practical wisdom from this sable brother.

FRIDAY, JUNE 19. Our ride to-day has been to the

Salt Lake, which lies some five miles west of the town, on the margin of the sea. It is cradled in the crater of an old volcano. You reach it by a steep ascent of one hundred feet, and rapid descent of as many more. It is the third of a mile in circuit; and, standing by its breathless margin, the rock-bound rim of the hollow cone soars above you in wild grandeur.

The lake is on a level with the sea, and is undoubtedly fed from it through unseen fissures. The salt is crystalized out of the water, through a rapid evaporation, occasioned by the intense heat to which it is subjected. It steams up as if the central fires, which once found an escape here, were again seeking for a vent. Should they burst forth, this lake will be thrown sky-high; and not only the geologist be bereaved of a rare curiosity, and the king deprived of an important source of revenue, but the kanacka will be obliged to eat his poi and fish without salt.

Nothing here has amused me more than the surf-sports of the young chiefs. Each takes a smooth board, of some eight feet in length, leads it over the coral shallows far out into the sea, and when a tremendous roller is coming in, jumps upon it, and the roller carries him upon its combing top, with the speed of an arrow, to the shore. A young American, who was among them, not liking to be outdone in a sport which seemed so simple, thought he would try the board and billow. He ventured out a short distance, watched his opportunity, and, as the roller came, jumped upon his plank, was capsized, and hove, half strangled, on the beach.

> "There, breathless, with his digging nails he clung
> Fast to the sand, lest the returning wave,
> From whose reluctant roar his life he wrung,
> Should suck him back to her insatiate grave."

The young females are as fond of the water as the men. We passed in a boat yesterday a group of them sitting on the coral reef a mile out at sea. They were enjoying the surf, which broke over them with each successive billow. Now and then a stronger wave would sweep some of them from their perch, and bear them to a great distance in its whirling foam. But they would soon swim back again amidst the laughter of their companions. They were without covering, and plunged under the water till our boat had got past, and then recovered their position on the reef; and there they sat like mermaids,

> Serene amid the breakers' roar,
> Their dark locks floating on the surge,
> Attuning shells, through which they pour
> The solemn ocean's mimic dirge.

SATURDAY, JUNE 20. Saturday here is a gala-day, especially the afternoon, when the natives give themselves up to amusement. Every horse is in requisition; and though often without saddle or bridle, has a rider on him, who is dashing about like an adjutant at a regimental training. The great plain at the eastern end of the town is alive with groups that have collected to witness or participate in the fun. The variety of colors, which blended their hues in Joseph's coat, hold no comparison with the motley dyes which flare up here in the costume of the crowd. They resemble the tints of the forest, when the autumn's breath has touched its leaves with frost; the foam of ocean breaking over their coral reef is not more tumultuous than the roar and rush of these living tides.

Here streams away a valetudinarian, whose puny frame has been borne to this shore like a bubble from some foreign clime. His light horse, fleet of foot, heeds his weight as little as if he were an elf that had left the forest to frolic on the green. His thin legs lie in the shadow of his stirrup-straps, while his sharp face peers up between the high pommel and stern of his saddle like a famished owl, watching between two old turrets a lunar eclipse.

Near him dashes on the wife of a chief, whose vast bulk shakes over the plunge of her strong horse as if the fat would fall from her sides in living flakes. The broad leaves of the koa tremble in the chaplet that encircles her head; her great shawl floats on the wind like a topsail, while the vast sweep of her garments rolls down over her courser's sides like the folds of an Arab's tent. By the side of her puny attendant she shows like the full-orbed moon with a little star twinkling near her rim; or like a giant oak with an alder in its shade; or like a ship-of-the-line with a cockle-boat under her lee.

Here sweeps past a compact figure on a horse half wild from the woods. His white trowsers, his blue roundabout, and tarpaulin with its yard of black ribbon streaming over the right ear, show him to be a tar fresh from the deck. His hammock-blanket, with its nettings for a girth, serve him for a saddle; while his bridle is a rope bent on a small anchor, which is wreathed with leaves and flowers, and which he can let go, when he would bring up his unkeeled craft. A shout follows wherever his unmanageable horse dashes,—unless it be among the crowd, and then there is such a scattering as there would be among sheep at the pounce of a wolf, or among pigeons at the swoop of the hawk.

Foremost in a gazing group bends an aged chief, who has come out to see one gala day more before he descends to the land of shadows. He erects his tall stature, but not in pride, and half forgets the tufted wand that has long sustained his tottering years. He thinks not of the feathered mantle which falls from his shoulders, or the badges of rank which glitter on his breast. His eyes are on a group of children wildly at play. Fourscore summers have shed their vernal honors since he was young as they, and yet their glee this day makes his pulses fly as if he were again a child. He watches their light footsteps, their laughing eyes, and timid hands as they garland with flowers the arching horns of the old patriarch of his flock.

"A band of children, round a snow-white ram,
There wreathe his venerable horns with flowers;
While peaceful as if still an unweaned lamb,
The patriarch of the flock all gently cowers
His sober head majestically tame,
Or eats from out the palm, or playful lowers
His brow as if in act to butt, and then,
Yielding to their small hands, draws back again."

Sunday, June 21. I exchanged with Mr. Damon this morning; he officiating on board the Congress, while I took his place in the Seamen's chapel. The frigate had the advantage in the arrangement, but I intend to look out for my floating parish. In the afternoon I was, by appointment, in the pulpit of the king's chapel. The spacious edifice was crowded. His majesty, the court, and chiefs were present, and an auditory of some three thousand. They had assembled under the vague expectation that Commodore Stockton might address them, for a report to that effect, without the commodore's knowledge, had been circulated through the town. I felt, in common with the missionaries, a desire that they should not be disappointed. But as the commodore was wholly unprepared, and averse to any arrangements that might seemingly trench upon proprieties, it was no easy matter to have their wishes realized.

Backed by the Rev. Mr. Armstrong, I made a bold push, and, having addressed the audience for half an hour, through him as interpreter, on the religious enterprises in our own country, which were throwing their light and influence into other lands, stated that I was aware of their desire that Commodore Stockton should address them, and that I would take the liberty of expressing the hope that he would gratify their wishes. He was sitting at the time by the side of the king; and while the choir were singing a hymn, Mr. Armstrong descended from the pulpit and urged with him the public expectation. He finally assented, and taking the platform under the pulpit, commenced a train of pertinent and eloquent remarks.

He spoke of the previous condition of those around him,—of the dark and cruel rites in which their ancestors were involved,—of the humanizing and elevating influences of that Christianity which had reached them,—of the philanthropy, faith, and devotedness of their missionaries,—of the destruction of nations where the true God was disowned, and of the stability of governments and institutions founded on the precepts and moral obligations of the Bible. He adjured them, by all the hopes and fears which betide humanity, to persevere in their great and good work of social, civil, and moral improvement. He urged upon them systematic industry, wholesome rules and regulations in their domestic economy, a respect for law and order, the advantages of education, the importance of the Sabbath-school system, the necessity of temperance; and assured them, that in all their good endeavors they would have the sympathy and support of the Christian world.

Such was the tenor of his remarks, which were delivered with as much freedom and force as if they had been well-considered and arranged. Their effect was obvious in the eager attention which pervaded the great assemblage. At the conclusion, the king and the chiefs came up, and, with undisguised emotion, thanked the commodore for his address. The commodore may win laurels on the deck, but none that can bloom more lastingly than these. If there be consolations in death, they flow from efforts made and triumphs won in the cause of humanity and God.

MONDAY, JUNE 22. The forcible introduction of the Roman Catholic faith into these islands was artfully disguised under the plea of religious toleration. The manifesto of La Place, acting under the authority of the French cabinet, sets forth, that, "Among civilized nations there is not one which does not permit in its territory the free toleration of all religions:" therefore he demands, under the batteries of his frigate, that the Roman Catholic faith shall have ample scope and verge here.

The basis of this demand is an assumption, contradicted by the most glaring facts. In countries no further removed than Chili and Peru, the organic laws of the land declare that "no religion except the Roman Catholic shall be tolerated;" and these laws are enforced. So much for universal toleration, in those countries where that religion is predominant, which La Place comes here, under the sanction of his government, to shoot down into the consciences of this people. A very expeditious mode this of making converts, and quite consonant with the theological tactics of a military propagandist. If you cannot reason your religion into a man, why, shoot it into him. You may, it is true, in doing this shoot his life out; but what of that, if you shoot your creed in. A dead man with your creed in him, is perhaps better than a living one without it.

This demand of La Place was accompanied by another, which would disparage the most petty prince in Christendom. It required the Hawaiian king to place on board the French frigate twenty thousand dollars, as a guarantee that Roman Catholic priests shall in future be undisturbed in propagating their faith. These priests, it was well known, were Jesuits, belonging to an order which France herself was at the time endeavoring to suppress. Perhaps she intended the Sandwich Islands as a sort of Botany Bay for these men, whom state policy had proscribed from her own soil. They had given the French monarch trouble enough, and it was time his Hawaiian majesty should take his turn.

Another demand, forced under the disguise of a treaty, was that French brandies should be admitted into all the Hawaiian ports, with only a duty of five cents on the gallon. It seemed to be thought that this liquor, among all its other wonderful achievements, would promote Christian charity, and open the way for the Jesuits among the natives. Brandy is good in cases of colic, but I never before heard of it as a specific against the evils of religious intolerance. But the French are a very sagacious people; and if they have found in it an antidote to bigotry, they ought not to be deprived of the honor and advantage of the discovery.

All these demands of the French government were compulsorily complied with under the batteries of an armed ship. The king had no alternative; he must either submit, or suffer Honolulu to be levelled with the ground, and its helpless inhabitants driven into the mountains. On the one hand lay rapine and massacre; on the other, Jesuits and brandy. Of the two evils, the king submitted to the latter. Mahomet propagated his religion with the sword; but he did not force on those whom he subjugated the elements of intoxication. It was reserved for the French, it seems, to discover this new ally, and give to shame its last blush.

The American missionaries were arraigned, and denounced by the French, on the charge of having stimulated the king and regent of the Hawaiian islands to measures of hostility against the introduction of the Roman Catholic faith. This accusation is met and annihilated by the well-known fact, that they who came here to preach that faith were supplied by these very missionaries with the books through which they obtained a knowledge of the native language. Fanatics, filled with intolerance, never supply their opponents with the means of propagating their faith. They may surround them with fagots, but never with books.

The truth is, the king and regent apprehended that the introduction of a new religion might produce dissensions among their people. They could not comprehend why a Protestant should not be permitted to marry a Roman Catholic, and very naturally dreaded the introduction of a system which set up such exclusive pretensions. Their untutored sagacity discovered the discord which this marriage prohibition must of itself create. Before Roman propagandists raise the cry of proscription, let them accommodate their antiquated faith to the more liberal and enlightened spirit of the age. Let them lift the ban from the sacred rights of marriage, and admit the possibility of a Protestant's getting into heaven, or at least of throwing his shadow in ; that will save the Swedenborgians !

But the king and regent were also apprehensive that the images used in the forms of the Romish worship might lead their people back again into idolatry. They could not see clearly any difference between praying to an image, or praying to a spirit through that image. They could not detach the substance from its seeming shadow, and worship the latter without an obtrusion of the former. My venerable friend, the bishop of New York, with his metaphysical acuteness, can undoubtedly accomplish this; but a poor kanacka here would be very apt to commit a blunder; and this, too,

> In that dread creed, in which a truth and blunder
> Are deemed as wide as heaven and hell asunder.

The crowning act of shame perpetrated here by La Place, was in his communication to the American consul, in which he informs that functionary, that in the havoc which will follow a non-compliance with his demands by the government, the missionaries, with their families, will not escape. They are singled out as objects of special vengeance. Their houses are delivered over to rapine, their wives and daughters to pollution. This communication our consul should have returned indignantly to its brutal author, and our government should have visited the insult which it conveyed with the rebuke and chastisement which it merited. If we would have our consular flag respected, we must not allow its sanctity to be trampled upon by every insolent bravado of the sea.

La Place, having achieved these triumphs, having bullied an unarmed government, menaced with massacre a helpless people, intimidated the wives and children of the missionaries, forced on a reluctant community his Jesuits and brandy, and filched all the small change in circulation, took his departure, much to the relief of all good men, and to the great disappointment, no doubt, of the devil, who had further work for him.

The officers of the American squadron, under the command of Commodore Reed, who arrived here a short time after the departure of La Place, issued a circular, from which the following is an extract :—

"Being most decidedly of opinion that the persons composing the Protestant mission of these islands are American citizens, and, as such, entitled to the protection which our government has never withheld ; and with unwavering confidence in the justice which has ever characterized it, we rest assured that any insult offered to this unoffending class, will be promptly redressed."

This circular, which honors the intelligence and moral justice in which it had its source, is signed by Commodore George A. Magruder ; Lieutenants Andrew H. Foot, John W. Livingston, Thomas Turner, James S. Palmer, Edward R. Thompson, Augustus H. Kelly, George B. Minor ; Surgeons John Hazlett, John A. Lockwood, Joseph Beale ; Purser Dangerfield Fauntleroy ; Chaplain, Fitch W. Taylor ; Professors of Mathematics, J. Henshaw Belcher, Alexander G. Pendleton.

Captain La Place having succeeded so brilliantly with his powder-and-shot diplomacy, Lord George

Paulet, the commander of her Britannic majesty's ship Carysfort, thought he would try his hand at the business. He arrived here a short time after his illustrious predecessor; but, having no Jesuits and brandy to introduce, it became necessary to find something else as a basis of action.

In this emergency, he drummed up a set of claims on the government, to which he deemed its resources unequal, and demanded for them immediate satisfaction. To his utter surprise, these claims were recognised: he had now no alternative but to bring in a new set, of such a magnitude as to render all adjustment impracticable. The government remonstrated against the injustice of the proceeding; but it was of no avail: payment must be made instanter, or the sovereignty of the islands surrendered. Lord George accordingly hauled down the Hawaiian flag, and run up that of her Britannic majesty. The little ships belonging to the government were all re-christened: one taking the name of Victoria; another the Adelaide; and even the old fort was honored with a Georgian title.

Dispatches were immediately sent by Lord George to the British ministry, informing them of the acquisition of all the Hawaiian islands to her Majesty's dominions. But in the mean time, Admiral Thomas, the senior officer of the English fleet in this sea, arrived here, in the Dublin, from Valparaiso. He requested an interview with the king: the real difficulties were at once amicably adjusted; the fictitious ones, which were the basis of Lord George's proceeding, were thrown by the Admiral to the wind, and the sovereignty of the islands restored. This was rather an imposing ceremony. The king and his chiefs appeared on the plain, east of the town, where fifteen or twenty thousand of the inhabitants had assembled. Admiral Thomas entered the grounds under a brilliant escort of marines from his squadron. The standard of the king was now unfurled, and his flag run up on the two forts. They were saluted by the guns of the Dublin and Carysfort, and Kamehameha III. was again on the throne of his ancestors.

Thus ended the brilliant conquest of Lord George, and thus vanished his dream of empire, when touched by the wand of moral rectitude. He was not only compelled to see the Hawaiian flag restored, but to salute it from his own ship, and with those very guns with which he had demanded its surrender under a threat that Honolulu should be blown sky-high. Verily, as the proverb hath it, "he that governs his own spirit, is greater than he that taketh a city." The conduct of Admiral Thomas was sustained by the British ministry, and Lord George went to the wall.

CHAPTER XIII.

PASSAGE FROM HONOLULU TO MONTEREY.

THE MORAL PHAROS.—THE MORMON SHIP.—BIBLE CLASS.—THE SEA-HEN.—OUR INSANE SAILOR.—FOURTH OF JULY.—PROFANENESS AT SEA.—EVENING PRAYER-MEETING.—FUNERAL.—TARGET FIRING.—RELIGIOUS CONDITION OF THE CREW.—ANCHOR UNDER MONTEREY

"The sea-bird wheels above the mast,
And the waters fly below,
And the foaming billows flashing fast
Are leaping up the prow."

TUESDAY, JUNE 23. We weighed anchor at daylight this morning, and stood out from the open bay of Honolulu. The breeze was fresh, and in a few hours Oahu presented only its volcanic peaks above the swell of the ocean. We cast a parting glance to those cliffs from which we had gazed in delighted wonder, and felt a sentiment allied to bereavement, as they faded on our vision.

The volcanoes which threw up these mountain-masses have long since rested from their labors; the flames which lit the savage grandeur of their craters are extinct; dim ages have swept over them, and only the bleak monuments of their terrific energy remain; but Christian philanthropy, without pomp and parade, and in the silence of that love which seeks only to solace and save, has here kindled a light that shall never wane. Centuries may come and go, and night rest upon other isles of the wide sea, but this light will still stream on in undying splendor. Beneath its beams generations will here go untremblingly down to the unbreathing sepulchre, and as this world darkens on their vision, discern those objects of faith which loom to light in the spirit-land. With the good, a shadow only falls between this world and the next.

Wednesday, June 24. We have been for the last twenty-four hours on our starboard tack, with the wind from the northeast. The jagged steeps of Kanie sunk this morning in the sea over our larboard quarter. We are again upon the wide ocean without an object on which the eye can rest. Our frigate has a heavy roll; she has in her six months' provisions, and lies too deep for the greatest speed. The heat is oppressive, but has been relieved by several refreshing showers. Our men jumped around in them like wild ducks in the foam of the cascade.

The ward-room of the Congress presents an orderly, well-regulated table. It has been so from the commencement of our cruise. Grace is said at our meals; not a glass of spirits has entered our mess; not a word of discord, petulance, or anger, has been heard. The officers are within the circle of that religious sentiment which more or less pervades the crew. It is religion alone that can bind passion, harmonize the elements of society, and render the obligations of mutual forbearance and love the abiding rules of action.

THURSDAY, JUNE 25. We left at Honolulu the American ship Brooklyn, with one hundred and seventy-five Mormon emigrants on board, bound to Monterey and San Francisco, where they propose to settle. They look to us for protection, and expect to land, if necessary, under our batteries. I spent the greater part of a day among them, and must say, I was much pleased with their deportment. The greater portion of them are young, and have been trained to habits of industry, frugality, and enterprise. Some have been recently married, and are accompanied by their parents. They are mostly from the Methodist and Baptist persuasions. Their Mormonism, so far as they have any, has been superinduced on their previous faith, as Millerism on the belief of some Christians. They are rigidly strict in their domestic morals; have their morning and evening prayers; and the wind and the weather have never suspended, during their long voyage, their exercises of devotion.

FRIDAY, JUNE 26. We have had since we left port

a head wind; but we are constantly working our way north through the trades into the variables; a few weeks since we were very anxious to get out of the variables, we are now equally anxious to get into them. But we were then sailing northwest; our course now lies northeast: such is the occupation of the sailor. He is forever crossing and retracing his own track, and well would it be for him if this crossing and retracing were confined to his track on the deep, but unhappily it enters into the pathway of his moral being. He plods back in penitence and remorse the space over which folly and passion blindly whirled him. "Facilis descensus averni, sed revocare hic labor, hoc opus est."

SATURDAY, JUNE 27. We have at last a slant of wind which has put us on our course. The Mormon ship must make haste if she expects to overtake us before we reach Monterey. It is a little singular that with a company of one hundred and seventy emigrants, confined in a vessel of only four hundred tons, depending on each other's activity and forbearance for comfort, unbroken harmony should have prevailed. They may have had their momentary jars, but I was assured by the captain, who is not of their persuasion, that no serious discord had occurred. They put their money into a joint stock, laid in their own provisions, and have every thing in common.

They chartered their vessel, for which they pay twelve hundred dollars per month. It will cost them for their passage alone some ten thousand dollars before they disembark in California.

SUNDAY, JUNE 28. We had divine service at the usual hour. The subject of the sermon was the aversion of the world to the meekness, humility, and forbearance which enter into the Christian character. Men of the world are too apt to consider these qualities incompatible with courage, resolution, firmness, and self-respect. But the most heroic virtues have been displayed in dungeons, on the rack, and at the stake, by martyrs to truth. He who suffered on the cross, triumphed over not only the malice of his foes, but the terrors of death. After service I met my Bible class, and spent an hour with them. Among them are some of the first seamen in the ship; men whose influence extend through the whole crew; several of these, there is reason to believe, have experienced religion since we started on the present cruise. God grant they may persevere with unshaken firmness.

I applied to-day to Captain Du Pont and Mr. Livingston for the apartment leading to the store-room, in which to hold our evening prayer-meeting. It was granted without any hesitation. This prayer-meeting commenced with three or four individuals;

it now embraces some fifteen or twenty, and it will not stop here.

MONDAY, JUNE 29. We have been in a dead calm all day,—the ocean slumbering about us without a ripple, and our dog-vane not lifting a feather. The lazy clouds piled themselves up in pyramids and castles on the sea, without a wave or breath to disturb their fantastic forms. The rays of the sun were quenched in their veils, and twilight spread over their summits her rosy charm. As night in her sable hues advanced, the moon came up and poured on turret and tower her tender light. Man rears his structures amid weariness and tumult; nature erects hers in silence. When the monuments of man decay, ages may sigh over their unreviving relics, but when those of nature are dissolved, others emerge from the ruin in more exulting beauty, as the bird of flame from the ashes of its parent.

TUESDAY, JUNE 30. When an aquatic fowl appears for which the sailor has no other name, he always calls it a sea-hen. Several of this brood have been about our ship to-day, circling through the air, and resting on the sleeping sea. The head is large, the neck strong, the wings long and arching, and the plumage dark brown. We tried to hook one of them with a tempting bait, but the fellow was too cunning.

The only purpose they seemingly serve is to relieve the monotony of a sea-life.

We have been lying now for two days in the same waveless berth; our motion has not been sufficient to straighten our log-line. Every cloud is watched, but it brings no breeze. It departs like the airy visions of childhood, and none knoweth the place of its rest. We are born in shadows; live in their aerial folds, and vanish at last into deep night. But the spark of the Divinity that glows within is quenchless evermore.

Wednesday, July 1. We caught to-day, with a hook, one of the sailor's sea-hens. It proved to be the brown albatros of the Pacific; and measured ten feet between the tips of its wings. When brought on board, the fellow threw his wild glances at the crew, and walked about as haughtily as if sole monarch of the peopled deck. One of the men attempted to trifle with his dignity, when he pounced upon him and severely chastised his impertinence. After being detained an hour, we let him go to join his female companion, who was waiting for him, on the wave, by the side of the ship. The albatros never deserts its consort in calamity.

The love which coldly wounds and kills,
Is that which care and sorrow chills.

Thursday, July 2. Our sailor, Lewis, who is touched with insanity, is again on deck. He moves around among the crew, but never participates in their amusements, or enters into conversation with any one. If questioned, his answers are so stern and brief they quell curiosity. He handles a rope as if there were a scorpion's fang in every strand. Only snatches of his history are known. He has borne arms; his last exploits were at San Jacinto. He has the air of one in whom the feelings of a better nature have been turned to apathy and scorn.

> "His features' deepening lines and varying hue
> At times attract, and yet perplex the view
> As if within that murkiness of mind
> Worked feeling, fearful and yet undefined.
> He has the skill, when cunning's gaze would seek
> To probe his heart and watch his changing cheek,
> At once the observer's purpose to espy,
> And on himself roll back his scrutiny."

Friday, July 3. We have at last a breeze from the northwest, which is leading us out of this region of calms. Our latitude is 35° n. Our thermometer ranges at seventy,—rather a cool temperature, considering that we are so near the vertical rays of a cloudless sun, wheeling around his northern bourne in his career of flame to the Line. But the temperature of the Pacific never undergoes those extreme changes to which that of the same latitude in the

Atlantic is subjected. The cause of this difference is probably found in the relative disproportion of sea and land over which the tides of the atmosphere pass in the two oceans.

Three seamen came into my state-room to-day to converse with me on the subject of religion. They stated that for several weeks their attention had been drawn to this subject, and that they had now resolved to renounce every sin, and seek an interest in Christ. I encouraged them in this good resolution, gave them books suited to their frame of mind, and invited them to our evening prayer-meeting. These are the bows of promise which span the dark tides of ocean.

SATURDAY, JULY 4. This is the anniversary of our national independence. The crew have been permitted to spend it as they pleased; no duty being required of them beyond what is essential to keep the ship on her course. Some collected themselves in groups, and spun patriotic yarns about naval actions in the last war; some sung the star-spangled banner; some waxed eloquent at the idea of a war with Mexico, and some sat quietly mending their old clothes. The young were generally the most eager for hostilities, and seemed to think they could hew their way with a cutlass and a pound of pork to the halls of the Montezumas.

Commodore Stockton gave an elegant dinner to his officers. Many sentiments, kindled by the examples of the glorious past, went round; and many thoughts of home and hearts left behind, melted in an under-tone through the festivities. How veneration, gratitude, and pride, will grow in the breast of an American, in a distant clime, over the memory of those who perilled their all in the Revolution! They rest in immortal remembrance amid the flowers and fragrant airs of earth:

> "By fairy hands their knell is rung,
> By forms unseen their dirge is sung."

SUNDAY, JULY 5. Though the morning has been overcast with flying clouds, from which dashes of rain have fallen, accompanied with sudden gusts of wind, giving every thing the air of discomfort, and rendering the ship rather uneasy, yet we have had our regular service. The subject of the discourse was, Profaneness—its degrading effects, its prohibition in the rules of the service, its violation of the laws of God.

This is the besetting sin of those who follow the seas,—of those who, in their helplessness, are surrounded by the most stupendous displays of omnipotent power. Yet let the ship in which it prevails most, be swept in a gale of shroud and mast, be driving amid breakers against the steep rock, her guilty crew will fall on their knees in prayer, and call on Him whose name they have profaned, whose worship they have derided, to have mercy and save.

Our prayer-meeting has increased, so that the small apartment in which we have been assembling will not accommodate us. Capt. Du Pont, on the suggestion of Mr. Livingston, has given us the use of the store-room. It has been so arranged that there is no interference with the public stores, and no increase of hazard from additional lights. It would have been easy for them to have suggested difficulties ; but, thank God, they are not so inclined. They have extended to me every facility and every encouragement in their power. Nor has any officer on board the ship cast an impediment in my way. Not a derisive remark from any one, either in or out of the ward-room, has fallen on my ear.

Monday, July 6. When we were receiving our crew at Norfolk, an old seaman, by the name of Barnard, applied to Capt. Du Pont to be shipped. He was told that he had not vigor for the hardships of another cruise, and kindly advised to make the Naval Asylum his home. But he plead the forty years of service which he had performed in our national ships so earnestly, that he was permitted to come on board. Though over sixty years of age, he has discharged the duties of quarter-master very well. But recently the springs of life have been giving way, till at last he has been obliged to relinquish his post at the wheel. He could not rally again, and has sunk to his last repose.

To-day we have consigned his remains to the deep. The body, wrapped in his hammock, was borne by his messmates up the main-hatch, along the line of the marine guard presenting arms, where it was met by the Commodore and Captain. As the band ceased its funeral air, the burial service was read, the plank on which the body lay was lifted, and Barnard glided down to his deep rest. Over him roll the waters of the Pacific.

> But when the last great trump shall thrill the grave,
> And earth's unnumbered myriads reappear,
> He too shall hear the summons 'neath the wave,
> That now in silence wraps his sunless bier.
> And coming forth, in trembling reverence bowed,
> Unfold the tongueless secrets of his shroud.

Tuesday, July 7. We have sailed since we left Callao about eight thousand miles without falling in with a single vessel, though the Pacific is said to be sprinkled with whalers and merchantmen. The former pursue their vocation without any reference to the customary tracks of other vessels; they set up their chase wherever the whale sweeps, be it to the Pole or the Line, and yet we have not encountered one of them. Out of the thousand, not one has come within the range of our vision. This gives one some idea of the immensity of the Pacific. A ship in it is like a meteor in the unconfined realms of space.

WEDNESDAY, JULY 8. We have had general quarters, with the exercise of the crew at the guns, almost every day since we left Honolulu. Mexican papers were received there, the day before our departure, stating that hostilities had commenced between that country and the United States, on the Texan line. We doubted the correctness of the information, but put to sea at once, that we might be off Monterey in season for any service which the possible exigency might require.

To-day we have been practising at target firing. This fictitious foe made his appearance on a platform buoyed up by eight empty casks at a distance, varying with the action of the sea and wind, of from one to two miles. The firing commenced on the larboard side, and was restricted to one round from each gun. It was found that the shot, though the guns had been elevated one degree, struck the water short of the mark. An order was therefore given to elevate the guns two degrees, and to be careful to fire on an even keel. This brought the target within a point-blank range ; and the shot whistled past it, grazing this side and that.

We now tacked ship, and gave the starboard lads a chance. Their shot struck with sufficient accuracy for all practical purposes in a naval engagement, and the target, though bobbing up and down on the sea as a frightened thing of life, very narrowly escaped. The whistling, whizzing sound made by a huge ball in its passage through the air, is like nothing else that I have ever heard. It seems to carry in its very tone an import of the destructive errand upon which it is sent. This ominous voice, however, in the excitement and thunders of an engagement, is never heard. The warning and the havoc come together, twins in life and death!

THURSDAY, JULY 9. We have made, for the last three days, but very little progress towards our port. The wind has been extremely light and baffling, breathing and dying away at all points of the compass. The atmosphere has had that peculiar property which magnifies every object of vision. The moon hung on the horizon this evening with a breadth of circle which attracted the attention of all on board; the stars seemed to have extended their glowing verge, the sea-bird to have enlarged its dusky form as it floated dimly in the pale light, while the wing of the cloud threw its vast shadow on the sleeping surface of the sea. We heard

"Not a sound, save the surge of the ship
As she lazily rolls to and fro,
And the sails as they listlessly flap,
And the creak of the rudder below."

Friday, July 10. We have had to-day a light but steady breeze on our starboard quarter. Our studding-sails have been set for the first time since we left Honolulu. We are now within nine hundred miles of our port. All are engaged, some in ship's duty, some in acquiring Spanish, some in writing letters home; while the crew, as they come off watch, occupy their time with books from the library. Sailors will read if you furnish them with books suited to their tastes and habits. Give them narratives, history, biography, and incidents of travel. In these sketches virtues may be shadowed forth that will win reverence and love, and the results of vice unfolded with repelling power. But all this requires care in the selection; this duty properly devolves on the chaplain; it is for him to elevate and mould the moral sentiments of those around him. If he is not equal to this, he should not put his foot on the decks of a man-of-war.

Saturday, July 11. Our light aft wind has left us, and we have in its stead a heavy sea, rolling in from the west. There must have been a tremendous blow in that quarter. Our ship rolled last night as she did off Cape Horn. Every thing in the ward-room and steerage which had not been secured, rushed about in crashing confusion. The candle-sticks leaped from the sideboard, a tray of knives and forks followed, while a water-tank flew from one bulkhead to another, as if determined to dash in its own staves. The front board of my berth had been taken out to admit more air, and I had no sooner dropped asleep, than out I rolled on the floor; and well was it for me that I did, for I was no sooner out of my berth than my library tumbled in. What singular feelings, half vexatious and half ludicrous, one has gathering himself up from such a tumble!

Sunday, July 12. The weather has been too stormy, and the roll of the ship too heavy, for religious service on deck. We have had a prayer-meeting in the store-room. The attendance was voluntary, but the large apartment was filled. A good number of our sailors are earnestly seeking religion, and several hope they have found it. I meet them every evening from eight to nine o'clock. They speak in these meetings with much frankness of their previous evil courses, and of their resolution to abandon them and seek Christ. Those who have obtained light and comfort, encourage others, and pray for them with an earnestness which shows their heart is in the work. Every evening some two or three new ones join us. Among them are some of the first sailors we have.

The effect of this on the discipline of the ship is too marked to escape observation. There is no disobedience and no punishment. Each performs with alacrity the duties of his station. It would seem as if we might throw every instrument of correction and coercion overboard; their requirement, for the present at least, has ceased. Give me the religious sentiment in a crew, and you may sink your handcuffs, cats, and colts in the depths of ocean. They who, under the hypocritical cry of church and state, would deprive our seamen of these influences, have steeled their hearts to the first instincts of humanity. Their religion, if they have any, is cruel as the grave.

MONDAY, JULY 13. The following note, which I received last evening from one of our quarter-gunners, a stanch sailor, derives its interest from the fact that he followed it up with an attendance at our prayer-meeting.

U. S. Frigate Congress, July 12, 1846.

DEAR SIR:—

With feelings of sincere regret for the error I made on the night of the 11th, by using profane language in your hearing, I do humbly crave your pardon, and I do assure you, had I known you were present at the time, such language would never have been used by me. I am aware I can make no excuse for the crime of swearing: it is, as you have truly said, the force of habit, which should have been checked by me years ago. No man inside this ship is more indebted to an all-merciful God than I am, for I have been totally shipwrecked in the course of my sea-life four different times, and been preserved when some of my shipmates met a watery grave; and still I sin greatly, daily, hourly, in spite of all my resolutions to the contrary.

Yours obediently.

Tuesday, July 14. We were tumbled out of our dead calm by a roaring northwester, and have been driven by it two hundred and thirty-five miles in the last twenty-four hours. We have six months' provisions, and four months' water, on board, and have been logging eleven and twelve knots. A ship that can do this under these circumstances, and close-hauled, must be a good sailer. We are now within two hundred and twenty miles of our port; and if this wind continues, shall probably anchor under Monterey to-morrow. Whether it be for hostilities or for peace, we know not; but we are prepared for either.

Wednesday, July 15. The wind continued very fresh through the night. Not wishing to make the land till daylight, we furled our top-gallant sails, hauled up our courses, double-reefed our topsails, and still run eight knots. As day dawned, Point Pinos rose fifteen miles directly ahead of us. But as the first rays of the sun tipped its forest-tops with flame, a bank of fog rolled between. Not a vestige of the coast was seen for hours; and we wore ship, and stood out to sea.

It was nearly noon before the fog lifted. We then made sail, and in two hours rounded Point Pinos, and entered the harbor of Monterey. We discovered at anchor the U. S. frigate Savannah, bearing the broad pennant of Commodore Sloat; the U. S. sloop-of-war Cyane, Captain Mervin; and the U. S. sloop-of-war Levant, Commander Page. We run up the red pennant, and saluted the blue of Commodore Sloat with thirteen guns, which were returned by the Savannah. As we rounded under her stern for our berth, her band struck up "Hail Columbia!" We came to anchor, in graceful style, outside the Cyane.

Here will we rest, and let the winds rave on

CHAPTER XIV.

GLANCES INTO CALIFORNIA.

SAILORS ON SHORE AS SOLDIERS.—THE BEAR FLAG.—CAPT. FREMONT AND HIS ARMED BAND.—DEPARTURE OF ADMIRAL SEYMOUR.—SAN FRANCISCO.—ASPECTS OF THE TOWN.—HABITS OF THE PEOPLE.—THE GOLD-DIGGER.—SPIRIT OF SPECULATION.—GAMBLING.—EFFECTS OF THE GOLD MINES.—PAST AND PRESENT CONDITION OF THE COUNTRY.

The peak where burns the blush of morn,
The glen in which a torrent rolled,
The crater where the Deil was born,
Are hemmed and stratified with gold;
And e'en the quartz, which bind the shore,
Sweat out at times the precious ore.

THURSDAY, JULY 16. The Cyane warped out of her berth this morning, and we warped into it. Our ships are now moored in line, command the anchorage, and present a very warlike appearance.

This afternoon a large ship was discovered rounding Point Pinos. She entered the harbor under a cloud of canvas, and proved to be the Collingwood, bearing the broad pennant of Admiral Seymour. She came to anchor outside the Congress and Savannah. Our band greeted her with "God save the Queen," which she returned with "Hail, Columbia." She is an 80 gun ship, and looks majestic on the wave. The Admiral was greatly surprised to find Monterey in possession of the Americans.

Commodore Sloat, having received information at

Mazatlan, through the public press, that our advanced posts on the Rio Grande had been attacked by a Mexican force, sailed immediately for this port. On his arrival the town was taken without any conflict, the flag run up and saluted with twenty-one guns from each ship of the squadron. A proclamation was then issued by the commodore, informing the inhabitants of the bases of his proceedings, and invoking quietude as the condition of security and repose; while our own men, who had been stationed on shore, were strictly enjoined not to molest the citizens in their lawful occupations.

Friday, July 17. The bay of Monterey circles up broad and deep into the coast. It is far from being land-locked, and yet the southern bend is sufficiently sheltered to afford a safe and quiet anchorage. The town is built within a circling range of forest-feathered hills, and on a plain that descends in easy slopes to the strand of the bay. A more inviting picturesque location for a city never entered a poet's dream. The buildings are reared of adobes, covered with a white layer of lime; they are seldom over one story and a half, and are ornamented with porticoes running the entire front. The streets are broad but irregular, and the hills around connect themselves with the gleaming walls of cottages which as yet exist only in your imagination.

The U. S. sloop-of-war Portsmouth, J. B. Montgomery commander, is at San Francisco; the Warren, J. B. Hull, commander, is at Mazatlan. Our flag is now flying over Monterey, San Francisco, Sonoma, and Sutter's Fort. No formidable attempt has been made by the Californians to recapture any of these positions. The great body of the inhabitants seem but little inclined to take up arms. They have no great affection for Mexico, or reverence for the military chieftains whom she has sent to govern them.

Our marine guard, commanded by Lieut. Zelin, and fifty sailors under the command of Lieut. Tilghman, left our ship to-day for duty on shore. It is amusing to see Jack with a carbine in his hand; he don't know what to do with it, whether to carry it in one hand or both, at his side or on his shoulder. When posted as a sentinel, he always forgets the countersign of course, and if a man looks pretty honest, allows him to pass; but if he comes in some mysterious shape, he may expect to be shot. One on an outpost last night, hearing a rumpling sound among the dry leaves, and catching glimpses, by the pale moonlight, of a form gliding behind this bush and that, instead of hailing, "Who comes there?" cried out, "A bloody Indian!" and let off his carbine. The guard, hearing the report, rushed immediately to the spot, where they found a bullock, which had narrowly escaped our sentinel's bullet. Jack, when shown his horned antagonist and rebuked for his precipitancy, gruffly replied, that it was impossible to make out, in the night and among the bushes, what sort of a craft was coming at him, and he thought it best to get the first fire.

SATURDAY, JULY 18. The whole of California is in a state of tumult, and was so before our squadron made a demonstration on Monterey. The jealousy of the government had been roused by the arrival of a fresh body of emigrants, who had located themselves on the Sacramento, and by the movements of Capt. Fremont, whose scientific projects a disturbed imagination had converted into revolutionary purposes. The emigrants were ordered out of the country, with Capt. Fremont and his exploring party; and measures adopted to enforce the mandate. But the indomitable captain and the emigrants were not thus to be ousted or overawed. They had the Anglo-Saxon blood in them, and decided that a man has a right to live where he pleases on this green earth of God's.

They ran up a flag sufficiently significant of their intentions,—a white field, red border, with a grizzly bear eyeing a single star, which threw its light on the motto, "The Republic of California." To this flag and its fortunes they pledged themselves in mutual confidence, and though a band of only two hundred, pushed their measures so vigorously that Gen. Castro, with a force of three times their numbers, retreated before their resolute positions. They are now within the department of Monterey, and their arrival is looked for hourly. Such in brief is the history of the Bear flag, and of that courageous organization which set the ball of Anglo-Saxon supremacy rolling in California.

Sunday, July 19. We had divine service at the usual hour. The object of the sermon was a plain illustration of the text, "The way of transgressors is hard." The every-day life of the sailor is a living commentary on the truth of this significant proverb. The hardships of his lot have generally been entailed upon him by a career of folly. The recitals of his errors, which are often poured into my ears, are full of painful interest. I greatly fear the novelties of the shore, and the excitements which reach us every day from all quarters, will dissipate that religious concern which has prevailed of late among our crew.

Monday, July 20. Captain Fremont and his armed band, with Lieut. Gillespie of the marine corps, arrived last evening from their pursuit of Gen. Castro. They are two hundred strong, all well mounted, and have some three hundred extra horses in their train. They defiled, two abreast, through the principal street of the town. The ground seemed to tremble under their heavy tramp. The citizens glanced at them through their grated windows. Their rifles, revolving pistols, and long knives, glittered over the dusky buckskin which enveloped their sinewy limbs, while their untrimmed locks, flowing out from under their foraging caps, and their black beards, with white teeth glittering through, gave them a wild savage aspect. They encamped in the skirts of the woods which overhang the town. The blaze of their watch-fires, as night came on, threw its quivering light into the forest glades, and far out at sea. Their sentinels were posted at every exposed point; they sleep in their blankets under the trees, with their arms at their side, ready for the signal shot or stir of the crackling leaf.

> For let a footstep, scarce as loud
> As falls the winter's flake,
> Approach their tents, they wake,
> And spring like lightning from the cloud.

TUESDAY, JULY 21. The Levant has been ordered to be ready for sea with all dispatch. She is to take Commodore Sloat to Panama, where he crosses the Isthmus for the United States. His measures here involve some responsibility, as no authentic intelligence of a declaration of war has reached us. But his motives have been high and patriotic, and his action opportune in the event of national hostilities. The command will now devolve on Commodore Stockton; what he will do with the California question, remains to be seen. Among the persons whose influence is felt in these affairs, stands T. O. Larkin, Esq., U. S. Consul for many years in this province, and of whose services I shall have occasion to speak hereafter.

Wednesday, July 22. Captain Fremont's band of riflemen visited our ship to-day, and lunched with us. Many of them are trappers from the interior wilds, who have never seen a man-of-war before. They looked at our frowning battery with a wonder for which their trap dialect had no expression. The Indians connected with the body, wanted to know how such an immense mass could be put on the *trail.* We pointed to our sails, clewed to the yards; they shook their heads in incredulity. They seemed to think there must be some invisible monster in the hold, whose terrific energies caused the ship to go. Our band played some of their most spirit-stirring airs, but they had as little effect on these children of the wild as the song of the grasshopper. The article which seemed to interest them most, was the rifle of Commodore Stockton; they handled it with that yearning fondness which a mother feels clasping her first-born.

THURSDAY, JULY 23. The Collingwood sailed to-day for the Sandwich Islands. Many of her officers had clothes on shore in the hands of washerwomen; they were hurried off, some half ironed, some half dry, and some in the suds. Such are the accidents which await the linen of one connected with a national ship. He may think himself fortunate if he recovers his clothes at all; they are often left as contingent remainders in a man's will.

The Collingwood has offered us no molestation: Admiral Seymour is an officer of great amenity of deportment,—has been several times on board the Congress: he was much impressed with the force of our battery, and says our ship is the most powerful frigate afloat in the world. The Admiral and most of his officers are connected with the English nobility, but assume no airs, and are boon companions wherever met. It has been often stated by American writers that the Admiral intended to raise the English flag in California, and would have done it had we not stolen the march on him. I believe nothing of the kind; the allegation is a mere assumption, unwarranted by a solitary fact. He had no such instructions from the British ministry: what the English *might* have done, had they been apprized of our designs, is another thing; what they *did* do, was to watch our movements. When we had harpooned the whale, they left us to make the most of its blubber and bones.

Friday, July 24. Capt. Du Pont left us to-day to take command of the Cyane—a fine ship, well officered and manned. We part with him with much regret; he has been with us in gale and calm, amidst the ice of the Cape and on the burning Line, and cheerfully shared, in his own person, every hardship and peril. His professional knowledge and efficiency, with his social qualities and unblemished character, have won our unmeasured confidence and esteem.

Mr. Livingston, our first lieutenant, succeeds to the command, under an appointment from Commodore Stockton, and combines, with the duties of this post, those of executive officer. His station is one of some difficulty, but he is the better qualified for it by his previous services and thorough knowledge of the crew. Capt. Mervin takes command of the Savannah—a post to which he is entitled by his experience and rank. The officers attached to this frigate are an ornament to the service; there are not wanting individuals among them whose religious example has been felt deep and wide.

Here the publication of my journal must rest; and be resumed in another volume, under the title of "Three Years in California." But without trenching on the incidents sketched in that volume, I may glance at a few local circumstances which recent events have thrown into remarkable prominency. The geographical features of the country will be described in their proper place; I turn from these to a point which looms up, in the fancy at least, like a headland on which a rosy twilight has poured its golden charm.

The bay of San Francisco resembles a broad inland lake, communicating by a narrow channel with the ocean. This channel, as the tradition of the aborigines runs, was opened by an earthquake which a few centuries since convulsed the continent. The town is built on the south bend of the bay, near its communication with the sea. Its site is a succession of barren sand-hills, tumbled up into every variety of shape. No levelling process, on a scale of any magnitude, has been attempted. The buildings roll up and over these sand ridges like a shoal of porpoises over the swell of a wave, only the fish has much the most order in the disposal of his head and tail. More incongruous combinations in architecture never danced in the dreams of men. Brick warehouses, wooden shanties, sheet-iron huts, and shaking tents, are blended in admirable confusion.

But these grotesque habitations have as much uniformity and sobriety as the habits of those who occupy them. Hazards are made in commercial transactions and projects of speculation, that would throw Wall-street into spasms. I have seen merchants purchase cargoes without having even glanced into the invoice. The conditions of the sale were a hundred per cent. profits to the owner, and costs. In one cargo, when tumbled out, were found twenty thousand dollars in the single article of red cotton handkerchiefs! "I'll get rid of those among the wild Indians," said the purchaser, with a shrug of his shoulders. "I've a water-lot which I will sell," cries another. "Which way does it stretch?" inquire half a a dozen. "Right under that craft there," is the reply. "And what do you ask for it?" "Fifteen thousand dollars." "I'll take it." "Then down with your dust." So the water-lot, which mortal eyes never yet beheld, changes its owners without changing its fish. "I have two shares in a gold mine," cries another. "Where are they?" inquire the crowd. "Under the south branch of the Yuba river, which we have almost turned," is the reply. "And what will you take?" "Fifteen thousand dollars." "I'll give ten." "Take them, stranger." So the two shares of a *possibility* of gold under a branch of the Yuba, where the water still rolls rapid and deep, are sold for ten thousand dollars paid down! Is there any thing in the Arabian Nights that surpasses this?

But glance at that large wooden building, which looks as if the winds had shingled it, and the powers of the air pinned its clapboards in a storm. Enter, and you find a great hall filled with tables, and a motley group gathered around each. Some are laying down hundreds and others thousands on the turn of a card. Each has a bag of grain-gold in his hand, which he must double or lose, and is only anxious to reach the table where he can make the experiment. You would advise him at least to purchase a suit of clothes, or repair his old ones, before he loses his all; but what cares he for his outward garb, when piles of the yellow dust swell and glitter in his excited imagination? Down goes his bag of gold—and is lost! But does he look around for a rope or pistol that he may end his ruin? No: the river bank, where he gathered that bag, has more; so he cheers his momentary despondency with a strong glass of brandy, and is off again for the mines. He found the gold by good fortune, and has lost it by bad, and now considers himself about even with the world. Such is the moral effect of gold hunting on a man whose principles are not as fixed and immoveable as the rock. It begins in a lottery and ends in a lottery, where the blanks outnumber the prizes ten to one.

But you are hungry—want a breakfast—turn into a restaurant—call for ham, eggs, and coffee—then your bill—six dollars! Your high boots, which have never seen a brush since you first put them on, have given out: you find a pair that can replace them—

they are a tolerable fit, and now what is the price—fifty dollars! Your beard has not felt a razor since you went to the mines—it must come off, and your frizzled hair be clipped. You find a barber: his dull shears hang in the knots of your hair like a sheep-shearer's in a fleece matted with burrs—his razor he straps on the leg of his boot, and then hauls away—starting at every pull some new fountain of tears. You vow you will let the beard go—but then one side is partly off, and you try the agony again to get the other side something like it; and now what is the charge for this torture—four dollars! Night is approaching, and you must have a place where you can sleep: to inquire for a bed would be as idle as to hunt a pearl in the jungle of a Greenland bear. You look around for the lee of some shanty or tent, and tumble down for the night; but a thousand fleas dispute the premises with you—the contest is hopeless—you tumble out as you tumbled in, and spend the remainder of the night in finding a place not occupied by these aborigines of the soil.

But you are not perhaps a gold-digger, as I had supposed; you are a supercargo, and have a valuable freight, which you wish to land. You have warped your vessel in till her keel rakes, and yet you are several hundred yards off. Some lighter must be found that can skim these shallows; your own boats will not do: after waiting two or three weeks, you get the use of a scow, called a lighter, for which you pay one hundred and fifty dollars a day.

To-morrow you are going to commence unloading, and wake betimes; but find that during the night every soul of your crew has escaped, and put out for the mines. You rush about on shore to find hands, and collect eight or ten loafers, who will assist you for fifteen dollars a day each. Your cargo must be landed, and you close the bargain, though your fresh hands are already half-seas over. The scow is shoved from shore, brought alongside, loaded with goods, which are tumbled in as an Irishman dumps a load of dirt, and then you up oars and poles and push for the landing; but the tide has ebbed too soon: you are only halfway, and there your scow sticks fast in the midst of a great mud bottom, from which the last ripple of water has retreated. You cannot get forward, and you are now too late to get back: night is setting in and the rain-clouds are gathering fast; down comes a deluge, drenching your goods, and filling your open scow. The returning tide will now be of no use, the scow won't float, except under water, and that is a sort of floating which don't suit you; skin for skin—though in this case not dry—what will a man not give for his own life? So out you jump, and by crawling and creeping, make your way through the mire to the landing, and bring up against a bin, where another sort of wallower gives you a grunt of welcome.

Your loafers must be paid off in the morning, and the scow recovered, or its loss will cost you half the profits of your voyage. But the storm last night has driven another brig into yours; and there they both are, like a bear and bull that have gored and crushed each other. But "misery loves company," and you have it. The storm which swamped your scow and stove your brig last night, has been busy on shore. Piles of goods heaped up in every street, are in a condition which requires wreckers as well as watchmen. But no one here is going to trouble himself about your misfortunes, nor much about his own. The reverses of to-day are to be more than repaired by the successes of to-morrow. These are only the broken pickaxes and spades by which the great mine is to be reached. What is the loss of a few thousands to one who is so soon to possess millions? Only a coon back in his hole, while the buffalo remains within rifle-shot,—only a periwinkle lost, while the whale is beneath the harpoon,—only a farthing candle consumed, while the dowered bride, blushing in beauty and bliss, is kneeling at the nuptial altar. But let that pass.

But you are not alone in your destitution and dirt. There are hundreds around you who were quite as daintily reared, and who are doing out here what they dodged at home. Do you see that youth in red flannel shirt and coarse brogans, rolling a wheelbarrow? He was once a clerk in a counting-house in New York, and came here to shovel up gold as you scoop up sand. He has been to the mines, gathered no gold, and returned, but now makes his ten dollars a day by rolling that wheelbarrow; it costs him six, however, to live, and the other four he loses at monté.

See you that young man with a long whip in his hand, cracking it over an ox-team? He was one of the most learned geologists, for his age, in the United States, and came out here to apply his science to the discovery of gold deposites; but some how his diving-rods always dipped wrong—and now he has taken a rod about which there is no mistake, so at least think his cattle. He would accumulate a fortune did he not lose it as fast as made in some phrensied speculation. But look yonder—do you see that young gentlemen with a string of fish, which he offers for sale. He was the best Greek and Latin scholar of his class in Yale College; and subsequently one of the most promising members of our bar. But he exchanged his Blackstone for a pick; and instead of picking fees out of his clients' pockets, he came here to pick gold out of the mines; but the deuce was in it, for whenever his pick struck close upon a deposite, it was no longer there! so he exchanged his pick for a hook and line, and now angles for pike, pickerel, and perch, and can describe each fish by some apt line from Catullus. He would do well at his new piscatory profession, but for the gilded hook of the gambler. He laughs at the trout for darting at a fictitious fly, and then chases a bait himself equally fanciful and false.

But look again—do you see that pulperia, with its gathered groups of soldiers and sailors, poets and politicians, merchants and mendicants, doctors and draymen, clerks and cobblers, trappers and tinkers. That little man who stands behind the bar and deals to each his dram of fire, was once a preacher, and deemed almost a prophet, as he depicted the pangs of that worm which dieth not; but now he has exchanged that *worm* for another, but preserved his consistency, for this worm, too, distilleth delirium and death. And that thick-set man who stands in the midst of the crowd, with ruby countenance and revelling eye, whose repartee sets the whole pulperia in a roar, and who is now watching the liquor in his glass to see if it stirreth itself aright, once lectured in the West on the temptations of those who tarry late at the wine; but now his teetotalism covers all liquors as goodly gifts graciously bestowed. But one brief year, and some dame Quickly may describe his pale exit as that of his delirious prototype,—"I saw him fumble with the sheets, and play with flowers, and smile upon his fingers' ends."

And yet with all these drawbacks—with all these gambling-tables, grog-shops, shanties, shavers, and fleas, San Francisco is swelling into a town of the highest commercial importance. She commands the trade of the great valleys through which the Sacramento and San Joaquin, with their numerous tributaries, roll. She gathers to her bosom the products and manufactures of the United States, of England, China, the shores and islands of the Pacific. But let us glance at California as she was a few years since, as she is now, and as she is fast becoming.

Three years ago the white population of California could not have exceeded ten thousand souls. She has now a population of two hundred thousand, and a resistless tide of emigration rolling in through the heart of Mexico, over the Isthmus of Panama, around Cape Horn, and over the steeps of the Rocky Mountains. Then the great staple of the country was confined to wild cattle; now it is found in exhaustless mines of quicksilver and gold. Then the shipping which frequented her waters was confined to a few drogers, that waddled along her coast in quest of hides and tallow; now the richest argosies of the commercial world are bound to her ports.

Three years ago the dwellings of her citizens were reared under the hands of Indians, from sun-baked adobes of mud and straw; now a thousand hammers are ringing on rafter and roof over walls of iron and brick. Then the plough which furrowed her fields was the crotch of a tree, which a stone or root might shiver; now the shares of the New-England farmer glitter in her soil. Then the wheels of her carts were cut from the butts of trees, with a hole in the centre for the rude axle; now the iron-bound wheel of the finished mechanic rolls over her hills and valleys. Then only the canoe of the Indian disturbed the sleeping surface of her waters; now a fleet of steamers traverse her ample rivers and bays. Then not a schoolhouse, public teacher, magazine, or newspaper, could be found in the whole territory; now they are met with in most of the larger towns. Then the tastes and passions of an idle throng ran on the guitar and the fandango; now the calculations of the busy multitudes turn to the cultured field and productive mine. Then California was a dependency of Mexico, and subject to revolutions with the success of every daring military chieftain; now she is an independent state, with an enlightened constitution, which guaranties equal rights and privileges to all. Then she was in arms against our flag; now she unrolls it on the breeze, with the star of her own being and pride glowing in the constellation which blazes on its folds.

Three years ago and San Francisco contained only three hundred souls; now she has a population of twenty-seven thousand. Then a building lot within her limits cost fifteen dollars; now the same lot cannot be purchased at a less sum than fifteen thousand. Then her commerce was confined to a few Indian blankets, and Mexican reboses and beads; now from two to three hundred merchantmen are unloading their costly cargoes on her quay. Then the famished whaler could hardly find a temporary relief in her markets; now she has phrensied the world with her wealth. Then Benicia was a pasture covered with lowing herds; now she is a commercial mart, threatening to rival her sister nearer the sea. Then Stockton and Sacramento City were covered with wild oats, where the elk and deer gambolled at will; now they are laced with streets, and walled with warehouses, through which the great tide of commerce rolls off into a hundred mountain glens. Then the banks of the Sacramento and San Joaquin were cheered only by the curling smoke of the Indian's hut; now they throw on the eye at every bend the cheerful aspect of some new hamlet or town. Then the silence of the Sierra Nevada was broken only by the voice of its streams; now every cavern and cliff is echoing under the blows of the sturdy miner. The wild horse, startled in his glen, leaves on the hill the clatter of his hoofs, while the huge bear, roused from his patrimonial jungle, grimly retires to some new mountain fastness.

But I must drop this contrast of the past with the present, and glance at a few facts which affect the future. The gold deposites, which have hitherto been discovered, are confined mainly to the banks and beds of perpetual streams, or the bottoms of ravines through which roll the waters of the transient freshet. These deposites are the natural results of the laws of gravitation; the treasures which they contain must have been washed from the slopes of the surrounding hills. The elevations, like spendthrifts, seem to have parted entirely with their golden inheritance, except what may linger still in the quartz. And these gold-containing quartz will be found to have their confined localities. They will crown the insular peaks of a mountain ridge, or fret the verge of some extinguished volcano. They have never been found in a continuous range, except in the dreams of enchantment. You might as well look for a wall of diamonds, or a solid bank of pearls. Nature has played off many a prodigal caprice in California, but a mountain of gold is not one of them.

The alluvial gold will at no distant day be measurably exhausted, and the miners be driven into the mountains. Here the work can be successfully prosecuted only by companies with heavy capitals. All the uncertainties which are connected with mining operations will gather around these enterprises. Wealth will reward the labors of the few, whose success was mainly the result of good fortune; while disappointment will attend the efforts of the many, equally skilful and persevering. These wide in-qualities, in the proceeds of the miner's labor, have exhibited themselves wherever a gold deposite has been hunted or found in California. The past is the reliable prophecy of the future.

Not one in ten of the thousands who have gone, or may go, to California to hunt for gold, will return with a fortune. Still the great tide of emigration will set there, till her valleys and mountain glens teem with a hardy, enterprising population. As the gold deposites diminish, or become more difficult of access, the quicksilver mines will call forth their unflagging energies. This metal slumbers in her mountain spurs in massive richness. The process is simple which converts it into that form through which the mechanic arts subserve the thousand purposes of science and social refinement, while the medical profession, through its strange abuse, keep up a carnival in the court of Death. But for this they who mine the ore are not responsible; they will find their reward in the wealth which will follow their labors. It will be in their power to silence the hammers in those mines which have hitherto monopolized the markets of the world.

But the enterprise and wealth of California are not confined to her mines. Her ample forests of oak, red-wood, and pine, only wait the requisite machinery to convert them into elegant residences and strong-ribbed ships. Her exhaustless quarries of granite and marble will yet pillar the domes of metropolitan splendor and pride. The hammer and drill will be relinquished by multitudes for the plough and sickle. Her arable land, stretching through her spacious valleys and along the broad banks of her rivers, will wave with the golden harvest. The raincloud may not visit her in the summer months, but the mountain stream will be induced to throw its showers over her thirsting plains.

Such was California a few years since—such is she now—and such will she become, even before they who now rush to her shores find their footsteps within the shadows of the pale realm.

In press, and will shortly be published,

THREE YEARS IN ALTA CALIFORNIA:

WITH

AN ACCOUNT OF THE GOLD MINES.

BY REV. WALTER COLTON, U.S.N.,

LATE ALCALDE OF MONTEREY.

THE MEXICAN WAR:

A History of its Origin, with a detailed Account of the Victories which terminated in the surrender of the Capital, with the Official Despatches of the Generals. By EDWARD D. MANSFIELD, Esq Illustrated with numerous Engravings.

From the Philadelphia North American.

Mr. Mansfield is a writer of superior merit. His style is clear, nervous, and impressive, and, while he does not encumber his narrative with useless ornament, his illustrations are singularly apt and striking. A graduate of West Point, he is of course familiar with military operations; a close and well-read student, he has omitted no sources of information necessary to the purposes of his work; and a shrewd and investigating observer, he sees in events not alone their outward aspects, but the germs which they contain of future development. Thus qualified, it need hardly be said that his history of the war with Mexico deserves the amplest commendation.

From the New York Tribune.

A clear, comprehensive, and manly history of the war, is needed; and we are glad to find this desideratum supplied by Mr. Mansfield's work.

From the New York Courier and Enquirer.

This is really a history, and not an adventurer's pamphlet destined to live for the hour and then be forgotten. It is a volume of some 360 pages, carefully written, from authorities weighed and collated by an experienced writer, educated at West Point, and therefore imbued with a just spirit and sound views, illustrated by plans of the battles, and authenticated by the chief official despatches.

The whole campaign on the Rio Grande, and that, unequalled in brilliancy in any annals, from Vera Cruz to the city of Mexico, are unrolled before the eyes of the reader, and he follows through the spirited pages of the narrative, the daring bands so inferior—in every thing but indomitable will and unwavering self-reliance, and military skill and arms—to the hosts that opposed them, but opposed in vain.

We commend this book cordially to our readers.

From the Baptist Register, Utica.

The military studies of the talented editor of the Cincinnati Chronicle, admirably qualified him to give a truthful history of the stirring events connected with the unhappy war now raging with a sister republic; and though he declares in his preface that he felt no pleasure in tracing the causes, or in contemplating the progress and final consequences of the conflict, yet his graphic pages give proof of his ability and disposition to do justice to the important portion of our nation's history he has recorded. The very respectable house publishing the book, have done great credit to the author and his work, as well as to themselves, in the handsome style in which they have sent it forth.

Miscellaneous Books.

POPE'S HOMER'S ILIAD. 32mo. sheep.

This edition of the translation of Homer is used not only as a volume for the Library, but as a text-book in grammar classes in Schools and Academies.

POLYMICRIAN NEW TESTAMENT. (Illustrated with Maps.)

This is the only edition of Polymicrian New Testament published in this country. It contains short explanatory Notes, and numerous references to illustrative and parallel passages, printed in a centre column.

WATTS ON THE IMPROVEMENT OF THE MIND. With Questions.

There is no book better adapted for the School Room, or more calculated to be useful to the youth of our country, than a familiar acquaintance with the sound instruction of this learned divine, given in this manual.

"An old substantial author in a new dress,—a little volume of 281 pages, in a neat but cheap form, worth its weight in gold; no sensible discriminating man would ever think of collecting a library without including this work. For a professing Christian to say that he has never read it, would argue that his reading had been superficial indeed. It is neither dry nor uninteresting, but it is filled with solid and useful truths." —*Western Paper.*

COLTON'S PUBLIC ECONOMY FOR THE UNITED STATES.

One Vol. 8vo.

"In this volume of 536 pages octavo, Mr. Colton, who is favorably known to the American public as the author of the 'Life of Clay,' the 'Junius Tracts,' and other popular works, has supplied the desideratum of a complete defence of the protective system, and an answer to the numerous works on the Free Trade side of the question. As far as we are able to judge from the opportunity we have had to examine the elaborate arguments of the author in the work before us, it appears to us that he has produced a work not only calculated to refute the points made by writers in favor of free trade, but sufficient to puzzle them to find ready answers to many of the positions he has taken. We rather think they will be disposed either to misrepresent him, or to pass over in silence some of his most potent arguments."—*New York Tribune.*

GOULD'S ABRIDGMENT OF ALISON'S EUROPE. One Vol. 8vo.

This work presents a comprehensive and perfect view of Europe during the stormy period from 1789 to 1815, in clear and perspicuous language, and in a beautiful style. Its publication supplies a desideratum in History, there being no work of a similar character attainable by the public, except at four times the expense. It is well adapted as a class-book in History for Colleges, Academies, and Schools, as well as for the general reader.

COLTON'S LIFE AND TIMES OF HENRY CLAY. In Two Vols. 8vo.

"Mr. Colton has done his work—a great work—bravely and well. This is the first successful life of Henry Clay yet written. This describes the man, not as a politician, orator, statesman, alone, but as all—and that honestly, candidly, thoughtfully, and the darkest and deepest passages intelligibly and philosophically. The chapters of his early life and personal character are beautiful, and the account of his political rise intensely interesting."—*Hunt's Merchant's Magazine.*

PROFESSOR BROOKS'S
GREEK AND LATIN CLASSICS.

THIS series of the GREEK and LATIN CLASSICS, by N. C. Brooks, of Baltimore, is on an improved plan, with peculiar adaptation to the wants of the American student. To secure accuracy of text in the works that are to appear, the latest and most approved European editions of the different classical authors will be consulted. Original illustrative and explanatory notes, prepared by the Editor, will accompany the text. These notes, though copious, will be intended to direct and assist the student in his labors, rather than by rendering every thing too simple, to supersede the necessity of due exertion on his own part, and thus induce indolent habits of study and reflection, and feebleness of intellect.

In the notes that accompany the text, care will be taken, on all proper occasions, to develop and promote in the mind of the student, sound principles of Criticism, Rhetoric, History, Political Science, Morals, and general Religion; so that he may contemplate the subject of the author he is reading, not within the circumscribed limits of a mere rendering of the text, but consider it in all its extended connections—and thus learn to *think*, as well as to *translate.*

BROOKS'S FIRST LATIN LESSONS.

This is adapted to any Grammar of the language. It consists of a Grammar, Reader, and Dictionary combined, and will enable any one to acquire a knowledge of the elements of the Latin Language, without an instructor. It has already passed through five editions. 18mo.

BROOKS'S CÆSAR'S COMMENTARIES. (*In press.*)

This edition of the Commentaries of Cæsar on the Gallic War, besides critical and explanatory notes embodying much information, of an historical, topographical, and military character, is illustrated by maps, portraits, views, plans of battles, &c. It has a good Clavis, containing all the words. Nearly ready. 12mo.

BROOKS'S OVID'S METAMORPHOSES. 8vo.

This edition of Ovid is expurgated, and freed from objectionable matter. It is elucidated by an analysis and explanation of the fables, together with original English notes, historical, mythological, and critical, and illustrated by pictorial embellishments; with a Clavis giving the meaning of all the words with critical exactness. Each fable contains a plate from an original design, and an illuminated initial letter.

BROOKS'S ECLOGUES AND GEORGICS OF VIRGIL. (*In press.*)

This edition of Virgil is elucidated by copious original notes, and extracts from ancient and modern pastoral poetry. It is illustrated by plates from original designs, and contains a Clavis giving the meaning of all the words. 8vo.

BROOKS'S FIRST GREEK LESSONS. 12mo.

This Greek elementary is on the same plan as the Latin Lessons, and affords equal facilities to the student. The paradigm of the Greek verb has been greatly simplified and valuable exercises in comparative philology introduced.

BROOKS'S GREEK COLLECTANEA EVANGELICA. 12mo.

This consists of portions of the Four Gospels in Greek, arranged in Chronological order; and forms a connected history of the principal events in the Saviour's life and ministry. It contains a Lexicon, and is illustrated and explained by notes.

BROOKS'S GREEK PASTORAL POETS. (*In press.*)

This contains the Greek Idyls of Theocritus, Bion, and Moschus, elucidated by notes and copious extracts from ancient and modern pastoral poetry. Each Idyl is illustrated by beautiful plates from original designs. It contains a good Lexicon.

THEORY AND PRACTICE OF TEACHING;

OR THE

MOTIVES OF GOOD SCHOOL-KEEPING.

BY DAVID PAGE, A.M.,

LATE PRINCIPAL OF THE STATE NORMAL SCHOOL, NEW YORK.

"I received a few days since your 'Theory and Practice, &c.,' and a capital *theory* and capital *practice* it is. I have read it with unmingled delight. Even if I should look through a critic's microscope, I should hardly find a single sentiment to dissent from, and certainly not one to condemn. The chapters on *Prizes* and on *Corporal Punishment* are truly admirable. They will exert a most salutary influence. So of the views *sparsim* on moral and religious instruction, which you so earnestly and feelingly insist upon, and yet within true Protestant limits. IT IS A GRAND BOOK, AND I THANK HEAVEN THAT YOU HAVE WRITTEN IT."—*Hon. Horace Mann, Secretary of the Board of Education in Massachusetts.*

"Were it our business to examine teachers, we would never dismiss a candidate without naming this book. Other things being equal, we would greatly prefer a teacher who has read it and speaks of it with enthusiasm. In one indifferent to such a work, we should certainly have little confidence, however he might appear in other respects. Would that every teacher employed in Vermont this winter had the spirit of this book in his bosom, its lessons impressed upon his heart!"—*Vermont Chronicle.*

"I am pleased with and commend this work to the attention of school teachers, and those who intend to embrace that most estimable profession, for light and instruction to guide and govern them in the discharge of their delicate and important duties."—*N. S. Benton, Superintendent of Common Schools, State of New York.*

Hon. S. Young says, "It is altogether the best book on this subject I have ever seen."

President North, of Hamilton College, says, "I have read it with all that absorbing self-denying interest, which in my younger days was reserved for fiction and poetry. I am delighted with the book."

Hon. Marcus S. Reynolds says, "It will do great good by showing the Teacher what should be his qualifications, and what may justly be required and expected of him."

"I wish you would send an agent through the several towns of this State with Page's 'Theory and Practice of Teaching,' or take some other way of bringing this valuable book to the notice of every family and of every teacher. I should be rejoiced to see the principles which it presents as to the motives and methods of good school-keeping carried out in every school-room; and as nearly as possible, in the style in which Mr. Page illustrates them in his own practice, as the devoted and accomplished Principal of your State Normal School."—*Henry Barnard, Superintendent of Common Schools for the State of Rhode Island.*

"The 'Theory and Practice of Teaching,' by D. P. Page, is one of the best books of the kind I have ever met with. In it the theory and practice of the teacher's duties are clearly explained and happily combined. The style is easy and familiar, and the suggestions it contains are plain, practical, and to the point. To teachers especially it will furnish very important aid in discharging the duties of their high and responsible profession."—*Roger S. Howard, Superintendent of Common Schools, Orange Co., Vt.*

ELOCUTIONARY WORKS,

BY CHARLES NORTHEND,

PRINCIPAL OF THE EPPES SCHOOL, SALEM, MASS.

I. NORTHEND'S LITTLE SPEAKER.
II. NORTHEND'S AMERICAN SPEAKER.
III. NORTHEND'S SCHOOL DIALOGUES.

I. NORTHEND'S LITTLE SPEAKER.

"THE LITTLE SPEAKER, AND JUVENILE READER.—Mr. Northend is known, both as an experienced teacher, and as the author of the 'American Speaker,' and other educational works. The object of this little work is, to provide the means for exercising quite young pupils in declamation. Mr. Northend justly remarks, that the longer exercises in declamation and composition are delayed, the more difficult it will be to awaken an interest in them. This little volume is well adapted to its purpose."—*Vermont Chronicle.*

II. NORTHEND'S AMERICAN SPEAKER.

"AMERICAN SPEAKER.—This is an admirable book—and as the exercise of declamation, of late, is considered essential to a good and finished education, and is introduced into our best schools as an important element, we hope that this volume of well-selected pieces, compiled with great care by the author from our best writers, will find its way into the hands of every school boy."—*Barnstable Patriot.*

"AMERICAN SPEAKER, by Charles Northend, Principal of the Eppes School, Salem.—In this work, Mr. Northend seems perfectly to have accomplished the object he had in view. The selections are made with perfect taste, and afford an ample variety, to meet all occasions. Wherever a work of this description is wanted, this may be safely recommended, as possessing every desirable attribute. It is for sale by all our booksellers."—*Salem (Mass.) Gazette.*

"It is the best compilation of the kind we have ever examined. The selections are of a high character, and an elevated moral tone is prominent throughout the work. The book is divided into three parts—the first being composed of sixty-two prose exercises; the second, of thirty-four interesting dialogues; and the last, of seventy short poems. We hope this book will soon be extensively introduced into our schools. The author truly remarks in the preface, 'The advantages of frequent practice in speaking are so many and so great, that it should receive more prominence in all our schools.'"—*Salem (Mass.) Advertiser.*

III. NORTHEND'S SCHOOL DIALOGUES.

"The character of the author of this work is a guarantee that it is a book of good practical common sense—one that will take hold of the youthful mind, and delight and interest it. A cursory examination has fully confirmed us in this favorable opinion. The author has selected such dialogues as contain good sentiments, and such as will have a salutary influence on the mind of the young."—*Teacher's Advocate.*

"The selections manifest an intimate knowledge of the wants of the young, a scrupulous regard to the sentiments inculcated, and an eye to combined instruction and amusement. They are preferable to any other books of the same character with which we are acquainted, from the greater variety of the selections, and from their being culled to a considerable extent from the works of modern authors. Children tire of old, threadbare pieces, however good they may be; and novelty has ever for them peculiar attraction."—*Gloucester Times.*

PARKER'S RHETORICAL READER. 12mo.

Exercises in Rhetorical Reading, designed to familiarize readers with the pauses and other marks in general use, and lead them to the practice of modulation and inflection of the voice. By R. G. PARKER, author of "Exercises in English Composition," "Compendium of Natural Philosophy," &c., &c.

This work possesses many advantages which commend it to favor, among which are the following:—It is adapted to all classes and schools, from the highest to the lowest. It contains a practical illustration of all the marks employed in written language; also lessons for the cultivation, improvement, and strengthening of the voice, and instructions as well as exercises in a great variety of the principles of Rhetorical Reading, which cannot fail to render it a valuable auxiliary in the hands of any teacher. Many of the exercises are of sufficient length to afford an opportunity for each member of any class, however numerous, to participate in the same exercise—a feature which renders it convenient to examining committees. The selections for exercises in reading are from the most approved sources, possessing a salutary moral and religious tone, without the slightest tincture of sectarianism.

"I have to acknowledge the reception through your kindness of several volumes. I have not as yet found time to examine minutely all the books. Of Mr. Parker's Rhetorical Reader, however, I am prepared to speak in the highest terms. I think it so well adapted to the wants of pupils, that I shall introduce it immediately in the Academy of which I am about to take charge at Madison, in this state. It is the best thing of the kind I have yet found. I cannot say too much in its favor."—*John G. Clark, Rector of the Madison Male Academy, Athens, Ga.*

"Mr. Parker has made the public his debtor by some of his former publications—especially the 'Aids to English Composition'—and by this he has greatly increased the obligation. There are reading books almost without number, but very few of them pretend to give instructions how to read, and, unluckily, few of our teachers are competent to supply the defect. If young persons are to be taught to read well, it must generally be done in the primary schools, as the collegiate term affords too little time to begin and accomplish that work. We have seen no other 'Reader' with which we have been so well pleased; and as an evidence of our appreciation of its worth, we shall lay it aside for the use of a certain juvenile specimen of humanity in whose affairs we are specially interested."—*Christian Advocate.*

"We cannot too often urge upon teachers the importance of reading, as a part of education, and we regard it as among the auspicious signs of the times, that so much more attention is given, by the best of teachers, to the cultivation of a power which is at once a most delightful accomplishment, and of the first importance as a means of discipline and progress. In this work, Mr. Parker's volume, we are sure, will be found a valuable aid."—*Vermont Chronicle.*

"The title of this work explains its character and design, which are well carried out by the manner in which it is executed. As a class-book for students in elocution, or as an ordinary reading book, we do not think we have seen any thing superior. The distinguishing characteristic of its plan is to assume some simple and familiar example, which will be readily understood by the pupil, and which Nature will tell him how to deliver properly, and refer more difficult passages to this, as a model. There is, however, another excellence in the work, which we take pleasure in commending; it is the progressiveness with which the introductory lessons are arranged. In teaching every art and science this is indispensable, and in none more so than in that of elocution. The pieces for exercise in reading are selected with much taste and judgment. We have no doubt that those who use this book will be satisfied with its success."—*Teacher's Advocate.*

Science of the English Language

CLARK'S NEW ENGLISH GRAMMAR.

A Practical Grammar, in which WORDS, PHRASES, and SENTENCES are classified, according to their offices, and their relation to each other: illustrated by a complete system of Diagrams. By S. W. CLARK, A. M. Price 50 cts.

"It is a most capital work, and well calculated, if we mistake not, to supersede, even in our best schools, works of much loftier pretension. The peculiarity of its *method* grew out of the best practice of its author (as he himself assures us in its preface) while engaged in communicating the science to an *adult* class; and his success was fully commensurate with the happy and philosophic design he has unfolded."—*Rahway Register.*

"This new work strikes us very favorably. Its deviations from older books of the kind are generally judicious and often important. We wish teachers would examine it."—*New York Tribune.*

"It is prepared upon a new plan, to meet difficulties which the author has encountered in practical instruction. Grammar and the structure of language are taught throughout by analysis, and in a way which renders their acquisition easy and satisfactory. From the slight examination, which is all we have been able to give it, we are convinced it has points of very decided superiority over any of the elementary works in common use. We commend it to the attention of all who are engaged in instruction."—*New York Courier and Enquirer.*

"From a thorough examination of your method of teaching the English language, I am prepared to give it my unqualified approbation. It is a plan original and beautiful—well adapted to the capacities of learners of every age and stage of advancement."—*A. R. Simmons, Ex-Superintendent of Bristol.*

"I have, under my immediate instruction in English Grammar, a class of more than fifty ladies and gentlemen from the Teachers' Department, who, having studied the grammars in common use, concur with me in expressing a decided preference for 'Clark's New Grammar,' which we have used as a text-book since its publication, and which will be retained as such in this school hereafter."—*Professor Brittan, Principal of Lyons Union School.*

"Clark's Grammar I have never seen equalled for *practicability*, which is of the utmost importance in all school-books."—*S. B. Clark, Principal of Scarborough Academy, Maine.*

"The Grammar is just such a book as I wanted, and I shall make it *the* text-book in my school."—*William Brickley, Teacher at Canastota, N. Y.*

"This original production will, doubtless, become an indispensable auxiliary to restore the English language to its appropriate rank in our systems of education. After a cursory perusal of its contents, we are tempted to assert that it foretells the dawn of a brighter age to our mother tongue."—*Southern Literary Gazette.*

"I have examined your work on Grammar, and do not hesitate to pronounce it superior to any work with which I am acquainted. I shall introduce it into the Mount Morris Union School at the first proper opportunity."—*H. G. Winslow, A. M., Principal of Mount Morris Union School.*

"Professor Clark's new work on Grammar, containing Diagrams illustrative of his system, is, in my opinion, a most excellent treatise on 'the Science of the English Language.' The author has studiously and properly excluded from his book the technicalities, jargon, and ambiguity which so often render attempts to teach grammar unpleasant, if not impracticable. The inductive plan which he has adopted, and of which he is, in teaching grammar, the originator, is admirably adapted to the great purposes of both teaching and learning the important science of our language."—*S. N. Sweet, Author of "Sweet's Elocution."*

MRS. EMMA WILLARD'S

SERIES OF SCHOOL HISTORIES AND CHARTS.

I. **WILLARD'S HISTORY OF THE UNITED STATES, OR REPUBLIC OF AMERICA.** 8vo. Price $1.50.

II. **WILLARD'S SCHOOL HISTORY OF THE UNITED STATES.** 63 cts.

III. **WILLARD'S AMERICAN CHRONOGRAPHER.** $1.50.

I. **WILLARD'S UNIVERSAL HISTORY IN PERSPECTIVE.** $1.50.

II. **WILLARD'S TEMPLE OF TIME.** Mounted, $1.25. Bound, 75 cts.

III. **WILLARD'S HISTORIC GUIDE.** 50 cts.

IV. **WILLARD'S ENGLISH CHRONOGRAPHER.**

WILLARD'S UNITED STATES.

The *Hon. Dan. Webster* says, of an early edition of the above work, in a letter to the author, "I KEEP IT NEAR ME, AS A BOOK OF REFERENCE, ACCURATE IN FACTS AND DATES."

"THE COMMITTEE ON BOOKS OF THE WARD SCHOOL ASSOCIATION RESPECTFULLY REPORT:

"That they have examined Mrs. Willard's History of the United States with peculiar interest, and are free to say, that it is in their opinion decidedly the best treatise on this interesting subject that they have seen. As a school-book, its proper place is among the first. The language is remarkable for simplicity, perspicuity, and neatness; youth could not be trained to a better taste for language than this is calculated to impart. It places at once, in the hands of American youth, the history of their country from the day of its discovery to the present time, and exhibits a clear arrangement of all the great and good deeds of their ancestors, of which they now enjoy the benefits, and inherit the renown. The struggles, sufferings, firmness, and piety of the first settlers are delineated with a masterly hand."—*Extract from a Report of the Ward School Teachers' Association of the City of New York.*

"We consider the work a remarkable one, in that it forms the best book for general reading and reference published, and at the same time has no equal, in our opinion, as a text-book. On this latter point, the profession which its author has so long followed with such signal success, rendered her peculiarly a fitting person to prepare a text-book."—*Boston Traveller.*

"MRS. WILLARD'S SCHOOL HISTORY OF THE UNITED STATES.—It is one of those rare things, a good school-book; infinitely better than any of the United States Histories fitted for schools, which we have at present."—*Cincinnati Gazette.*

"We think we are warranted in saying, that it is better adapted to meet the wants of our schools and academies in which history is pursued, than any other work of the kind now before the public. The style is perspicuous and flowing, and the prominent points of our history are presented in such a manner as to make a deep and lasting impression on the mind. We could conscientiously say much more in praise of this book, but must content ourselves by heartily commending it to the attention of those who are anxious to find a good text-book of American history for the use of schools."—*Newburyport Watchman.*

Fulton & Eastman's Book-keeping.

A PRACTICAL SYSTEM OF BOOK-KEEPING.

BY LEVI S. FULTON & G. W. EASTMAN.

Containing three distinct forms of Books, adapted for the Farmer, Mechanic, and Merchant—to which is added a variety of useful forms for practical use, viz.: Notes, Bills, Drafts, Receipts, &c., &c. Also a Compendium of Rules of Evidence applicable to Books of Account, and of Law in reference to the Collection of Promissory Notes, &c.

BOOK-KEEPING BLANKS. (Two Nos. in a set.)

Adapted to Fulton & Eastman's Book-keeping.

The use of these Blank Books will be found very important in familiarizing the scholar with the forms requisite to the keeping of accounts according to Fulton & Eastman's system.

"I have examined with much satisfaction Fulton & Eastman's System of *Book-Keeping*, and take pleasure in recommending its adoption to my immediate friends and others. It is simple and easily reduced to practice, and possesses a peculiar adaptation to the wants of the community for which it is designed. The plan for Merchants' Books, which I examined more critically than other portions of the work, is very neat, compact, and economical, and must ensure a great degree of accuracy in keeping accounts."—*Elijah Bottom, Book-keeper for John M. French & Co., Rochester, N. Y.*

"I have examined Messrs. Fulton & Eastman's 'Practical System of Book-Keeping,' and am pleased with the work. As a branch of Education, Book-Keeping is well deserving a high estimation; and, I will add, there is none of equal importance and utility more generally neglected, particularly in our public schools. The work is plain, simple, and comprehensive, and well adapted to meet the wants of the business community. In many respects I deem it superior to any other work of the kind with which I am acquainted. I shall recommend it to the schools under my charge."—*John T. Mackenzie, Town Superintendent.*

"Fulton & Eastman's Book-Keeping.—We had supposed that, in the multiplicity of works on Book-Keeping, hardly any thing valuable remained to be suggested by later authors, should any such present themselves. But we have been convinced of our short-sightedness in examining the work with the above title, now before us. The work is principally designed for schools—for common schools—but should be in the hands of every Farmer, Mechanic, and Merchant in the land. It opens with a system of account-keeping for farmers, followed by one for mechanics, and this, in turn, by an admirable and comprehensive system of mercantile Book-keeping, which, for its simplicity, and time and labor saving properties, possesses advantages over all other systems with which we are acquainted."—*Wayne Co. Whig.*

"We are very much pleased with the design and execution of this work. It is exceedingly practical; being by single entry, containing three different forms of books, for the Farmer, the Merchant, and Mechanic. To these are added notes, bills, drafts, receipts, and a compendium of rules of evidence applicable to books of account, and of law in reference to the collection of promissory notes. A work of such a character, and of so much practical value, speaks for itself, and stands in need of no commendation from us to ensure it a large sale among all classes."—*Albany Spectator.*

"I should think it admirably adapted as a Text-Book for schools, and the study of it of much greater importance than it has hitherto been considered. I hardly know whether the Book is of more importance to scholars in school, or to Farmers, Mechanics, or business men. The system, to which is added a variety of useful 'Forms,' which most business men have occasion to use more or less, is certainly well worth the price of the Book, to any man transacting business to the amount of twenty-five dollars a year."—*E. L. Jones, Book-keeper, Michigan.*

Gillespie's Manual of Road-Making.

GILLESPIE ON ROADS AND RAILROADS.

A MANUAL OF ROAD-MAKING.

Comprising the principles and practice of the Location, Construction, and Improvement of ROADS, (common, macadam, paved, plank, &c.,) and RAILROADS. By W. M. GILLESPIE, A. M., Professor of Civil Engineering in Union College. Price $1.50.

"I have very carefully looked over Professor Gillespie's Manual of Road-Making. It is, in all respects, the best work on this subject with which I am acquainted; being, from its arrangement, comprehensiveness, and clearness, equally adapted to the wants of Students of Civil Engineering, and the purposes of persons in any way engaged in the construction or supervision of roads. The appearance of such a work, twenty years earlier, would have been a truly national benefit, and it is to be hoped that its introduction into our seminaries may be so general as to make a knowledge of the principles and practice of this branch of engineering, as popular as is its importance to all classes of the community."—*Professor Mahan, of the Military Academy.*

"This work contains in a condensed form, all the principles, both ancient and modern, of this most important art; and almost every thing useful in the great mass of writers on this subject...... Such a work as this performs a great service for those who are destined to construct roads—by showing not only what ought to be done, but what ought not to be done; thus saving immense outlay of money, and loss of time in experiments...... The committee, therefore, recommend it to the public."—*Report of a Committee of the American Institute.*

"The views of the author are sound and practical, and should be read by the people throughout the entire length and breadth of the land...... We recommend this Manual to the perusal of every tax-payer for road-making, and to the young men of the country, as they will find useful information in relation to each department of road-making, which will surely be useful to them in after-life."—*American Railroad Journal.*

"If the well-established principles of Road-Making, which are so plainly set forth in Prof. Gillespie's valuable work, and so well illustrated, could be once put into general use in this country, every traveller would bear testimony to the fact that the author is a great public benefactor."—*Silliman's American Journal of Science.*

"This small volume contains much valuable matter, derived from the best authorities, and set forth in a clear and simple style. For the want of information which is contained in this Manual, serious mistakes are frequently made, and roads are badly located and badly constructed by persons ignorant of the true principles which ought to govern in such cases."—*Journal of the Franklin Institute.*

"It would astonish many 'path-masters' to see how much they don't know with regard to the very business they have considered themselves such adepts in. Yet all is so simple, so lucid, so straightforward, so manifestly true, that the most ordinary and least instructed mind cannot fail to profit by it. We trust this useful and excellent volume may find its way into every village library if not into every school library, as well as into the hands of every man interested in road-making."—*New York Tribune.*

"This elaborate and admirable work combines in a systematic and symmetrical form the results of an engineering experience in all parts of the Union, and of an examination of the great roads of Europe, with a careful digestion of all accessible authorities. The six chapters into which it is divided comprehend a methodical treatise upon every part of the whole subject; showing what roads ought to be in the vital points of direction, slope, shape, surface, and cost, and giving methods of performing all the necessary measurements of distances, directions, and heights, without the use of any instruments but such as any mechanic can make, and any farmer can use."—*Newark Daily Advertiser.*

NATURAL AND EXPERIMENTAL PHILOSOPHY.

BY R. G. PARKER, A. M.,

AUTHOR OF "RHETORICAL READER," "EXERCISES IN ENGLISH COMPOSITION," "OUTLINES OF HISTORY," ETC., ETC.

I. PARKER'S FIRST LESSONS IN NATURAL PHILOSOPHY.

II. PARKER'S SCHOOL COMPENDIUM OF NATURAL PHILOSOPHY.

The use of school apparatus for illustrating and exemplifying the principles of Natural and Experimental Philosophy, has, within the last few years, become so general as to render necessary a work which should combine, in the same course of instruction, the theory, with a full description of the apparatus necessary for illustration and experiment. The work of Professor Parker, it is confidently believed, fully meets that requirement. It is also very full in the general facts which it presents—clear and concise in its style—and entirely scientific and natural in its arrangement.

"This work is better adapted to the present state of natural science than any other similar production with which we are acquainted."—*Wayne Co. Whig.*

"This is a school book of no mean pretensions and no ordinary value."—*Albany Spectator.*

"We predict for this valuable and beautifully-printed work the utmost success."—*Newark Daily Advertiser.*

"The present volume strikes us as having very marked merit."—*N. Y. Courier.*

"It seems to me to have hit a happy medium between the too simple and the too abstract."—*B. A. Smith, Principal of Leicester Academy, Mass.*

"I have no hesitation in saying that Parker's Natural Philosophy is the most valuable elementary work I have seen."—*Gilbert Langdon Hume, Prof. Nat. Phil. N.Y. City.*

"I am happy to say that Parker's Philosophy will be introduced and adopted in "Victoria College" at the commencement of the next collegiate year in autumn, and I hope that will be but the commencement of the use of so valuable an elementary work in our schools in this country. The small work of Parker's (Parker's First Lessons) was introduced the last term in a primary class of the institution referred to, and that with great success. I intend to recommend its use shortly into the *model* school in this city, and the larger work to the students of the provincial Normal school."—*E. Ryerson, Superintendent of Public Instruction of Upper Canada.*

"I have examined Parker's First Lessons and Compendium of Natural and Experimental Philosophy, and am much pleased with them. I have long felt dissatisfaction with the Text-Books on this subject most in use in this section, and am happy now to find books that I can recommend. I shall immediately introduce them into my school."—*Hiram Orcutt, Principal of Thetford Academy, Vermont.*

"I have no hesitation in pronouncing it the *best work on the subject now published.* We shall use it here, and I have already secured its adoption in some of the high-schools and academies in our vicinity."—*M. D. Leggett, Sup. of Warren Public Schools.*

CHAMBERS' EDUCATIONAL COURSE.

THE SCIENTIFIC SECTION.

The Messrs. Chambers have employed the first professors in Scotland in the preparation of these works. They are now offered to the schools of the United States, under the American revision of D. M. REESE, M. D., LL. D., *late Superintendent of Public Schools in the city and county of New York.*

I. **CHAMBERS' TREASURY OF KNOWLEDGE.**
II. **CLARK'S ELEMENTS OF DRAWING AND PERSPECTIVE.**
III. **CHAMBERS' ELEMENTS OF NATURAL PHILOSOPHY.**
IV. **REID & BAIN'S CHEMISTRY AND ELECTRICITY.**
V. **HAMILTON'S VEGETABLE AND ANIMAL PHYSIOLOGY.**
VI. **CHAMBERS' ELEMENTS OF ZOOLOGY.**
VII. **PAGE'S ELEMENTS OF GEOLOGY.**

"It is well known that the original publishers of these works (the Messrs. Chambers of Edinburgh) are able to command the best talent in the preparation of their books, and that it is their practice to deal faithfully with the public. This series will not disappoint the reasonable expectations thus excited. They are elementary works prepared by authors in every way capable of doing justice to their respective undertakings, and who have evidently bestowed upon them the necessary time and labor to adapt them to their purpose. We recommend them to teachers and parents with confidence. If not introduced as class-books in the school, they may be used to excellent advantage in general exercises, and occasional class exercises, for which every teacher ought to provide himself with an ample store of materials. The volumes may be had separately; and the one first named, in the hands of a teacher of the younger classes, might furnish an inexhaustible fund of amusement and instruction. Together, they would constitute a rich treasure to a family of intelligent children, and impart a thirst for knowledge."—*Vermont Chronicle.*

"Of all the numerous works of this class that have been published, there are none that have acquired a more thoroughly deserved and high reputation than this series. The Chambers, of Edinburgh, well known as the careful and intelligent publishers of a vast number of works of much importance in the educational world, are the fathers of this series of books, and the American editor has exercised an unusual degree of judgment in their preparation for the use of schools as well as private families in this country."—*Philad. Bulletin.*

"The titles furnish a key to the contents, and it is only necessary for us to say, that the material of each volume is admirably worked up, presenting with sufficient fulness and with much clearness of method the several subjects which are treated."—*Cin. Gazette.*

"We notice these works, not merely because they are *school books*, but for the purpose of expressing our thanks, as the 'advocate' of the educational interests of the people and their children, to the enterprising publishers of these and many other valuable works of the same character, the tendency of which is to diffuse useful knowledge throughout the masses, for the good work they are doing, and the hope that their reward may be commensurate with their deserts."—*Maine School Advocate.*

Chambers' Educational Course.

I. CHAMBERS' TREASURY OF KNOWLEDGE.

PART I. *Embraces Elementary Lessons in Common Things*—or things which lie most immediately around us, and first attract the attention of the young mind.

PART II. *Embraces Practical Lessons on Common Objects*—such as articles or objects from the Mineral, Vegetable, and Animal Kingdoms, manufactured articles, miscellaneous substances and objects, &c.

PART III. *Embraces Introduction to the Sciences.* This presents a systematic view of nature, under the various sciences. Care is taken that the information given should not be a superficial view of a few unconnected phenomena, but a chain of principles calculated, in combination, to impress a distinct and comprehensive idea on the mind of a very young child.

This volume is designed for an early reading book, that the scholar may be exercised in reading, and at the same time acquire knowledge of such subjects as his capacity will enable him to understand. It contains much useful information upon common objects of life.

"The American editor, in bringing the above excellent reading book in its present enlarged and improved shape before the American public, has done great service, in our opinion, to the cause of education. He has, in fact, rendered it one of those rare school readers, which, while affording rational *amusement* to the youthful mind, is, at the same time, calculated to excite its *thinking* and reasoning powers, thereby accomplishing the grand object of intellectual education, which is nothing more, as the poet has tersely told us, than teaching the 'young idea how to shoot.'"—*Rahway Register.*

"This volume is very happily adapted to the capacities of children, as soon as they can read with facility, and designed to present some new truth in nature or art to their opening minds, exemplified with beautiful illustrations drawn from familiar objects."—*Christian Observer.*

"All that the title-page promises, the book contains. It is indeed a treasury, full of knowledge for the information of the young."—*Richmond Christian Advocate.*

"The intention of the writers was to furnish a reading book for children, which might be used at an early period, and at the same time furnish a vast amount of knowledge. In this they have admirably succeeded. The volume contains a simple survey of the mineral, vegetable, and animal kingdoms, and an introduction to the sciences. We commend it to families who are seeking elementary works for their children."—*Western Christian Advocate.*

II. ELEMENTS OF DRAWING AND PERSPECTIVE. (By JOHN CLARK.)

PART I. *Embraces Exercises, for the Slate.*
PART II. *Embraces the Principles of Drawing and Perspective.*

With but very few exceptions, children are fond of making efforts in Drawing. Furnished with a black-lead pencil and sheet of paper, or slate and pencil, they are delighted to scribble whatever their fancy suggests. Followed up methodically by the teacher, their infant aspirations may lead to the development of much valuable talent. This volume is on a new branch introduced into the common studies in the pursuit of knowledge. It contains diagrams and illustrations, exhibiting the style and manner of drawing, from the first rudiments of outline to the finished sketches of landscape and scenery. This is a useful branch of education, heretofore studied but little, but which will be better appreciated as more understood.

III. CHAMBERS' ELEMENTS OF NATURAL PHILOSOPHY.

PART I. *Embraces Laws of Matter and Motion.* PART II. *Embraces Mechanics.* PART III. *Embraces Hydrostatics, Hydraulics, and Pneumatics.*

In the treatment of the several subjects, great care has been taken to render the language simple and intelligible. Illustrated by wood engravings.

Chambers' Educational Course.

IV. REID & BAIN'S CHEMISTRY AND ELECTRICITY.

PART I. *Embraces Illustrations*, and Experiments of the Chemical Phenomena of Daily Life. By D. B. REID, M. D., F. R. S. E.
PART II. *Embraces Electricity*, (statical and current.) By ALEXANDER BAIN, the original inventor of Electric and Telegraphic clocks.

This work is designed to facilitate the introduction of Chemistry as an elementary branch of education in schools. Illustrated by engravings.

"We have met with no works of the same character, which present the facts pertaining to these interesting sciences in a style so simple and attractive, so well adapted for use in schools, and for the wants of those who have not the time to spare for the perusal and study of more elaborate treatises."—*Maine Common School Journal.*

"A knowledge of chemistry has become almost indispensable to a successful prosecution of most of the avocations of society. As far as possible, therefore, should it become one of the studies of the schools. For that purpose, this treatise appears to be as well adapted, to say the least, as any text-book that has yet been prepared. It has the advantage, which is no trifle, of all the recent discoveries and improvements in the science; and through the whole there is a constant illustration of the text by neat and appropriate engravings. It should receive, as it deserves, attention from teachers and others charged with the superintendence of education."—*Worcester Palladium.*

"The above work constitutes No. IV. of Chambers' Educational Course, and is here presented in a suitable shape for the use of schools. The kindred phenomena of electricity and chemistry are illustrated, and clear as sunlight, to those who will study the book—which is not only convenient, as to size and arrangement, but is ornamented with a large number of the most ingenious wood-cuts."—*Chillicothe Gazette.*

"Chemistry is one of the most profitable studies, because it bears directly upon our interests in almost every pursuit in life. We have reviewed this excellent work for schools, and we are gratified to say that it is one of the latest and best improvements we have seen. In truth, it may afford valuable information to many whose school-days are past."—*Mississippian.*

"The appearance of this work in Chambers' admirable Educational Series, and Dr. Reese's imprimatur as editor, will probably be taken in lieu of any commendation our brief acquaintance with it could furnish. Its arrangement strikes us as very clear and scientific; its illustrations are full; and though the work is brief, and designed to be only elementary, it is yet comprehensive and able."—*N. Y. Evangelist.*

"It treats of the subject in a plain and common-sense manner, suited to the comprehension of the young, and adapted to the wants of the student who plods his way up the hill of science unaided by the living teacher."—*Western Citizen.*

"The first part of this work appears, from the examination we have given it, to be less encumbered with the mere mention of chemical compounds that are rarely seen, and more devoted to matters of primary and practical interest to the tyro in Chemistry, than some of the American treatises that are extensively in vogue. It will be found also to furnish directions to the student for performing experiments; and one good experiment, thoroughly wrought out by the student, is worth more than the perusal of a whole volume without it.

"Part II., on Electricity, is more full than usual for the subordinate place that this branch of Natural Philosophy is made to take in the midst of a treatise on Chemistry. It will enable the student to understand a science to which mankind are indebted, at the present day, for what we conceive to be the most remarkable and important invention of the age, viz. the Electro-Magnetic Telegraph; and no one can fail to perceive the superiority of the invention by our distinguished countryman over those that have had their origin abroad. To those who are desirous to find a good text-book for classes in our common schools and academies, we think we may safely recommend this."—*Rome Sentinel.*

Chambers' Educational Course.

V. HAMILTON'S VEGETABLE AND ANIMAL PHYSIOLOGY.

PART I. *Embraces the General Structure and Functions of Plants.*
PART II. *Embraces the Organization of Animals.*

The object of this work is to unite Vegetable and Animal Physiology, and bring both systems under one head, as properly connected and adapted to the mind of the student.

"This is the best treatise adapted to educational purposes, which we have seen upon that subject. We cordially commend it to the special attention of parents and school committees."—*Teacher's Advocate.*

"This should be made a branch of common-school education, in order that the laws of health may be universally understood."—*Vermont Chronicle.*

VI. CHAMBERS' ELEMENTS OF ZOOLOGY. (ILLUSTRATED.)

Presenting a complete view of the Animal Kingdom as a portion of external nature. As the composition of one of the most eminent physiologists of our age, it possesses an authority not attributable to such treatises in general.

"This is a treasure for the poor man's home, and the hope is not unfounded, that many a poor man's son may, from the pleasure derived from its perusal, be induced to cultivate a taste for the study of nature and her laws. We admire all the works published by the Chambers, and seize them like the hand of a tried friend. There seems to be a desire to do good as well as sell the book, exhibited on every page. The present, in some 500 pages, gives a rapid but scientific view of the animal kingdom. It is admirably adapted for schools and as a reading book for young naturalists. We should judge its perusal by general readers an almost necessary preparation to that of a popular treatise on geology."—*Literary World.*

VII. ELEMENTS OF GEOLOGY. (BY DAVID PAGE.)

The subject is here presented in its two aspects of *interesting* and *important.* Interesting, inasmuch as it exhibits the progressive conditions of the earth from the remotest periods, and reveals the character of the plants and animals which have successively adorned and peopled its surface; and important, as it determines the position of those metals and minerals upon which the arts and manufactures so intimately depend.

"This is the most explicit and concise work on the above subject with which we are acquainted. In style it is simple and interesting, and may be readily understood by persons unacquainted with the science. It is admirably adapted as a text-book for those who wish to obtain a knowledge of Geology by studying nature. Appended, is a brief geological description of each country in the world."—*Young Student.*

"In this volume, facts and suppositions are given with clear method; concisely, and yet with sufficient distinctness to be easily mastered by the pupil or the general reader. Numerous engravings throw much light upon the text; and help, not only to form, but to fix impressions. It is well adapted for use in high-schools; and numerous questions facilitate the learner's progress."—*Worcester Palladium.*

"This work gives an outline of the science in a very small compass. It is lucid, comprehensive, attractive, and admirably arranged as a text-book for the use of academies and colleges."—*H. S. Thrall, Professor of Chemistry and the Physical Sciences, Kenyon College, Ohio.*

Davies' System of Mathematics.

MATHEMATICAL WORKS,

IN A SERIES OF THREE PARTS:

ARITHMETICAL, ACADEMICAL, AND COLLEGIATE.

BY CHARLES DAVIES, L.L.D.

I. THE ARITHMETICAL COURSE FOR SCHOOLS.

1. PRIMARY TABLE-BOOK.
2. FIRST LESSONS IN ARITHMETIC.
3. SCHOOL ARITHMETIC. (Key separate.)
4. GRAMMAR OF ARITHMETIC.

II. THE ACADEMIC COURSE.

1. THE UNIVERSITY ARITHMETIC. (Key separate.)
2. PRACTICAL GEOMETRY AND MENSURATION.
3. ELEMENTARY ALGEBRA. (Key separate.)
4. ELEMENTARY GEOMETRY.
5. ELEMENTS OF SURVEYING.

III. THE COLLEGIATE COURSE.

1. DAVIES' BOURDON'S ALGEBRA.
2. DAVIES' LEGENDRE'S GEOMETRY AND TRIGONOMETRY.
3. DAVIES' ANALYTICAL GEOMETRY.
4. DAVIES' DESCRIPTIVE GEOMETRY.
5. DAVIES' SHADES, SHADOWS, AND PERSPECTIVE.
6. DAVIES' DIFFERENTIAL AND INTEGRAL CALCULUS.

---

7. **DAVIES' LOGIC AND UTILITY OF MATHEMATICS.**

This series, combining all that is most valuable in the various methods of European instruction, improved and matured by the suggestions of more than thirty years' experience, now forms the only complete consecutive course of Mathematics. Its methods, harmonizing as the works of one mind, carry the student onward by the same analogies and the same laws of association, and are calculated to impart a comprehensive knowledge of the science, combining clearness in the several branches, and unity and proportion in the whole. Being the system so long in use at West Point, through which so many men, eminent for their scientific attainments, have passed, and having been adopted, as Text Books, by most of the colleges in the United States, it may be justly regarded as our

NATIONAL SYSTEM OF MATHEMATICS.

THE ARITHMETICAL COURSE FOR SCHOOLS.

1. Davies' Primary Table-Book.

The leading feature of the plan of this work is to teach the reading of figures; that is, so to train the mind that it shall, by the aid of the eye alone, catch instantly the idea which any combination of figures is intended to express.

The method heretofore pursued has aimed only at presenting the combinations by means of our common language: this method proposes to present them purely through the arithmetical symbols, so that the pupil shall not be obliged to pause at every step and translate his conceptions into common language, and then retranslate them into the language of Arithmetic.

For example, when he sees two numbers, as 4 and 8, to be added, he shall not pause and say, 4 and 8 are 12, but shall be so trained as to repeat 12 at once, as is always done by an experienced accountant. So, if the difference of these numbers is to be found, he shall at once say 4, and not 4 from 8 leaves 4. If he desires their product, he will say 32; if their quotient, 2: and the same in all similar cases.

2. Davies' First Lessons in Arithmetic.

The First Lessons in Arithmetic begin with counting, and advance step by step through all the simple combinations of numbers. In order that the pupil may be impressed with the fact that numbers express a collection of units, or things of the same kind, the unit, in the beginning, is represented by a star, and the child should be made to count the stars in all cases where they are used. Having once fixed in the mind a correct impression of numbers, it was deemed no longer necessary to represent the unit by a symbol; and hence the use of the star was discontinued. In adding 1 to each number from 1 to 10, we have the first ten combinations in arithmetic. Then by adding 2 in the same way, we have the second ten combinations, and so on. Each ten combinations is arranged in a separate lesson, throughout the four ground rules, and each is illustrated either by unit marks or a simple example. Thus the four hundred elementary combinations are presented, in succession, in forty lessons,—a plan not adopted in any other elementary book. The author has embodied in a recent edition of this work the general principles contained in the Primary Table-book, so that the scholar can, if desired, commence the study of arithmetical tables with this second book.

3. Davies' School Arithmetic.

This work begins with the simplest combination of numbers, and contains all that is supposed to be necessary for the average grade of classes in schools. It is strictly scientific and entirely practical in its plan. Each idea is first presented to the mind either by an example or an illustration, and then the principle, or abstract idea, is stated in general terms. Great care has been taken to attain simplicity and accuracy in the definitions and rules, and at the same time so to frame them as to make them introductory to the higher branches of mathematical science. No definition or rule is given until the mind of the pupil has been brought to it by a series of simple inductions, so that mental training may begin with the first intellectual efforts in numbers.

THE ACADEMIC COURSE.

1. Davies' University Arithmetic.

The scholar in commencing this work, is supposed to be familiar with the operations in the four ground rules, which are fully taught both in the *First Lessons* and in the *School Arithmetic.*

In developing the properties of numbers, from their elementary to their highest combinations, great labor has been bestowed on classification and arrangement. It has been a leading object to present the entire subject of arithmetic as forming a series of dependent and connected propositions; so that the pupil, while acquiring useful and practical knowledge, may at the same time be introduced to those beautiful methods of exact reasoning which science alone can teach.

Extract of a Letter from the Professors (Mahan, Bartlett, & Church) of the Mathematical Department of the United States Military Academy.

In the distinctness with which the various definitions are given—the clear and strictly mathematical demonstration of the rules—the convenient form and well-chosen matter of the tables, as well as in the complete and much-desired application of all to the business of the country, the "University Arithmetic" of Prof Davies is superior to any other work of the kind with which we are acquainted.

2. Davies' Practical Geometry and Mensuration.

In this work all the truths of Geometry are made accessible to the general reader, by omitting the demonstrations altogether, and relying for the impression of each particular truth on a pointed question and an illustration by a diagram. In this way it is believed that all the important properties of the geometrical figures may be learned in a few weeks; and after these properties have been once applied, the mind receives a conviction of their truth little short of what is afforded by rigorous demonstration.

3. Davies' Elementary Algebra.

This work is intended to form a connecting link between Arithmetic and Algebra, and to unite and blend, as far as possible, the reasoning on numbers with the more abstract method of analysis. It begins with an introduction, in which the subject is first treated mentally, in order to accustom the mind of the pupil to the first processes; after which, the system of instruction assumes a practical form. The definitions and rules are as concise and simple as they can be made, and the reasonings are as clear and concise as the nature of the subject will admit. The strictest scientific methods are always adopted, for the double reason, that what is learned should be learned in the right way, and because the scientific methods are generally the most simple.

4. Davies' Elementary Geometry.

This work is designed for those whose education extends beyond the acquisition of facts and practical knowledge, but who have not the time to go through a full course of mathematical studies. It is intended to present the striking and important truths of Geometry in a form more simple and concise than is adopted in Legendre, and yet preserve the exactness of rigorous reasoning. In this system, nothing has been omitted in the chain of exact reasoning, nothing has been taken for granted, and nothing passed over without being fully demonstrated. The work also contains the applications of Geometry to the Mensuration of Surfaces and Solids.

5. Davies' Elements of Surveying.

In this work it was the intention of the author to begin with the very elements of the subject, and to combine those elements in the simplest manner, so as to render the higher branches of Plane Surveying comparatively easy. All the instruments needed for plotting have been carefully described, and the uses of those required for the measurement of angles are fully explained.

Davies' System of Mathematics.

THE COLLEGIATE COURSE.

The series of works here presented, form a full and complete course of mathematical instruction, beginning with the first combinations of arithmetic, and terminating in the higher applications of the Differential Calculus. Each part is adapted to all the others. The Definitions and Rules in the Arithmetic, have reference to those in the Elementary Algebra, and these to similar ones in the higher books. A pupil, therefore, who begins this course in the primary school, passes into the academy, and then into the college, under the very same system of scientific instruction.

---

1. Davies' Bourdon's Algebra.

The Treatise on Algebra by M. Bourdon, is a work of singular excellence and merit. In France it is one of the leading text-books. Shortly after its first publication it passed through several editions, and has formed the basis of every subsequent work on the subject of Algebra.

The original work is, however, a full and complete treatise on the subject of Algebra, the later editions containing about eight hundred pages octavo. The time given to the study of Algebra in this country, even in those seminaries where the course of mathematics is the fullest, is too short to accomplish so voluminous a work, and hence it has been found necessary either to modify it, or to abandon it altogether. The Algebra of M. Bourdon, however, has been regarded only as a standard or model, and it would perhaps not be just to regard him as responsible for the work in its present form.

2. Davies' Legendre's Geometry, etc.

Legendre's Geometry has taken the place of Euclid, to a great extent, both in Europe and in this country. In the original work the propositions are not enunciated in general terms, but with reference to, and by the aid of, the particular diagrams used for the demonstrations. It was supposed that this departure from the method of Euclid had been generally regretted, and among the many alterations made in the original work, to adapt it to the systems of instruction in this country, that of enunciating the propositions in general terms should be particularly named; and this change has met with universal acceptance.

3. Davies' Analytical Geometry.

This work embraces the investigation of the properties of geometrical figures by means of analysis. It commences with the elementary principles of the science, discusses the Equation of the Straight Line and Circle—the Properties of the Conic Sections—the Equation of the Plane—the Positions of Lines in Space, and the Properties of Surfaces.

4. Davies' Descriptive Geometry.

Descriptive Geometry is intimately connected with Architecture and Civil Engineering, and affords great facilities in all the operations of Construction.

As a mental discipline, the study of it holds the first place among the various branches of Mathematics.

5. Davies' Shades, Shadows, and Perspective.

This work embraces the various applications of Descriptive Geometry to Drawing and Linear Perspective.

6. Davies' Differential and Integral Calculus.

This treatise on the Differential and Integral Calculus, was intended to supply the higher seminaries of learning with a text-book on that branch of science. It is a work after the French methods of teaching, and in which the notation of the French school is adopted.

www.ingramcontent.com/pod-product-compliance
Lightning Source LLC
LaVergne TN
LVHW021137110826
845150LV00005B/1052

* 9 7 8 1 4 2 5 5 4 8 6 7 4 *